Soaring and Crashing:
My Bipolar Adventures

by Holly Hollan

7010 Grove Crest Drive, Austin, TX 78736
Work Phone: (512) 389-4497
Cell Phone: (512) 771-2615
Home Phone: (512) 288-9457
E-mail: hollysusan@gmail.com
Web site: http://www.holly-holy.com

Austin, Texas

ISBN-13: 978-1-934248-76-8
ISBN-10: 1-934248-76-2

Cover Design by Meghan Gale and Joe Schaffer
Interior Design by Peggy LeTrent

Printed in the United States of America

Table of Contents

Acknowledgements

Often I believe I owe my life to those who have provided encouragement and support throughout this roller coaster ride. This is not meant to be an all-inclusive list, but these individuals have been among the most influential. Of course, my parents; my sisters Heather Nicely and Heidi Grether and their gracious husbands, Vince Nicely and Tim Grether; my sweet nieces Eliana Grether and Shala Nicely; precious girlfriends, Deborah (Deb) Fries; Joan Boyer; Dolores (Dee) Rice; Maria Emerson; Andrea Donio; Lorene Moore; Patsy Curtis; Trena Barnett and daughter, Megan; Becky Cottrell; and Estella Casarez; my team leader, Kathleen Martin; coworkers, Kathy Keller, Alan King, Susan Marks and Sara Persoff; ex-husband, Wesley Peurasaari and his spunky wife, Marcy; departed drum teacher, Jimmy Boyer; departed paralyzed lover, Danny Smith; departed husband, Kenneth Joe Hollan; departed preacher friend, Harold Sims; dear, healing priest, Father Jack Sheffield and his lovely wife, Anna Marie; steadfast friends, Robert C. Brooks ("Troll") and Lew and Terry Gordon; Neil Diamond; all of my friends on the "I Am, I Said" Message Board, especially Tom Sadge, Joan Nurczyk, Kate Mirah, Soma, Sherry, Revvie Bob and Jeanie Washer and others too numerous to mention; genius stepdaughter and her husband, Katherine and Erich Pelletier; friend and supporter, Dr. Rich Patrock; friends, Robert Mobley, Chuck Siercks and Ricky Campbell; gracious editor, Pamela Baggett-Wallis; encouraging agent, Sally Hill-McMillan; and the doctors: Dr. Roger Callahan, Dr. William C. Lawrence, Dr. Lee M. Shulman, Dr. Robert D. Handlesman, Dr. Gary Aitcheson, Dr. Tracy Gordy; and my ultimate fabulous team, Dr. Robert E. Cantu and the most brilliant, patient, encouraging and efficacious of them all, Dr. William J. Dubin of Psychological ARTS, Austin, Texas.

Foreward
William J. Dubin, PhD

I am a psychologist and was at one time Chief of Service of the Intensive Care Unit of Manhattan State Hospital, and extreme examples of madness had been the focus of my early career. There is much to learn from looking at things from the perspective of a human with different wiring. Unfortunately, much of the popular literature has gotten it wrong. The portrayal of mania and psychotic episodes tends to be developed by individuals who have not personally experienced it, and those who have are rarely able to write about it coherently or insightfully.

The readers of "Soaring and Crashing" have an opportunity to vicariously experience some of the frontiers of human perception and interpretation. Holly Hollan meets the diagnostic criteria of Bipolar Disorder – personally riding an unusually steep version of this roller coaster – and is also a fine writer with the technical skills to be our charming and light-hearted tour guide as she takes us on an exciting trip to the limits of madness.

Perhaps due to her wonderful disposition, Holly has, surprisingly, gotten what she wants, however unlikely such outcomes might be. More than 15 years ago I told her, with a degree of certainty, "You will never marry Neil Diamond!" I would have been surprised at that time to discover that one day Neil Diamond would announce: "I love you Holly," on national radio. If you like the thrill of fast action, unpredictable ups and downs, and yet a long-term coherent story and willful influence over the unfolding of events, hang on, you are in for a treat. Ahead is a fabulous adventure tale of a journey to the edge and back again.

But there is another audience for this book, an audience which I believe is Holly's primary target: Bipolars. A great achievement of this work is a description of a realistic path to a good long-term outcome, described clearly and coherently in the last four chapters.

Introduction

I'm not a famous actress like Patty Duke (Anna Marie in *They Call Me Anna*) or Carrie Fisher (in *The Best Awful*); or a gifted psychiatrist like Dr. Kay Redfield Jamison (in *An Unquiet Mind*); or a flamboyant, young journalist like Lizzie Simon (in *Detour: My Bipolar Road Trip in 4-D*); or a notorious newswoman like Jane Pauley (in *Skywriting: A Life Out of the Blue*). I'm simply a Web developer for the state of Texas, in my late 50s, and have been diagnosed as bipolar since 1980. However, I have known secretly of my condition since I was seven years old.

I've actually dealt with the bipolar condition all my life. I say "dealt with" and "condition" rather than "suffered from" and "disorder" because the former presents a sense of being in control; whereas, the latter conveys the image of a helpless victim. Actually, the brilliant psychologist (therapist) whom I see, Dr. William J. Dubin of Austin, Texas, prefers to call it the "bipolar **trait**." His belief is being bipolar merely means "a different organization of the mind having its advantages and disadvantages." Again, the emphasis is on self-control of one's thought processes and on insightful encouragement rather than on illness or disease.

With that being said, I shall refer to this condition throughout these pages interchangeably as the bipolar characteristic, bipolar disorder (BPD, not to be confused with Borderline Personality Disorder), the bipolar trait or the bipolar experience. In years past, it was referred to as manic depression because that terminology more adequately depicts the polarity of the condition. That is why Dr. Kay Redfeld Jamison, psychologist and staff member at Johns Hopkins University, and author of "*An Unquiet Mind*," among other texts, prefers to reference the condition as manic depression. It is a disorder in the degree to which one's relationship with oneself is disruptive; when one can dispassionately experience manic depression, one knows there are tremendously positive elements few people are able to achieve.

There have been untold numbers of books written about this disorder that affects one percent of the population, or about two million people. Much research has been done, yet actually very little progress has been made in determining its exact causes and in finding solutions. There is no real cure; the condition is generally life-long and chronic. Many believe it gets worse as one grows older. There is no iron-clad medical test that can be performed to determine whether one has bipolar disorder. The diagnosis generally is based on demonstrated symptoms, all of which can be revealed readily by reading the materials resulting from a "Google" search on the Internet.

Numerous studies have tried to identify a genetic predisposition to BPD. However, in many cases, one identical twin will have it and the other does not. Environmental factors such as one's upbringing, experiences in school and interpersonal relationships greatly influence the manifestation of this condition. Brain mapping experiments reveal bipolar persons appear to have small pools of water in their brains (*An Unquiet Mind* by Dr. Kay Redfeld Jamison).

It is widely accepted that a significant contributing factor revolves around three neurotransmitter activities in the brain: serotonin, acetylcholine and dopamine. Additionally, levels of the hormones cortisol and adrenaline play a key role in the anxiety component of the condition. From my own experiences, I believe the disruptive nature of the bipolar existence is based upon energy imbalance. Either the serotonin-neurotransmitter process is intensified to a biochemical excess, which creates the manic, scattered energy; or it is impeded to an abnormal level which creates the depressive, "half-of-my-mind-is-dead" disillusionment.

This energy imbalance manifests in what I experience as a "right-and-left-brain" conflict. Our left brain tends to be logical, meticulous, organized and responsible. Our right brain facilitates creativity, spontaneity and playfulness. I experience depression when I feel as though my creative right brain has not received enough stimulation, or when the serotonin activity has decreased so much I couldn't be creative no matter how hard I try. Conversely, I experience mania when it seems as though my right brain, under the influence of excessive serotonin release rates, takes over in wildly imaginative creativity and activity that can become delusional and psychotic.

Another significant aspect of life as a bipolar individual is hyperthymia, meaning too much emotion, or moods that are too intense. Good things are experienced as intensely energizing boosts to one's morale, beyond what the situation calls for; and likewise, disappointments are registered as major letdowns leading to futility, despair and utter hopelessness.

Perhaps this memoir will provide insights for others who may be struggling to come to grips with a diagnosis of bipolar disorder — manic-depression. I unequivocally state Jimi Hendrix was correct when he sang, *"Manic-depression's a frustrating mess."* As one who has dealt with this frustration, and who has spent thousands of dollars in therapy trying to untangle the mess, my intent is to expose bipolor emotions and experiences. I hope to provide fresh insights and rays of hope to professionals trying to get a better handle on the condition for treating their patients, as well as to those dealing with the condition, be they newcomers to the diagnosis or old hands at it.

The first several chapters of this book are about growing up bipolar. This series of chronological vignettes helps readers develop insights into the roots of the bipolar existence as I have experienced it. It is not meant to be an all-inclusive narrative, but rather a summary of pertinent events and scenarios to enlighten the reader about the bipolar roller coaster. It will illustrate key components leading up to my eventual diagnosis of "296.44 Bipolar I Disorder, Most Recent Episode Manic, Severe With Psychotic Features." In particular, I hope mothers will be able to recognize and understand their bipolar children. It also provides assistive insights for friends, family and coworkers who interact with bipolar individuals.

The remaining few chapters explore methods of dealing with the bipolar condition from a cognitive approach as gleaned from intensive psychotherapy and hypnotherapy with a gifted and compassionate psychotherapist. Medications also are discussed. I consider myself an expert on the subject because I have tried my entire life to understand it and ultimately to view the bipolar condition as a gift from which I can offer understanding to others, rather than to view it as a cross to bear.

Chapter 1: The "Glowing Bush"

Whenever you encounter stress or temptation ask yourself:
What is the best use of my attention right now?

– William J. Dubin, PhD

"*Do not worry my little child,*" I distinctly heard in a loud, deep, but gentle voice. "*You will be great some day. You will be famous. You will help a large number of people.*" As I stood before the spirea bush that bleak November day when I was seven years old with my eyes tightly closed, praying for the first time in my life, "*Dear Father God, what must I do to make Mother love me?*" I heard my answer, and when I opened my eyes, my entire body heaved in a huge convulsion, while the bush, stripped of its leaves for winter, burst aglow in shimmering tiny white blossoms of spring.

This vision was my first remembered break with reality. The religious overtone was the refrain that played out in all my serious manic episodes for decades, well into middle age. Religion, in the form of agape—the unconditional love of others—also has played a role in my ability today to accept my condition, exercise control over my feelings and even revel in my uniqueness.

I didn't get to this point, however, without serious emotional and physical pain. And I didn't get to this point without the extraordinary intervention of caring family, friends and medical professionals.

I endured decades of irrational terrors, depressions and isolation before I learned the patterns of my illness and how to anchor my racing thoughts. My childhood memories are exceptionally clear to me and particularly painful because I felt unloved and unlovable. The vision of the glowing bush became my first "secret" and sense of "mission." For the first time, I realized I was somehow different. Our family was far from religious and I had no reference to biblical tales at that age. Knowing that, and knowing what we do today about mental illness, that experience could be nothing other than my first manic moment. But no one in our immediate world recognized it as such, least of all me.

None of the conventional wisdom at the time prepared my mother to recognize or deal with my condition. Her reactions to my odd behaviors added to the fears and self-loathing of my childhood. I did not, could not, please my mother. I now know that although Mother loved me, her exasperation with my despair and despondency, interspersed with exhilarating moments of intense glee over nothing, was caused by her not knowing how to interact with me.

Mother had her own problems. Her first husband and father of my older sister Heather was killed in a freak army base accident during World War II just months before he was due for discharge. Mother was an only child, daughter of a working, twice-divorced mom, which was a bizarre exception back in the 20s when being from a broken home was scandalous.

My grandmother had significant mental problems, too. When Mother was five, she was mysteriously sent to Florida to live with her grandmother while her own mother spent a year in a mental hospital. This raises the question of genetics versus environment that plagues many illnesses.

By the time Mother met Daddy, she likely was eager for a new life. My parents purchased a farm so Heather and I could grow up in the country and enjoy all the wonders of nature. I learned later the former owner of the old farmhouse died in my bedroom and often wondered if his ghost haunted our house. Shortly after we moved there, while I was still a baby and Mother was home alone, lightning struck the fuse box and caught the floorboards under my bedroom on fire. These facts would take on mysterious meaning during my future manic episodes.

Mother soon realized there was something radically different about me from Heather who was quiet and agreeable. I can remember as a small child standing in my playpen, unable to occupy myself with my toys and reaching for someone to pick me up and offer comfort. I was forever uncomfortable. Mother couldn't understand my behavior. She was frustrated and unable to provide the nurturing I felt I needed to be accepted.

When I was about four or five years old, I became hysterical when Heather and I couldn't be in the same ballet class. I couldn't stand the thought of being in a room full of strangers. This happened again when we attended a Bible school. When we played the game "Red Rover, Red Rover, Let Johnny Come Over" I was horrified because I could see the potential for children getting hurt as they tried to break through the arms of the kids trying to block them. I refused to play.

I recall being lonely in my early years because while Heather was at school, I found all of the things I tried to entertain myself with, such as paper dolls, to be boring. Nothing held my attention for long. I was restless and often felt lost and in another world. I also cried a lot which annoyed Mother as she kept telling me not to cry ("Nobody wants to be around a crybaby!") and I needed to learn how to entertain myself. Again, I experienced isolation and that sense of being different.

Heather and I attended a one-room country school that housed kindergarten through 8th grade, taught by Mrs. Frasier, a gifted teacher and close family friend. She was one person who understood me.

There were only four children in my kindergarten class, and I would often get my work done rapidly and then go bother the older students to find out what they were doing. Mrs. Frasier called me "Little Charlie Chipmunk" because I chattered and talked every chance I got. When she promoted me to first grade, she wrote in her report: *She is a fine student, and often will begin writing on her paper, and as soon as she makes one mistake, she will wad the paper up in a ball, throw it away, and start over again until she has a perfect project to turn in. She amazes us with her vocabulary and is generally a very likable sweet little girl. She is most definitely ready to be promoted to the first grade.* It is interesting I adopted such a perfectionistic approach to anything I would engage in – it had to be just right or it wasn't comfortable or acceptable.

The summer I was six I went to a Bible school with our neighbors to the south. I astounded the teacher when I could recite from memory every single book of the Old and New Testaments. To this day, my memory – near total recall – has been one of my saving graces.

In these early years, I suffered several nightmares that would wake me, screaming. A couple of times Mother would come into my room and yell at me for disturbing the household. I began to fear my mother and to believe the world was not a safe place. I felt rejected by the very person who should have lovingly provided me with a sense of safety and encouragement.

We had an ill-tempered Shetland pony named Playtime who would allow Heather and her friend, Jacque, to ride him; however, he repeatedly threw me off. But I was single-minded in my determination to ride that pony. One afternoon he threw me seven times, and each time I climbed back up. Stubbornness became one of my dominant traits—just one of many my mother found difficult to deal with. The events of that afternoon revealed my tenacity and perseverance—traits that saw me through difficult times.

Later Jacque got a horse of her own and rode him to our house which inspired Heather to want a real horse instead of the wimpy, cantankerous pony! Daddy was just about ready to pursue Heather's desire, but my actions unintentionally sabotaged that.

Daddy left some Vicks cough drops out on the bookcase and I helped myself to one without asking. Our parents fed us only nutritional food that included no refined white sugar, white flour, chocolate, etc. We were on the J.I. Rodale and Adele Davis *"Let's Eat Right to Keep Fit"* programs long before "eating right" and being nutrition conscious was fashionable. We would take handfuls of vitamins and mineral supplements twice a day.

After putting the cough drop in my mouth, I approached Mother and said, "I'm going outside until supper is ready." She replied, "What's in your mouth?" I said, "Nothing." She admonished, "Don't lie to me. I know you have something in your mouth. What is it?"

"A cough drop," I shakily replied. Then came the clincher, "Where did you get it?" My fatal answer, "Daddy gave it to me."

I went outside, feeling about two inches tall, but not knowing what was in store for me. Within a few minutes of Daddy coming home from work, I was beckoned into the house. Mother's eyes were like fire and she was shaking she was so furious: "One thing I HATE is a LIAR. You not only told ONE, but you told TWO lies. Now for that, you and Heather CANNOT have your horse."

Talk about GUILT! MY actions denied my blessed sister HER heart's desire. I emphatically learned the TRUTH should be my guide, no matter what. I learned to seek and tell the truth, even though my perception of the truth may have been far from reality, it nonetheless was my truth.

The reverse of this episode revealed Mother was a woman of strong principles. Daddy asked me to dump bushel-baskets of cut-up corn cobs on our sizable garden to minimize the weeds. I spent a while mulching about one row of the vegetables while Daddy followed my efforts, covering several more rows. He arranged for a friend from the village to come get some of the corn cobs for his garden.

When he arrived, Mr. Ball said to me, "Did you put all of those corn cobs down for your daddy?"

I said, "No, sir. I just did some of it; he did a lot more than I did."

"Well," he said, "I'll bet you did a whole lot, so here's a quarter."

I promptly went to Mother, handed her the quarter and said, "Here's a quarter Mr. Ball gave me for putting those corn cobs down. I told him I didn't do hardly any of it." Mother took the quarter and I went back outside.

When I came in for supper, she gave me two quarters saying, "Here's the quarter back that Mr. Ball gave you and here's another one for telling the truth. I'm proud of you."

She rewarded me for good behavior. While I was still terrified of her, I knew I had finally done something that pleased her. I felt a glimmer of hope that I wasn't worthless.

In the fall of 1955, Mother was pregnant with my little sister Heidi. It was close to Thanksgiving and Mother and Heather had gone shopping for petticoats to wear with our square dance dresses. Mother and Daddy started dancing and teaching dance lessons during Mother's pregnancy with me. Dancing was their primary passion.

While Heather and Mother were gone shopping, I was left with Grandma Davis to help her with some fall gardening. I assisted Grandma for a couple of hours in planting a large garden of tulip and narcissus bulbs and put leaves over them to protect them for winter. Two hours was a long time of dedicated focus for the attention span of a seven-year-old. But it wasn't enough.

Daddy asked Grandma to pick up the bricks the remodeling crew had thrown out the upstairs window. Heather's bedroom was in the process of being converted to allow me to share the room with her since baby Heidi would be taking over my bedroom.

After all the work in the garden, I took my red wagon over to the pile of bricks and picked one up. It had a centipede on it. Tossing the brick aside, I screamed, "Ewwww, there's BUGS on these!"

Grandma Davis got angry at me, and when Mother and Heather arrived home, she told Mother I had been a brat. Mother punished me by putting the petticoat she purchased away in the upper reaches of a closet, saying I couldn't have it for a whole year! One of Mother's trademarks was her punishments were often too severe for the crime. It was at this time that I went out to the spirea bush, prayed and received my "glowing-bush answer."

Because Mother criticized and chastised me so relentlessly for my tears and constant dissatisfaction, I believed she didn't love me. Yet she tried her hardest to help teach me self-control, never knowing anything was "wrong" with me. She was continually annoyed by my outbursts of temper and tears because I wasn't like Heather, who was agreeable, quiet and read books constantly.

I remember long periods of feeling a deep despondency as if I were a stranger to myself. I wondered why I wasn't a happy little girl, and then there were times of total elation over nothing! I experienced a high energy level and felt almost wild. Mother would make me sit on the window seat if she perceived me as being "bad" until I thought over what I had done. If I wiggled my foot, she'd smack me on the knee in reprimand saying, "Hold still. Stop your wiggling. People will think you don't know how to be still." And I can remember thinking, *Who cares if I can't sit still? What does it matter to them? It's better than kicking Mother which is what I feel like doing.*

A particularly happy time came when we got our collie puppy, Boots. Daddy built a huge, two-room doghouse complete with siding and a hinged, sloped roof with shingles. It was large enough I could crawl through the staggered doors into the large back room and sit there with our new puppy. Often, as I was growing up, I would literally sit "in the doghouse" to hide from my mother and cry because I felt so lost and unappreciated.

Baby sister Heidi came into the world Feb. 16, 1956, the birthday of our great grandmother. Unfortunately, I had the chicken pox and Daddy didn't know how to take care of me. Since Mother was fearful of losing another man in her life, she let baby Heidi stay at the hospital and came home to take care of me. It was one more time I felt terribly guilty, believing it was my fault my baby sister had to stay at the hospital without her mother because I was sick.

The day they brought Heidi home from the hospital was particularly memorable. As Mother held her on her lap, Heather, Grandmother Davis and Daddy all smiled at her, and Heidi smiled a radiant baby smile back at them. But when I went over to her, she cried! Not knowing any better, I immediately believed she hated me and knew it had been my fault she had to stay at the hospital! Again, I felt like an abandoned outcast.

This was further enhanced because Mother would not let me hold my baby sister, which gave me the distinct sense she didn't trust me with her. Older sister Heather got to do all of the help tending to the baby, and I felt I lost my place in the family. Everyone doted on little baby Heidi and suddenly I was no longer "cute and little."

I remember my eighth birthday as if it were yesterday. I received four gifts that year, and they all started with the letter "B." I got a baby doll, a blue baby buggy, a baby doll bed Mother made and a blue bicycle. Later that summer, a significant event took place. We had a long lane that led through the back yard down toward the middle section of our property, which was a woods with a small creek running through it and a pond at each end of the land. I used to take walks through the woods and spend many hours making little boats to float down the small rapids in the creek. I believe escaping to the woods at times helped me find myself because I bonded with nature, and the birds' songs, especially the wood thrush, which sang so melodically. Walking among the trees and wildflowers and listening to the birds sing gave me a sense of peace much like listening to classical music did.

One day I decided to take my doll in the baby buggy for a walk to the woods. The grass was long and as I tried to push the buggy through it, the wheels and axles got tangled up in the grass and it got stuck. I tried my hardest to dislodge it, but it kept getting ever more entangled. I became so frustrated I started screaming and stomping my feet. Mother heard me back at the house and came flying out the kitchen door, down the rickety porch steps and charging down the lane toward me. She ripped down my pants and spanked me severely, yelling, "I'll not have you out here behaving like a spoiled brat. You will stop this screaming immediately. You ought to be ashamed of yourself for carrying on like that. How do I know you're not really in trouble?" She hit me so hard my knees buckled, and then turned around and stormed back to the house.

At that moment, I became terrified of my mother and believed I could never trust her. I viewed her as my mortal enemy and I was doomed to a state of eternal damnation by her. I felt like something was terribly wrong with me that I aroused such an intense degree of wrath from my own mother.

*   *   *

Daddy, My Sometimes Ally

My memories of my father are much warmer than my memories of my mother. Whether that is the difference between my parents' personalities or the typical father-daughter closeness is something to think about. As my sense of alienation from Mother was set in cement, my father was doing his best to bond with me. I can remember going out to the dance hall he built and him turning on waltz music, teaching me how to waltz by having me stand on his feet as he did the steps. It was a deep sense of protection and love, and I developed a remote glimmer of confidence that I had an ally in Daddy.

Daddy endeared himself to me by how thoroughly involved he got with Christmas festivities. We were not a religious family and only attended church a couple of times at Easter—I remember wearing white gloves and a fancy hat and dress. But Daddy had a Christmas spirit that rivaled almost any child's holiday enthusiasm. My parents were generous at Christmas. Daddy woke us up early on Christmas morning, joyfully announcing throughout the house, "Merry Christmas! Merry Christmas! Come down and see what Santa Claus has brought us!"

I always felt self-conscious at Christmas and strange – like a dark cloud surrounding me because of the song, *"He knows if you've been bad or good so be good for goodness' sake!"* I never felt I'd been "good enough" to deserve my gifts because Mother constantly gave me the message I was "bad" for all of my crying and stubbornness. I consistently perceived the world as a bewildering, unfriendly place.

One afternoon playtime, Daddy turned me loose with his classical music 78 RPM record collection. My entire world changed because I discovered music! Tchaikovsky's "Nutcracker Suite," "Swan Lake Ballet," "Italian Caprice," and the "1812 Overture" became my favorites, as well as Ravel's "Bolero," Beethoven's "Fifth Symphony," and Strauss waltzes. I suddenly discovered a whole new universe where I became enraptured and felt safe and uplifted. It was almost a religious experience, as being engulfed in music became for me in the future. Over the years, this passion for music became inexplicably entwined with religious convictions during my manic phases.

I remember trying to seek an ally in my father as a haven from Mother's constant annoyance with me. However, my dad worked long hours and I only saw him briefly in the mornings before school and on the weekends. He was a third-year pre-med student at the University of Michigan with a 4.0 grade point average when he met and fell in love with Mother. When he learned he could not continue his medical school pursuit because he was colorblind, he was bitterly disappointed. At

Chapter 2: "My Firsts And 'I Know Stuff'"

Emotional experiences elicited by external events – depression resulting from genuine loss or fear resulting from genuine threat – have information value. Emotional experiences – primary symptoms of bipolar disorder – have no information value.

– William J. Dubin, PhD

I could hardly wait for my tenth birthday as it felt magical to finally move into double digits in age which meant I was that much closer to adulthood. I hated being a kid because I felt I was always being controlled by Mother. I couldn't wait to grow up and leave home so I could make my own rules. I thought maybe once I became an adult, the tears, silent desperation and sense of never fitting in would subside. Little did I know what lay in store for me once that day came.

My entire focus in life was on trying to be good so I could have the sense that Mother loved me, yet I always came up short. There were many times I'd wander off in our woods especially at spring time and gather wildflowers for Mother, assembling charming little bouquets for her birthday or Mother's Day. I would give them to her and she would say, "You do a lot of nice things around here, but that doesn't undo all of the unpleasantness you cause." It would have been helpful if she had merely said, "Thank you."

Mother and Daddy did work hard to instill proper values in us such as following the Golden Rule and getting our work done before we played. At an early age, I developed a meticulous sense of responsibility, both toward myself and others. I definitely knew right from wrong and I tried diligently to do right. Yet somehow, I sensed there was an ongoing battle inside me that I could never win.

No one appeared to understand my sensitivities; no one knew of the battle, the darkness I constantly fought. I would sit down to dinner and begin to eat the soup Mother prepared, which was delicious, but too hot. I'd take a sip and then have to guzzle water, which we had at every meal – never soda pop or anything else, to cool my tongue. Mother would say to me, "Your soup is the same temperature as everyone else's. It's not too hot for them. What do you think I did? Make your soup hotter just to burn your tongue?" I'd start to cry and she would be angry. *"Yes, the soup IS too hot for me,"* I'd think, wondering what was wrong with me, and feeling chagrined I annoyed Mother once again through no obvious misbehaving I was aware of.

The summer after I turned ten, my parents enrolled me in a 4-H camp. I was excited to go because I finally felt like a "big girl like Heather" who had been to camp annually for the previous few years. She always came back so happy, and I wanted to be part of the fun, too. It was a long drive to the camp location during which my excitement turned into a huge, gnawing hole in my soul, and I didn't know it at the time, but I was having my first panic attack. I didn't want to go. My head was spinning with thoughts of, *"Will I cause the same unpleasantness here that I cause at home? Will I be able to keep from crying? Will I sleep okay?"* Mother and Daddy checked me in and we found my cabin, which was located directly across the trail from an immediate drop-off into a steep and deep ravine with a stream running below. The counselors assigned me to a top bunk. My enthusiasm returned because I'd never slept in bunk beds before.

After my parents left, I sat and cried. That familiar sense of darkness fell upon me and I felt helpless and completely alone. I tried to participate in the evening's events. I tried to make new friends yet I felt like a gangling misfit. That night was a disaster because while asleep, I climbed out of the bunk bed and began walking out the door. Someone rescued me just seconds before I stepped into the ravine.

I cried all the next day and the counselor called my parents who told her to simply put me on a bottom bunk and that I had to stay there for the rest of the week. I wanted to go home to my familiar surroundings where I could hide in my collie Boots' doghouse where I felt safe. I tried, however, to do what they expected of me and found I did enjoy swimming. Our afternoon swimming sessions were the one salvation of the entire week. At the end of that week, I was never so glad to see my parents in my life. They were not thrilled I had been such a "baby." I never went back to 4-H camp.

Our neighbors had a swimming pool put in. They lived about a quarter mile south of our house, with our cornfield separating the two homes. I would walk through the cornfield every day to go swimming with them. However, Mother would not let me go on weekends because she said their family didn't need me there to interrupt their family time together. During the summers, I couldn't wait for Monday to come so I could go back down and swim for most of the day.

One time, a thunderstorm came up rather suddenly. Mother had a rule I was not to go inside the Thorntons' house. She kept telling me she didn't want me to wear out my welcome. So I had to hurry home and try to beat the thunderstorm. I already had a keen respect for lightning because I'd seen it strike the tree across the field from our front porch and strike one of the trees in our orchard. I ran as fast as I could, but a huge bolt of lightning with its resultant thunder hit so close it knocked me to the ground. At that point, my respect for lightning turned into a gigantic fear.

Every time a thunderstorm brewed after that, I would become almost hysterical. Mother would chastise me telling me I shouldn't show my fear because little sister Heidi wasn't afraid, and Mother didn't want her to be. I began to learn how to be somebody I wasn't.

I remember starting sixth grade and being moved from the regular elementary school to the second floor of a very old, hot, rickety former high school. My sole motivation in my studies was to get better grades than my older sister Heather had because I thought if I did, my parents would love me and finally be proud of me. I spent the first six weeks of that school year studying world history as our social studies class. Just before the end of the first six weeks, I was moved to the far end of the new high school to a class with a strange male teacher. His students were studying world geography instead of history, and we were given a six-week exam for which I received a "D." I was appalled and terrified to bring that grade home to Mother and Daddy. I did the best I could with no exposure to the subject matter, but felt I failed miserably. I was so upset that I got sick to my stomach and couldn't stop crying. I tried to tell my parents what happened and they didn't seem too bothered by it. I was much more concerned than they were.

Mr. Fruhman insisted we read the newspaper. Mother would not let me read the paper, nor did we have a television. She confronted my teacher stating she wanted me to be able to remain a little girl because I would be exposed to the trauma of the world soon enough and she would not allow me to read the paper. This caused an uncomfortable gap between my teacher and me.

He would spend hours talking about ancient forms of capital punishment and the Salem Witch Trials and elaborate upon how each instrument of torture was used. I had nightmares every night that someone put me in an iron maiden, or that I was being drawn and quartered, or my head was going to be chopped off in a guillotine. I didn't dare tell Mother what he was teaching us because I was afraid that would cause a further rift between him and her with its resulting discomfort to me.

That year, for one of my book reports, I read "*Where the Red Fern Grows,*" a story about a boy and his two red hunting hounds. I used to sit inside during lunch recess and read instead of going out to play with the kids because I was much more comfortable reading animal stories than being around other people. One day, at lunch time, I finished the book that ended with the two dogs dying. I put my head on my arms on the desk and sobbed unceasingly. I went to the lavatory at the end of lunch time so the kids wouldn't see me crying, but someone came down and said I had to come back to class. Everyone thought I was a weird basket case because of my ongoing tears. The sorrow in that book triggered a sense of excessive emotion (hyperthymia) that I could not control, one of the blueprint symptoms of bipolar disorder.

I had never been glad to see a school year end, but that year had been the most uncomfortable because I felt hated both at home and at school. Even though summers were long and boring, aside from swimming at the neighbors, I was glad to anticipate seventh grade and junior high school.

A few times each year, Daddy and Mother would go away for a week or ten days to various parts of the country to square dance conventions. They would leave us in the care of Grandma Davis or our teacher friend, Mrs. Frasier. Every time, before they left, Mother would say, "Now be good. Make me proud of you." I would think to myself, *"I'll do the best I can, but I really don't know what it is I do that's so bad. What if they don't come back? What if something happens to them?"* When I'd get up the first day they were gone, I felt a gaping sense of abandonment and a nagging fear that somehow I would not make Mother proud.

Finally, that summer was over with and it was time to start junior high school. One thing Mother did at the start of each school year was to make her girls "first-day-of-school" dresses. She was a gifted seamstress who always wanted our school year to start off with something new fashioned by her own hands. I was so proud to wear the dresses she worked so hard to complete that often she was up until the wee hours the night before finishing her projects.

I liked seventh grade because I was in band that year, playing the coronet. There was a special bond between the students in band – we were all aspiring musicians. It gave me an opportunity to express that deep part of my soul that longed to come out. Our bandleader was extremely hot-headed. One student, Jerry, was red-headed and the class clown. Mr. Talbot had no tolerance for any horseplay in his classroom and because of this, I was extremely fearful of him. One time, he got so angry with the class clown that he slapped him across the side of the head. I felt so sorry for Jerry because he wasn't really bad and he made me laugh. It wasn't long before Mr. Talbot was released of his duties.

An incident occurred that year which further demonstrated my excessive emotions. Every child had to have a tuberculosis test that the school arranged to be performed at school. I was terrified of needles and already had one TB test done that didn't "take." When it was time to get in line, I ran screaming down the hall to the girls' lavatory, hysterically shaking. One of the teachers came in and admonished me telling me to get in line like everyone else. They accused me of "just trying to get attention." I was ashamed and embarrassed that I was so afraid and was unable to hide it. The other students thought it was quite amusing and laughed at me which caused my first glimmer of wanting to leave this world.

Later that fall, I suffered my first loss. We were keeping our collie Boots tied up because he insisted on chasing the gravel trucks that constantly ran up and down our country road to the gravel pits a few miles north of our house. One day Daddy noticed the collar had completely eaten its way through the hide on Boots' neck as he strained and barked at the trucks. Since Daddy was a humane individual, he made a vow that no dog of ours was going to be chained again and he let Boots run loose. No longer did my collie sleep in his dog house but rather on the door mat by our front door, waiting for us to come outside and play.

One day, just as the bus picked us up to take us to school, Boots chased after it because he didn't want us to leave. In the opposite direction came a gravel truck that hit Boots. I saw it all and screamed at the top of my lungs so piercingly that the bus driver thought I had been hit by the truck. When he realized I was okay, he accelerated and I kept screaming and trembling because I saw my beloved dog lying at the edge of the road.

When I got to school, between two of my classes, I called Mother who told me she saw no sign of Boots and maybe he had gone back to the woods because injured animals will often seek a place of cool mud to soothe their wounds and be alone. I called her back and she said she had not seen him. I cried much of the day and dreaded going home.

Mother met me at the door and hugged me with tears in her eyes. This was the first time I saw any visible emotion from her other than annoyance at me. She told me that around mid-morning, the truck driver stopped by the house and told her of the accident, and that he removed Boots from the road and into the weeds at the edge so he wouldn't keep getting hit. He offered to buy us another dog. Mother said she didn't want to tell me until I got home because she wanted me to complete my day at school. That evening, Daddy buried Boots and I cried myself to sleep, wondering how I would ever get over the loss of my dear pet and friend.

During the rest of that school year, I started a ritual upstairs while doing my homework. I could not concentrate because my mind was always absorbed with thoughts of suicide and wanting to escape the confusion and turmoil I felt almost constantly. I began playing the classical music Daddy introduced me to at age seven that I loved so much. Somehow the distraction of the music allowed me to focus on my homework and get it done much faster. Mother used to wonder how I could concentrate and get my schoolwork done with the music playing, but I brought home all As and Bs, so she decided I must be doing something right and let me continue my own studying methods.

When I came home from school, I began talking incessantly to Mother while she sewed about "this girl at school." I told her all about how "this girl" cried all of the time and how the kids teased her and tried to make her life miserable. This began my first sense of disassociation because as I would talk, I'd feel happy and joyful and like I was someone else. I was able to interact with Mother at a level of detachment from the battle that raged within. Of course, "this girl" was me I was talking about.

The next year, in eighth grade, two rather bizarre things occurred leaving me certain something was curiously strange within me. My Grandpa Ralph was diabetic and was sick. One evening while doing my homework, I was listening to an album by the Seekers when the song, *"I'll Never Find Another You"* came on. I stood up and looked in the mirror when suddenly, my whole body went into a tremor, and I started crying as I "heard" a voice tell me: *"Your Grandpa Ralph has died."* Shaking, trembling and in a hot flash, I sat down and buried my face in my hands and sobbed. The next morning, the phone rang and Daddy answered it only to be told the news that his father had passed away that night. I never did tell anyone I already had that foreknowledge, but I was terrified it happened.

Several months later, this scene repeated itself. I was again listening to the Seekers and heard *"I'll Never Find Another You:"* *"There's a new world somewhere...and I know I'll never find another you ...."* Again, my entire body trembled all over and I started crying. Again, I heard that "voice" say, *"Your beloved school teacher, Mrs. Frasier, has just died."* She had been battling cancer and we were all concerned she was in decline and suffering. The following morning, again the phone rang with her husband Archie calling us to give us his sad news. I was mortified because I thought, *"Why is it I know these things? Nobody else seems to know people have died before receiving a phone call informing them of the news."* And again, this secret stayed with me as I never told anyone because I was afraid something was seriously wrong.

I remember going to Mrs. Frasier's funeral, which was a Catholic Mass. This was the first time I'd ever been to a Roman Catholic Church and I was amazed at the sense of holiness I felt in that sanctuary. I felt a presence I at once bonded with, and I knew "something" was there that was much bigger than I was. Daddy acted immature and condescending during the whole service because during the preparation of the Eucharist for Holy Communion he asked as the bells rang, "What are they doing? Making a cake?" I was appalled at his lack of holiness and respect for what I was experiencing as deeply sacred and comforting. I felt safe in that church service and I know I felt the presence of God and the Holy Spirit for the first time. I was awe-stricken and wanted to punch my father to shut his mouth with his snide remarks.

Later that school year, I became more and more despondent. I only had two friends, because everyone else thought I was strange. I wanted to die because I believed I would never be any good. I hurt so badly. I wanted to try to shock Mother into knowing how isolated and rejected I felt most of the time. So one night, I found a razor blade and took a slice out of my left wrist. It bled some and I suddenly realized I diverted my constant inner pain to something that hurt worse and I found some relief. However, I immediately became petrified Mother might even get angrier with me, so I hid my cut wrist from her. It was a little tricky doing dishes that night because the soapy water made it really smart.

The next day at school, my friend Margaret asked me what happened, and I told her I wanted to kill myself. She went home and told her mother who forbade her to be my friend any longer. I rather abruptly learned wanting to die was not acceptable, yet I couldn't keep those thoughts out of my mind.

Another interesting thing occurred the year I was 13. This was when I realized my older sister Heather was 17 years old and Mother and Daddy had just celebrated their fourteenth wedding anniversary. I couldn't figure out how Heather could be 17 and Mother and Daddy were married for 14 years! I was scared to ask them, so I asked my biology teacher who asked the school counselor to contact Mother, which created quite an embarrassing scene for her.

I also speculated about it with our neighbor because being naive and afraid of Mother, I thought some strange scientific or miraculous event had occurred! Well, Barbara "talked" and the whole thing blew up into a most unfortunate set of events for Mother that she forbade me from going down to the Thorntons' again. I hated myself for my curiosity but I felt I hadn't done anything wrong. It would have helped if I was informed.

The following evening, I had to use the bathroom (we had one for the family of five) and Daddy came marching in nude to take a bath, something he did frequently, thinking nothing of exposing his maleness to us young girls, which made me distinctly uncomfortable. As he bathed, he told me Heather's father was killed in the war before he met Mother and fell in love with her and her daughter, married Mother and adopted Heather as his own. I always wished it had been Mother who told me that sad story, not Daddy. I felt a deep pang of sadness and compassion for what Mother must have endured in the loss of her husband.

The following summer, the Thorntons moved and a new family, Dr. Watkins and his five children moved in. He was a psychiatrist who terrified me because I was certain he could see right through me and knew how disturbed I really was. He would stand at a distance with his hands behind his back and watch me as I interacted with his children. I desperately wanted to talk to him, yet I knew he worked out of the mental hospital and when he came home, he was not doing "doctor stuff." The good thing about this change in neighbors was that finally my mother would let me go down and play with their children, even though their oldest was five years younger than I was. No longer did I have to isolate myself all of the time because of the incident with Barbara Thornton telling people there was something wrong with our family because of Heather being my half-sister. No longer was I being punished for someone else's misunderstanding of the events regarding my sister's heritage.

The Watkins family had a Shetland pony named Mickey and we all would ride him down the lane through the woods, around the back field and back up to the gate. One day while I was taking my turn, Mickey bolted and left me lying on the ground. My back hit a stone leaving me in searing pain. I limped up to the Watkins' house and Mrs. Watkins asked me what happened. When I told her, she, who was a nurse, immediately helped me upstairs to her girls' bedroom and had me lie down. Dr. Watkins came in to ask me how I was feeling. I remember experiencing an intense combination of embarrassment that I was hurt along with a sense of gratitude that someone was finally concerned about my well being.

Later that evening, Dr. Watkins drove me home and told Mother and Daddy what happened. Daddy took me to the bone doctor who operated on his back, where they took X-rays and discovered my right leg was 3/8" shorter than my left. The doctor cautioned Daddy I had his bad back – an "S" curve or something which I did not understand and told him I should be cautious to avoid falls or further injury. He instructed my parents to put a lift in my right shoes in an effort to straighten out my spine, which made me feel more bothersome.

Another incident occurred during that last year of junior high school (in our school system, 9th grade was considered high school) that further alienated me from all of the students and my family. Little sister Heidi was in kindergarten and one day, as we were riding home on the bus, I decided to tease her a bit. I meant no harm, but just felt like teasing her. I told her she had to get off the bus one stop earlier than our house and stay with Dr. Jackson, the obstetrician who lived two houses north of us. I told her Mother was not going to be home and that she didn't want us to be home alone together. It was a joke, and I just wanted to see if she would believe me. She got off the bus and then I told her, "No, I was just teasing." She went home, crying to Mother that I lied to her, and Mother became furious with me for upsetting my little sister. Her punishment was that I could not wear nylon stockings or use makeup for the whole next school year. This meant I would appear radically different from all of the other girls in the ninth grade and would be further taunted and teased as my schooling progressed. I would experience more rejection and isolation and became more introverted and despondent, wishing more fervently that I were dead because it seemed as though I could do nothing right.

One summer in my early teens, we took another family vacation. This time, it was to College Station, Texas so Mother and Daddy could attend a round dance workshop. Daddy owned a 1956 Lincoln Continental, claiming it was the best traveling car he'd ever owned. I remember he tried on and off to quit smoking, which was an ongoing point of contention between Mother and him. I observed with curiosity how hard it was for him to quit. Before we left for the trip, he gave up the cigarettes. After we were on the road for about an hour or so, he stopped at a Texaco station to get gas and came back with a couple packages of cigarettes – Lucky Strikes. Mother launched a tirade upon him that he had reneged on his commitment. I remember him saying, "You don't expect me to drive all the way to Texas without smoking, do you?"

On the way to Texas, I was in awe at the beauty of Memphis, Tennessee – the huge, ornate, beautiful homes and mansions I had only seen in "*Gone with the Wind*." It was breathtaking to see for real what I had only seen in the movie. I was mesmerized by the majesty of the homes in that city. I was also overtly enthusiastic about eating at a restaurant in Texarkana situated on the corners of four adjoining states.

When we arrived in Texas and our hosts greeted my parents with effusive hugs and hospitality, I became aware of the welcoming warmth of people in the South. I was impressed with their overall affection, almost gushing kindness and laid-back attitude. At the hotel, I immediately was able to make friends with the other kids who were close to my age and I found myself comfortable and enjoying the kids' planned activities of horseback riding, swimming, hiking and eating together. One older girl, Elaine, was a pianist who had composed a beautiful piece. She played the piano in the hotel for us each night while we sang along to favorite songs. But the piece she wrote had a hauntingly beautiful melody that captured my spirit so richly, I asked her to teach me how to play it. I learned the first several chords and realized I was making music while becoming absorbed and lost in her moving melody. Again, the mystic peace I discovered in music enraptured my spirit and soul.

After that trip to Texas, I had a profound sense that *"I will go back there again some day. There's something special about Texas and I want MORE!"*

Another interesting incident occurred to close out my junior high years. About half-way through the year, the new band leader realized I did not have the most effective teeth structure (embouchure) for playing the $400 coronet my parents had purchased for me, so he recommended I take up the French horn. Mother and Daddy were adamant that they had spent their money on the coronet so they were NOT going to allow me to play the French horn. I felt confused and conflicted because one authority (the teacher) was making his informed recommendation and they were being stubborn because of their investment in my instrument. Thus, during class, I studied and played the French horn and at home, I practiced the coronet. It felt good to have a secret.

It came time for the spring concert and I was feeling traumatized because the band leader wanted me to play the French horn the school provided. Mother and Daddy were coming to the concert. What would I do? The night of the concert arrived, a sultry, hot night with storms brewing. When I decided to proudly sit as first-chair French horn instead of third chair coronet and play as if my parents were not there, a strange thing happened: An electrical storm came up with all of its fury, lightning and thunder crashing all around us. Suddenly, the lights went out in the auditorium at the very moment of my French horn solo!

I knew my part, and the thrill of playing it vanquished my deep fear of lightning. I kept right on playing, while the rest of the band stopped! I was the only one who had my part memorized, so I proudly played my solo until the lights came back on and the rest of the band members joined in as we finished the piece. I was ecstatic—elated—that I carried the show. It lit a spark within me that I was so completely in my element, performing and engaging in an artistic, creative expression. I was so absorbed in the music and felt such a sense of joy and peace, I realized I'd not yet experienced that kind of comfort. After the concert, my parents never said one word about how well I played the French horn. But this time, I knew, and that was all that mattered. It was a significant triumph I never felt before. I finally realized I could do something right, and I felt whole.

Chapter 3: Teachers' Pet

*A professional boxer will hire sparing partners to improve
his skills of responding to difficult and painful situations.
Primary symptom episodes can be your sparring partners.*

— *William J. Dubin, PhD*

During the summer before ninth grade, which was considered high school in the Dexter, Michigan school district, we acquired two Border collie puppies we named Duke and Duchess. We grieved the loss of our collie Boots and Daddy did considerable research about the Border collie breed. It was funny because we set out to get one male puppy. However, Daddy fell in love with Duchess because she had so much white on her and was adorable. I could tell that in this one instance, his overwhelming desire superseded Mother's admonitions. Usually, he gave in to Mother and her regimented ideas and demands; however, this time, I was happy he won!

He built a 40-foot by 40-foot pen for them and moved the two-room, hinged-roof doghouse into it so the dogs would not have to be tied. Later on that fall, the puppies both got sick while Mother and Dad were on one of their square dance vacations. Even at fourteen years old, I was aware enough to know something was quite wrong. Their noses were hot; they were listless. I felt responsible for their well-being and didn't know what to do. Suddenly, I felt like an adult as I talked to Grandma Davis and told her I thought we should call the veterinarian, to which she agreed. The vet came out and gave them shots and gave me pills to administer to the pups, showing me how to do it. I had no idea what he charged my parents, but for the first time upon their arrival home from a trip, they were proud of me for how I handled the situation which caused me elation beyond the situation.

I embarked upon a program of obedience training when the pups were about four months old having obtained a simple, step-by-step approach book to follow. I got so engrossed in this project, while at the same time reading a book about a young man who was blinded by a firecracker accident on the Fourth of July, and his experiences in getting and bonding with a leader dog. I decided at once the career I wanted was training leader dogs to help the blind. I wrote to the Rochester School for the Blind, inquiring as to what courses I should take during high school to prepare me for future education in training leader dogs. Breathless, I awaited their reply.

Several days later, I was ecstatic to find their letter in the mail and ripped it open only to find their disheartening words: *We do not allow women to train our dogs because they get too attached to them.* Sadly, I was ill-prepared to deal with this form of rejection. I screamed; I cried; I pounded a tree; and I went running in to Mother, not caring if she saw my tears and desperation. I believed this devastation was based on something she would understand. She didn't hug me as she had when Boots died, but she listened and told me she felt badly I was so deeply disappointed. She encouragingly suggested I might want to investigate becoming a veterinarian instead.

That incident became a defining pivotal point in the years to come because at that juncture, I began hating that I was a girl. I wanted nothing to do with femininity – I had already been deprived of makeup, nylon stockings and ladylike shoes (had to wear bobby socks and saddle shoes) because of teasing Heidi to get off the bus early the year before. I told Mother over and over, "I hate being a girl; I don't want to get married and have children; I want to be a career woman; I want nothing to do with men." She was supportive of me saying, "That's okay. Nobody is expecting you to get married and have children; lots of women make their lives by embarking upon careers."

When I began ninth grade, however, she clobbered me with another significant deprivation. I wanted to continue my passion of playing in the band. I desperately needed the camaraderie and fellowship I found among the band members in the two previous years. It was the sense of family and the spirit of belonging I never achieved before. She removed me from band because it entailed after-school practice sessions saying, "I will not be a glorified taxi service." I went to my room and wept feeling a huge, gaping hole in my soul that was impossible to fill. I cried numerous times over the next several days.

Of course, my emotionality again became the laughing stock of the school when one day, during typing class, as I sat in the row directly beneath the windows, a severe electrical storm occurred. With the first FLASH-CRACK of the very close lightning, I screamed and ran from the room to the girls' lavatory, shaking and crying, which the other students found quite amusing. After that incident, for days I felt engulfed by much more than the dark thunderclouds of the rain storm because somehow I knew my reaction was unacceptable, yet there was no way I could contain it. I had a force operating within acting like a formidable foe.

As a substitute for band participation, I enrolled in home economics and even though I hated being female, I particularly enjoyed the sewing portion of the course. I wanted to learn how to do what Mother excelled at. That year at Christmas, I chose to make Mother a muumuu as my gift to her. I wanted it to turn out perfectly, as pristine as the beautiful dresses she fashioned to wear while square dancing and as lovely as the dresses she always made for us for the first day of school each year.

We had an old treadle sewing machine in the hallway to our upstairs bedroom and I spent the first part of our Christmas vacation diligently working on her surprise. I had a tiny transistor radio tuned to CKLW which played almost non-stop Beatles' music. I remember one cold, gray Saturday afternoon, as I sewed, feeling a growing anticipation of presenting my gift to her, hearing John Lennon sing, "So This Is Christmas." Suddenly, a flood of tears enveloped my being and I could not stop sobbing. I wanted to die. I wanted out. I felt like I lost not only the battle but the war that raged constantly at my core. Just as suddenly, I shuddered as I tried to understand what could possibly be causing this outburst, and the only thing I could think of was one of Mother's admonishments, *"If the teachers knew what I know about you, you'd flunk."*

I was inducted into the National Honor Society as a provisional member in the ninth grade. The day of the ceremony occurred after one of my not-so-successful evenings whereby I experienced more tears in my bedroom and felt like the gloom would never lift. I didn't know if Mother and Dad even cared enough to come to the assembly the next day, and I realized this achievement didn't make me feel any more loved, wanted or accepted.

We had a new superintendent of the school system that year and while each class was small and everyone knew each other, he hadn't yet learned who the students were. I was surprised when the ceremony began because there sat both of my parents, causing me to feel both a sense of fear and of gratification and pride. My maiden name was "Ralph" so when the superintendent announced the inductees and came to my name, he said, "Now I'm not sure if I have this right: RALPH HOLLY." The whole auditorium burst into an uproarious cacophony of laughter as I turned beet red, wishing I could melt into the floor, my legs like rubber, and rose to go to the stage to claim my certificate. My one opportunity to achieve a solemn mark of distinction was eradicated by an educated man making an ill-informed assumption about my name. I was humiliated and chagrined beyond words.

At the end of ninth grade, I was so determined to earn an "A" on my exams in each class that I studied for hours, reading and reviewing the typed notes I prepared from each presentation.

I was so deeply concerned I might fail (because to me, a "B" was failing since Mother said repeatedly, "All we expect is that you do your best," and I knew "my best" was an "A"), that I developed severe, sharp, gripping pains in my lower right side. I couldn't stand up, the pain was so bad, and Mother rushed me to the doctor, thinking I might be having an appendicitis attack. The doctor found nothing wrong and told her I might be experiencing a case of nerves because of pressures from school. She assured me I would do just fine. I do believe I did get "As" on each of my exams, but due to averaging of the grades for the entire year, the final result was "B-or-Better" honor roll. I vowed, *"I have three more years to achieve a four-point grade point average at least once – that's better than Heather ever did."* High scholarship became my identity. Academic achievement brought about my highs.

During the summer after ninth grade, two of the neighbor children were undergoing Confirmation classes in their Catholic faith. I became interested in Catholicism especially after having attended the funeral mass for our friend Mrs. Frasier. The girls would share their course material with me and I became so enthralled with the idea of becoming Catholic that I went behind Mother's back one day while she and I attended one of the many estate sales she pursued in her efforts to collect antique furniture to refinish. I purchased a gorgeous purple bead Rosary and a white leather-bound Catholic Missal and Bible. I learned how to pray the Rosary, collected the prayer cards from the neighbor girls and began to give myself Mass while sitting on my bedroom floor between the bed and the closet. At the same time, Heather was dating a young man of the Christian Science Faith and was going to meetings and reading everything Mary Baker Eddy wrote.

As I would ride on the lawn mower, cutting our nearly one acre of lawn, I would pray the Rosary over and over again feeling a connection to something much bigger than I was and deriving a rather remarkable sense of peace very similar to what I found when indulging in music or wandering through the woods and gazing into the burbling creek.

One night, I announced to my parents that I wanted to become Catholic and that the neighbor girls would help me, that their mom gladly offered to take me to Catechism and it would mean no extraneous transportation to them. I may as well have fired the shot that commenced World War III because they both hit the ceiling, becoming vehemently angry stating, "You WOULD pick the one we hate the most!" They had a hostility and hatred of the Roman Catholic Church which they literally poured out upon me with a vengeance, almost as if I deliberately set out to offend them. Their animosity had something to do with the wealth of the church and despising the Pope. I sheepishly trudged up to my room where I sobbed myself to sleep thinking, *"What ELSE can I do wrong? I can't even love God in the way my heart is calling me to."* I continued to pray the Rosary and give myself Mass knowing the peace I found could not be snatched away or minimized by their prejudice.

The summer I was 15, just before 10th grade, my parents did one of the most amazing things of my life. They enrolled me in horseback riding school in preparation for getting me my very own horse, Suzie-Q. I had begged them to get me a horse, saying I would forego all of the feminine things Heather had indulged in: formal dresses for proms, class rings, class pictures, yearbooks, even my senior trip. I was shocked when they agreed to purchase Suzie-Q, a 15-year-old quarter horse and Morgan mare from one of their friends. Suzie would be my sole responsibility along with intensive initial preparation by Daddy who built a special box stall with insulation and a sloped roof inside our rickety, leaky one-hundred-year-old barn.

I saved my allowance and lawn mowing money and purchased a beautiful English saddle, riding boots, bridle, curry comb, hoof pick and brushes. Now, in addition to our Border collies, I had another endearing project into which I could throw all of my energies and passion. I read everything I could about horsemanship and riding, jumping, grooming, stall maintenance and feeding. I willingly worked from dawn to dusk piling bales of hay and straw into the barn for Suzie.

Finally the day came for her to arrive! I had a minor setback: I had been very slow to develop and that was the first day of my menstrual period. I had cramps that doubled me up, which scared me because I often saw Mother experience a similar discomfort, one time so badly that I found her lying on the kitchen floor completely doubled up in pain. She gave me a Bufferin and told me they would pass.

I treated Suzie-Q like the queen of my life. For the next three years, she was my friend, my confidante, my shoulder to cry on as I would hug her neck after getting her all groomed and her stall cleaned, sobbing into her mane as she munched on her hay and Beatles' music filled the barn. *"They sing of love ... something I know not ... why is it so elusive?"* Little did I realize the object of my parents' love for me stood right before my eyes. That in getting Suzie-Q, they were showing me love in the best way they knew how.

One of the significant results of having Suzie-Q was the opportunity to bond with my little sister Heidi. She was too young to ride such a spirited horse by herself, yet she sincerely wanted to be involved with horsemanship at a limited level. I went out of my way to be kind to her and allowed her to sit on Suzie's back while she was tied in the crossties and I groomed her. This was very special for Heidi and helped us to be involved with something together. I would take Suzie out in her fenced pasture and put her on a 20-foot lunge line and let Heidi get on and ride around in a circle at the end of the line so Suzie would be in my control and not take off in a manner which Heidi could not control. The delight this brought Heidi made me feel a sense of "connectedness" to something positive.

As I progressed into 10th grade, I noticed I was developing intensely rigid and militant values. A couple of girls from our class had gotten pregnant, which disgusted me. I had no boyfriends, went on no dates nor did I socialize. I was adamantly against sex, smoking and drinking. It's almost as if I to take a definitive stand about morality to begin to find some kind of identity. This sense of righteousness would intensify and take a different form as time progressed.

I had few friends except the teachers who all liked me because I contributed to class discussions, asked questions revealing an interest in the subject matter, and I consistently performed well on all quizzes, tests and examinations. One thing I did do which endeared me to my classmates would be to wait until just before the end of class and then ask an insightful question which resulted in the teachers holding the class after the bell rang to answer my question in a meaningful way. Then they would forget to assign our homework!

I began reading rather intensely and supplementing my already precocious vocabulary. I'll never forget the trouble I caused one time in English class when someone said something rather inane and I spouted off with, "That was asinine!" The student was highly offended and whined to the teacher, "Are you going to let her talk like that? She just said I was an ass!" The teacher laughed and said I used a completely appropriate word and told the complaining student to look it up in the dictionary. I experienced a rather smug sense of victory.

Likewise, my classmates could not understand my choice of literature. When I read George Orwell's *Animal Farm*, they mercilessly teased me thinking I was still hung up in reading my animal stories. With confidence, I stood up and presented my book report and clearly instructed the class it was not a juvenile animal story. At this point, I was beginning to convert my sense of alienation, confusion, ongoing sorrow and anger into a rather defined outward self-righteousness and tendency toward being highly judgmental. I believed if I became more like my parents, especially my mother, perhaps they would accept my emotionality with less annoyance.

I was wrong. I tried to embark upon sewing projects. Since Mother was the expert seamstress, I would assemble a garment and then go downstairs to receive her approval. One time in particular, she commented that the plaid on a particular skirt wasn't quite matched on the side seam. I abruptly turned around and stormed up the stairs, slamming the door behind me. She shouted, "You come back down here and shut that door right"! I wanted to kill her. I was so angry that she had nothing positive to say, I went back down to gently shut the door behind me only to hear more of her criticism. "If you didn't want my opinion, then why did you ask? I'm sick and tired of your childish tantrums and I don't want to hear another word out of you." I never asked her for her opinion on my sewing projects again.

The summer before 11th grade, I tried to follow in my parents' footsteps down a new path. They had read Ayn Rand's *"The Fountainhead," "We the Living"* and *"Atlas Shrugged,"* and finally discovered an ideology that embodied their own rigid values and self-righteousness. Ayn Rand and her intellectual peer, Dr. Nathaniel Branden, were atheists. Dr. Branden would say during his national lecture tours, in response to God as the Creator of the Universe, "Existence exists. You cannot go around it; you cannot go under it; you cannot go over it; existence exists; it has always existed. The forms of existence have changed and evolved; the tree is the result of the seed of the parent tree. To posit a God as the Creator of all things is to push the argument back one step farther. You cannot have an infinite series of antecedent causes."

My parents became the business representatives for the Nathaniel Branden Institute for the Ann Arbor, Michigan and surrounding area. In this capacity, they held taped lecture series about philosophy, psychology and everything else the philosophy of Objectivism as purported in Ms. Rand's books was based on. Objectivism became their religion, and they presented me with a Christmas present of a five-year subscription to *"The Objectivist,"* a newsletter developed by NBI, as well as obtaining all of the back issues for me.

I read everything I could and tried to understand this new mode of thinking in an attempt to make sense out of the chaos in my mind. I became even more militant in my beliefs among my peers at school, trying to turn them all into atheistic capitalists. I found a certain degree of security in this new form of righteousness simply because for once I felt like I was on the same side of the fence as my parents, and I was indoctrinating myself in what appeared to make more sense than anything else I encountered. My sole objective was to try and calm the monster that kept turning me into a tearful, hostile, lonely, alienated misfit.

However, there were several aspects of Dr. Branden's psychological approach that perplexed me. One was his assertion that "emotions are automatic value responses." I tried to understand what he meant by that, yet I could never comprehend to what values I was responding when I would feel as if my whole body was exploding, as if there was fire running through my veins, and the incessant tears. Another claim Dr. Branden made was that "feelings are not tools of cognition." I agonized over how he would respond to my experiences of knowing Mrs. Frasier and Grandpa Ralph died before the family had been notified of those events.

Another affirmation Dr. Branden proclaimed continuously was that "actions have consequences." I never could understand how my parents would always hold that up to my face, yet when I would take actions such as working hard to get good grades, or take my mother out to lunch with my allowance money, or responsibly take care of my horse, I never experienced any "consequences" of good behavior. I never received any kind of "well done," or "we love you and cherish you" kind of feedback. I always felt under the gun for my flaws and defects that I somehow knew were not directly within my control.

As I progressed into 11th grade, four significant scenarios unfolded that made it a rather momentous year. The first was my United States history teacher. He was the most animated, dynamic teacher I ever had. He was able to bring the history of our country alive in a way that made one realize history is not about dates and events but rather, about people, personalities and their interactions. He employed a learning tool called the "group test" whereby he would select the four or five brightest kids in the class as team leaders and then would divide up the rest of the class into those four or five groups. He would present the same questions to each group, who would discuss and compile the answers. I was always the "A" student, so everyone wanted to be in my group and thus receive an "A." Suddenly, I had friends! It was rewarding to feel wanted and needed.

Mr. Torp exuded kindness and concern and took a special interest in me. He became the first person I could truly bond with and confide in. I spent hours during the school year, meeting him before classes started, talking to him about how awful I felt most of the time, how I wanted to kill myself, how confused and alienated I was and how I believed something was wrong with me. I was able to have my emotions without judgment or chastisement. He kept our conversations confidential and didn't reveal what I said to my parents or counselors. Although the summer following my junior year, he did go to work at Ford Motor Company where he met my father and had some interesting discussions with him about Objectivism, capitalism and other such philosophical pursuits.

The second interesting and formulating situation occurred when the school brought in an exchange student from Budapest, Hungary, Marta Rubin. Because I was receiving all "As" in my English class, I was exempted from having to write a term paper and instead was allowed to spend my English classes sitting in the lobby and talking to Marta in an effort to teach her English. This was a cultural exchange I found so immensely rewarding that when the semester concluded, we began writing letters to each other and have stayed in contact ever since. My affiliation with Marta, who was from a Communist country, would later result in a stressful conflict once I arrived at college.

What I discovered during these exchanges with Mr. Torp and Marta was that even though I was extremely troubled, knowing they were interested in what I had to say and were concerned about my well-being, allowed me to reach out and dispel some of the despair that lurked at my core.

The third rather powerful event that took place in my junior year was the junior play. Instead of presenting one three-act play as they always had, they produced three one-act plays. I auditioned for and received the leading role in the play, "*Sorry, Wrong Number!*" When I announced to Mother I had landed the starring role, she retorted, "Well, I don't think you can hardly compete with Agnes Morehead. I highly doubt you'll be able to pull that one off." Such confidence ... more negativity ... no encouragement.

The weekend after we received our playbooks, we had one of the most intense snowstorms of my life (February 1965) which resulted in two "snow days" off school. I took that opportunity to learn all my lines – remember my memory I've alluded to? Dear little sister Heidi patiently helped me, which I thought was so gracious of a nine-year-old. She spent hours with me, reading the lines preceding mine while I memorized my lines.

When we had the first play practice, the director was amazed I knew all my lines. We were practicing in the biology room and the concluding part of the play included the lines: "*He's coming; he's coming up the stairs; he's going to get me ...*" and then the leading character screams in stark terror at the realization she's going to be murdered. I screamed with everything I had in me and terrified myself that I was able to scream with such a vengeance. I knew that scream represented much more than merely acting the part in the play. It was so shrill and devastating that people from all over the school came down to the biology room to see what was going on. The director merely told them I had seriously gotten into my part.

On opening night of the play, older sister Heather, who was studying speech and dramatic arts in college, brought her drama coach with her. After the play, this drama professor, the dean of the dramatic arts department at Albion College, told my parents, sisters and me she had never seen someone so young able to incite such fear within an audience. I never received any praise from my parents. At that time, I had not heard of Arthur Janov and his book, *"Primal Scream,"* but acting that part in the play allowed me to get something out that had been festering inside me for years.

The fourth event occurred during the summer after my junior year and was another tragedy – another loss. At my mother's insistence a couple of years earlier, we gave one of our Border collie dogs, Duchess, away because she insisted on biting at and trying to herd Suzie-Q as I was riding. Herding is a Border collie's natural instinct, but Mother thought I might get hurt. Duke remained our only dog, a loyal sweetheart. One day he disappeared and I was devastated. I rode my bicycle for miles around the countryside, calling and looking for him. My father heard the University of Michigan was doing experiments on dogs and were picking up strays and cutting off their feet to keep them from escaping while they performed their inhumane experiments. Dad thought that since Duke was so friendly, he would have easily gotten in a stranger's car. I almost vomited when I thought that may have been his fate. I cried for nights when I realized Duke was not coming back.

During my senior year, I thought I had begun making some friends. However, when it came time to select a homecoming queen, remember I was skinny, had straight and stringy hair because my mother only allowed me to wash it once a week. She was afraid more frequent washings would make it more oily and she didn't want the inconvenience of moving her clothes in the laundry room. As a joke, the class nominated me to be homecoming queen, and I was selected. Then they told me this was just a joke and selected one of the more beautiful girls in the class. This mean-spirited contrivance only served to make me hate myself more and set in motion a general distrust of people that I found to be a major obstacle in the coming years.

I embarked on extemporaneous speaking and won several awards. I won a dictionary for taking first place in one impromptu speaking event. I achieved a four-point-zero grade point average for the entire year, thus meeting the most important goal of my schooling. I missed no school that year and my ranking in the class was tied at third place with a 3.834 overall grade point average. I was even able to go on the senior trip to Washington, D.C. and felt like I belonged with the group who went.

At the end of my senior year, I went to the eye doctor to have my glasses adjusted. He sternly warned my mother I would never make it through college because he could somehow see through the nerves of my eyes that I was a highly agitated, unstable young girl. He told Mother he thought I had serious problems that should be attended to. She disregarded his cautions.

A week before graduation, we sold Suzie-Q because I was going to be working at Ford Motor Company the summer before college to help defray some of the cost; thus, I could not take care of her effectively. I was extremely sad to see her go, but equally pleased that for once, the following fall, I could leave home and make new friends and embark upon the challenge of college all of the teachers warned us of – that it would be much more difficult than high school.

I met a gentleman, Bob ("Boz") Berning who was 6 feet, 9 inches tall, at the Nathaniel Branden Institute lectures and we went on one date to a James Bond movie, which I hated. We were chaperoned by his father because he lost his license due to speeding. I was desperate to "belong" and attend my senior prom. But Mother adhered strictly to the "girls-don't-call-boys" rule and I had no way of letting Boz know about the senior prom. So one night while Mother and Daddy were out at our dance hall teaching a dance lesson, I called a girlfriend and asked her to call Boz and let him know of our prom so in this way, if he wanted to ask me, at least he'd know about it. I felt conniving and manipulating, but I was desperate.

He did call and asked me to go. Since I promised my parents I wouldn't request them to buy me any formals, I borrowed a prom dress from my sister Heather. It was about two inches too short and looked ridiculous, but at least I got to dress up like a lady, which was extremely foreign to me. However, I was determined to override my awkwardness and fears and try to fit in with the rest of my class.

We went to the dance, but he didn't know how and we stepped on each other's toes. At the end of the evening, when he brought me home, he kissed me. In the process, he bit my upper lip rather hard. That further served to make me despise men and see them as bumbling idiots.

Two nights before graduation, the school held an awards night. I was supposed to receive three awards and I asked my parents to please take me. They refused because they had to attend to a Nathaniel Branden Institute lecture that night and told me if I wanted to go, I'd have to find a ride. Fortunately, one of the girls in the village of Delhi was going, had her drivers' license and agreed to take me. The emptiness I felt that night as I received my awards with my parents absent was something I grappled with for numerous years.

Then came the big night: graduation. I was so ready to leave high school and all of its painful and frustrating memories and move on to the new life of college. My one girlfriend picked me up and took me to graduation, but my parents did attend. After the ceremony, Pat and I drove around to many of the after-parties being held and I had my first drink of alcohol: Southern Comfort. I loved it! And I had a second drink at the next party.

By dawn, we closed out the night's events by going out to the farm where the girl who bought Suzie-Q lived. I was appalled by what I saw. Suzie no longer had a nice box stall to protect her from the severe elements of Michigan winters but rather, only a little rickety lean-to for shelter. She came trotting over to the fence and whinnied in recognition of me and I fed her a carrot and petted her. I felt sorrow she was no longer my companion and friend.

During the summer after graduation before I started college, I worked on the assembly line at Ford Motor Company and heard language I never heard before! I began having an awful dream about Suzie-Q that a huge snowstorm had come and I couldn't get in the barn to give her food and water. And that I forgot about her. When I finally got the barn door opened, there was nothing left of Suzie but the skeleton of her bones. That nightmare continued for at least 30 years.

That summer the family was entirely engrossed in another event: Older sister Heather was getting married. During the excitement of the planning for Heather's wedding, I was admitted to Eastern Michigan University (EMU) in Ypsilanti, Michigan for the fall semester. The family went from one transition to another because after the wedding, the primary focus became getting me ready for college. I was thrilled that finally I would enter the doors of higher education; however, the earlier caution of my eye doctor that I would most likely have a breakdown once I left home lurked in the back of my mind as a potentially impossible obstacle to overcome. I only hoped he was wrong.

Chapter 4: Dismissed During Darkness

While you may not think so you are playing it well. Winston Churchill wrote a book about Britain in 1940 and called it Their Finest Hour. *When I was young I thought it was a stupid title, because at that time Britain was losing the war. How could getting blitzed be their finest hour? Now as an adult I understand. Even though things were not going well for them, they played well and eventually won. It is at these times when you have to rise to the occasion. I know it is no fun, but you can only be heroic when you are up against it.*

– William J. Dubin, PhD

While I was rather concerned about leaving home and moving into the dorm at EMU, I was also quite excited to begin this new life. I saw college as a privilege and challenge, and was eager to leave my old self behind, as well as to get out from under the stringent watchful eye of my mother. My roommate was a sophomore who smoked Newport menthol cigarettes and was well established in her social life. I didn't see much of her, but it wasn't long after classes began that I tried puffing on one of her cigarettes, although I didn't inhale.

One of the regrets of my life occurred during the first few days of orientation of freshmen. I indicated on my application an interest in track and field because I ran the quarter mile in several track meets during my junior and senior years in high school. I also ran in the first women's cross country track meet in the state of Michigan, after which I developed walking pneumonia. Because of this interest, the track coach at EMU sent me an invitation addressed to RALPH HOLLY to meet at the field house for a reception for entering freshmen who may be interested in track. I should have shown up and introduced myself as "HOLLY RALPH – are you still interested?" But I didn't – I could have had fun with that.

I had no problems getting to my classes and carrying out my assignments as I was motivated to learn as much as I could to make the dean's list for scholastic aptitude, again, to do better than Heather had in college. My writing skills greatly impressed the freshman English composition instructor who gave me an "A" therefore exempting me from second semester composition during which freshman students had to prepare a term paper. The meteorology aspect of my earth science class fascinated me, so college was fulfilling.

My dormitory, Wise Hall, was a magnet to house most of the Jewish girls from the Jewish sections in the Detroit area. I made friends easily and found the Jewish girls to be bright, humorous and down to earth. They weren't "catty" like so many of the girls in high school had been. I also made friends with a brilliant Jewish young man. All of the girls tried to tell me Barry was "strange," and that his father died and he never got over it. They also told me he was gay. Barry and I developed a rather strange bond. He designed jewelry and gave me a beautiful hand-crafted gold ring in friendship. I found myself developing an attraction for him I'd never felt before – I was turned on. It wasn't long before I found myself wanting to experience him sexually, but he showed no such interest.

He had a friend who tried to take me under his wing and explain to me Barry was rather disturbed and I shouldn't have expectations of him. One night, I learned just how disoriented and mixed up Barry was. He wanted to take me outside on a hike late one full-moon winter night because he told me he was waiting for his relatives to show up from Venus. The really sad thing was I believed him! I finally felt like I had found someone who was as disconnected from others as I was and I felt safe with him. He understood my ongoing sadness and he held my hand as we walked and talked, neither of us making much sense. Yet the comfort I felt with him was profound.

About the middle of that first semester, my roommate joined a sorority and moved out so I was alone. My best friend from high school was also going to EMU and stayed in another dorm in the complex. When Barbara moved out, Pat moved into my room. I was always saddened during the weekends because she went home to visit her family, yet my parents would not let me come home. I had to wait until Thanksgiving before they came to get me for the holiday weekend.

This visit proved to be a disaster. I tried to tell my parents I was bored with my studies because they were too easy, that I didn't know if I wanted to stay with my declared history major following in my high school history teacher's footsteps, and I was confused. I wanted to change my major to speech and dramatic arts, which I implemented at the beginning of the second semester.

During the Thanksgiving weekend, I got up feeling despondent and Mother would say, "Well look who got up on the wrong side of the bed this morning!" I tried to be cheerful, but I missed Barry and the comfort I felt with him, while I felt unwelcome at home.

I got in an argument with Mother about something and she tried to take the upper hand. As she did, I made a facial expression to her whereby I rolled my eyes like, "Here we go again." She hit me as hard as she could and I ducked, causing her to land a sharp slap on the left side of my head, rupturing my eardrum, while snapping at me, "You can at least act like you respect me, even if you don't." I wanted to choke her, but I was effective at restraint.

As they took me back to the dorm at the end of the weekend, I got my mail and among the letters was one from my girlfriend Marta Rubin in Budapest, Hungary. Daddy looked at me with fire and hostility and said to me, "You will NOT write letters to that Communist girl. If I catch you writing any her more letters your college funds will be CUT OFF. Do you hear me? The Communists have killed millions of people and I'll not have you in cohorts with one."

I replied, "But Daddy, SHE hasn't killed anybody; she's just a pianist and is interested in teaching other children how to play the piano. You have Catholic friends and the Roman Catholics killed hundreds of people during the Spanish Inquisition, but that doesn't keep you from having them as friends, does it?"

He said, "That's different – it was hundreds of years ago. The Communists are usurping freedom and taking lives the world over and I refuse to permit you to write to one." My familiar sense of "somehow I'm in trouble again" intensified with a force that would become seriously destructive in the coming weeks and months.

I completed the first semester with a 3.5 grade point average yet I was restless, sad and bored. Shortly after the Christmas holidays, a friend of my older sister's, who was a junior at EMU, told me about this gentleman who was in the hospital having had major intestinal surgery from which he almost died. He was recovering well, but was quite despondent over how sick he had been and what a long road he had ahead of him. Louise gave me his number at the hospital and told me I should call him to brighten his spirits, which I did.

For the next several days, we would call each other and spend hours on the phone each evening. He had an extremely sexy voice and I learned he was in my English literature class of several hundred students. Upon his discharge from the hospital, he told me he'd meet me before the literature class. Upon first glance, I was stunned at how dashingly handsome he was and I was instantly attracted to him. I wanted to go out with this man – I wanted ALL of him! We talked after class that day and on several successive days the class convened.

I had a job working Friday and Saturday nights at the front desk for one of the men's dorms. It was lonely and quiet during the weekends because most of the students went home; whereas, I could not because it was too much effort for my parents to travel the whole 30 miles to come and get me and take me back. I felt like I was out of sight and out of mind.

As I'd sit there doing my homework reading during the long weekend hours, I'd fantasize about being with Ron and how wonderful it would be to have a date with him. I felt rather empty and confused as to why he hadn't asked me out. One night, I read a movie review of the thriller, "*Psycho*," which was being held somewhere on campus during the coming weeks. In the review, it stated, "*Not to be seen by persons who are emotionally disturbed.*" I thought, "*Well, I guess I'd better see it then because that way I'll <u>know</u> if I'm 'emotionally disturbed' for once and for all*"!

I didn't see Ron for the whole following week. I found myself slipping deeper and deeper into depression, and I wore all black and sunglasses everywhere, day and night, so people couldn't see my eyes. I knew they were beginning to appear dark, and I was afraid I looked crazy. I felt as though I were slowly falling; time began to feel warped and an intensely dark storm was closing in around me. All sense of joy and light-heartedness escaped and I kept feeling as though something awful was about to happen. I somehow knew something quite bad was surrounding me, but nothing in my objective reality was actually harmful or dangerous. I was experiencing a deep sense of grief, like someone very close to me died, and I wandered aimlessly around campus, feeling hopelessly lost.

On the Friday before the showing of "*Psycho*," after literature class, the fatal event took place. I saw Ron outside the lecture hall talking to a very attractive brunette and they hugged and walked off hand-in-hand together. I later learned she had been his girlfriend all along. He never mentioned her and I felt I had been played for a freshman fool. I felt used and abused and ... ABANDONED! I had been tossed aside with not so much as a "good-bye" or a "thank you."

I skipped my next class and went back to my dorm, crawled up onto my top bunk, buried my head in my pillow, pounded it and sobbed and cried deeper than I ever had before. All of my fantasies and hopes were dashed, scattered to the wind. I felt like I was suddenly NOTHING. I wanted to die, to slice my wrists for real this time. But I started writing poetry instead. All night long, I wrote poetry and began assembling it into a book, cutting out pictures from magazines that matched the themes in the poems. I couldn't sleep; I cried and wrote and cut out pictures and glued the whole thing together. This focus kept me from killing myself.

The following weekend I went to see "Psycho." Of course, the movie was terrifying, but I had to stay and see how it turned out. I realized I did possess a trait that would often serve me well in the —following years – an unending curiosity about what tomorrow might bring. I am convinced I incorporated the old saying, "curiosity killed the cat" as a reverse-motivation mantra to which I responded, "*Not me!*"

After experiencing the gut-wrenching, gripping trauma of that movie, I began to have more and worse nightmares while my depression, hopelessness and devastation grew ever deeper. At the time, the Black Power movement had taken on significant impact in every area of college life, and our literature professor asked us to attend a rally. I refused to go saying, "*Nobody really wants to be white; otherwise they wouldn't have invented suntan lotion!*" I was simply growing more hostile to everything.

We had to read numerous books in the literature class. I found myself making judgments about the books merely from their titles. Eric Hoffer's "*The Ordeal of Change*" I found particularly depressing, but even more so was "*The Stranger*" by Albert Camus. The professor insisted on referring to the candle imagery in that book as a phallic symbol that evoked passionate hostility and intolerance in me. I wrote an essay refuting his assertion and made a similar presentation in my public speaking class. I became vehemently opposed to any attempts by the professors to manipulate my thoughts, impressions or ideas.

For the remainder of the semester just prior to mid-term exams, I again participated in extemporaneous speaking, attending several forensic events around the state. An upper-classman from Sierra Leone, son of a dignitary, took a distinct liking to me. He appreciated and was attracted to my fiery presentations and my gutsy personality. There was no sense of romance, just mutual appreciation. For reasons I did not comprehend, I felt a sense of safety in his presence. That would dramatically change the following summer.

By a strange stroke of genius, I completed my mid-term exams and embarked upon spring break carrying a 4.0 grade point average for the first half of my second semester as a freshman. While home during the break, I contemplated suicide and wrote more dark poetry. I stayed in my room almost the entire time, realizing this awful, foreboding, black mood was lasting longer than it ever had and was growing deeper with each passing day.

My parents met a psychologist named Dr. Roger Callahan through their affiliation with the Objectivist philosophy and the Nathaniel Branden Institute (NBI). His practice was about an hour's drive from Ann Arbor and I spent my spring break trying to figure out how I might be able to see Dr. Callahan to get some help from this "thing" I knew was much bigger and more powerful than I was. I prayed; I cried; I dreaded going back to campus, yet I didn't want to stay home.

Shortly after the second semester began, Ron, the upper classman who dumped me in favor of his real girlfriend, agreed to meet me in his car after literature class. I tried to talk to him about the sinister, oppressive feelings I was having, and how I felt I was losing my mind. When I opened my mouth and tried to talk, all that came out were screams of the same intensity I uttered during the play, "*Sorry, Wrong Number.*" I could not stop screaming as he held me and acted totally helpless. He told me I should go to the student health center and try to talk to someone there but I was terrified to talk to anyone whom I did not explicitly know or trust.

A few days later, I wrote a suicide note in which I told anyone who might read it that I was in too much pain to go on living, that

I could no longer function in the academic environment, that I could not think any more, and that I embraced the arms of death as the only viable solution to the depths of despair and misery to which I had plummeted. I left the note on the dashboard of Ron's car and resolutely walked down the railroad tracks in the hope that a train would come and demolish me.

I walked and cried for well over an hour as darkness began to settle. Feeling futile that I couldn't even be destroyed by a train, I turned around and slowly made my way back to my dorm. When I walked in, the entire lobby was in a bustle and the first thing I saw was my father standing there, talking to the dorm's house mother. They both turned and saw me and immediately escorted me to my room, commanding me to pack up all of my things so my father could take me home. The house mother said, "You are being dismissed from this university because we are not a baby sitter." Solemnly, I helped my father load the car with all my possessions and rode home in silence.

When we arrived my father said, "Go sit down at the kitchen table and don't do or say anything until I get back inside." He had to go out to the dance hall and turn the NBI tape over for the attendees at one of the Objectivist lecture series. I remember thinking, *"Something else is always more important than I am. I am nothing to them, never have been and never will be. I am just plain NOTHING"*! He came back into the house several minutes later and sat down at the table with me and asked Mother to join us. The first words out of his mouth were, "Now that you've ruined your chances for higher education, what do you plan to do with yourself?"

I replied, "Well, I guess I'd better get a job so I can pay you rent." They responded that I should research all of my Objectivist literature by Dr. Nathaniel Branden and Ayn Rand and that through those writings, I would find out how to think appropriately and I would be able to live effectively. They believed that literature would solve all my problems. What they didn't realize is that thinking rationally while in the midst of a bipolar depressive episode is generally unlikely without competent psychotherapeutic assistance.

That was the end of that conversation as they told me to go upstairs to bed while Daddy unloaded my belongings from the car. As I slowly made my way up to my bedroom, my mind screamed at me, *"Ask them if you can please see Dr. Callahan ... you have nothing to lose ... you've lost everything ... remember the song,* "Turn, Turn, Turn" – *to everything there is a season, a time for every purpose under heaven" ... maybe it's time they will see you really do need help; maybe now they will understand. Pray for the strength to ask them ..."*

I knew the next day my father was returning to campus to speak with the dean of student affairs who had made the recommendation that I be dismissed. All day I sat on the window seat in our front room and tried to read the Objectivist literature but the words swam before my eyes. I felt like a frightened, caged bird in desperate need of freedom. I couldn't talk to Mother; I was numb.

Late in the afternoon, little sister Heidi came home from school and bounced through the door. Upon seeing me, she said, "Holly, what are you doing home?"

I replied, "Because I'm sick."

She quipped back, "You don't look sick – sick in the head, maybe."

Mother, from the living room laughed and chided, "Not a bad observation for a 10-year-old, wouldn't you say?"

I wanted to kill them both. Breathless, I awaited Daddy's arrival, hoping against all odds that Dr. Lawrence would inspire him to do something to help me. He was late getting home, and when he did, he asked Mother and me to come to the kitchen. We all sat down and he asked me, "Well, has any of your reading today set you straight?"

"No, Daddy, I can't concentrate. I don't even know what I'm reading. None of it makes any sense to me..." I stopped, gulped, and terrified, made myself continue. "I was hoping maybe you could take me to see Dr. Callahan."

Almost before I finished speaking, he bellowed, "If you think your mother and I are going to spend that kind of money, you have another thing coming." I could not believe my ears. He might as well have beaten me with a stick.

The next day they departed for one of their square dancing sojourns to another part of the country, leaving Heidi and me in the care of Grandma Davis. I was consumed with guilt, confusion and desperation. In an effort to do something beneficial and occupy myself, I volunteered to make Heidi a dress for a special occasion to which she'd been invited. I measured her and laid out the pattern upstairs and cut out the dress. Over the next few days, I made good progress in sewing her dress and it came time to try it on her for various fittings.

She had put her hair in rollers and the dress had to be put on over her head. We were in the bathroom where there was a mirror so she could see herself in the dress, and I tried to gently pull it over her head and face so I wouldn't disturb the rollers. I had no earthly idea Heidi had a fear of anything covering her face and my taking my time was solely out of consideration for the efforts she had made to curl her hair.

Heidi started crying and threw a fit that both startled and angered me and somehow, I flipped my hand back and knocked the light fixture cover off. As it crashed down to the sink, Grandma Davis marched into the bathroom shouting at me, "I HATE you." I was completely defenseless because one more time, my actions somehow caused an uproar and further unpleasantness. I did not know where there were any razor blades, or I would have gone upstairs and slit my wrists. As it was, I found a bottle of Midol and took several of them, hoping they would dull the pain that engulfed my entire being.

I went upstairs and hibernated in my room not even caring if I ate any supper. Soon, my ears started ringing in an awful tinnitus because of the pills and I felt even worse. The next day I went down to our neighbors' and asked their daughter if I could speak to their mother. I knew Mrs. Watkins was a nurse, and thought maybe she could help me. I had to talk to someone. I knew her husband was a psychiatrist and believed she would at least be able to listen to me without hurting me further. I told her everything that happened and I told her I believed the time had come for me to leave home. She was extremely kind but rather noncommittal and told me that if there was anything she could do to help to let her know.

Just her presence as an external ear was more helpful than she could ever have imagined because it provided a sounding board upon which I could get outside the raging storm inside my head and hear myself at least making some sense. I realized as I talked to her that I was nothing but an irritant in our family's household and I believed remaining there would only serve to exacerbate my depression, desperation and desolation. I decided that as soon as my parents came home from their trip, I would not even give them time to reprimand me for trying to suffocate Heidi; I would tell them I wanted to get out immediately.

They arrived home late in the evening after I had gone to bed so Grandma Davis had plenty of time to tell them how badly I behaved. When I got up the next day and told them I wanted to move out and support myself, I have never seen two people act so fast on my behalf in my life. Daddy got me a paper and I found several jobs I thought I could do. Mother took me on a job interview and I was hired by the first employer with whom I interviewed. In one week I would start working at the University of Michigan Horace H. Rackham Graduate School, filing transcripts and answering telephones, making $365 per month.

The next day, I again reviewed the paper and found a tiny, furnished, efficiency two-room apartment on the second floor of an old house next to the Handicraft Furniture right in the center of town within walking distance from the graduate school. Mother took me to see it, and paid my first month's rent of $65 and a deposit. The house had five tenants, four of whom shared the one bathroom upstairs.

She then took me shopping and bought me everything I would need to set up housekeeping such as an electric frying pan, as there were no kitchen privileges; silverware; iron and ironing board; and food for the shared refrigerator. Grandma Davis gave me a set of dishes, bedding and towels. Within a week, they moved me in to my own place and I was left to support myself. Daddy's parting words to me after I was settled in were, "If you lose your job because of your own idiotic actions, you are on your own. We will NOT help you; you CANNOT come home. If you lose your job because of economic conditions or things beyond your control, we will be here to help."

As they drove off, I thought, *"There is no way I will EVER ask them for ANYTHING. As God is my witness, I WILL take care of myself."*

Chapter 5: Dazzle Them With Brilliance

One of the problems of bipolar is the polarization of self image: "I am the greatest person who ever lived or I am the worst person who ever lived." The primary problem is that these over reactions mask the truth. Don't get sidetracked by taking the "I'm worthless, it's hopeless" beliefs seriously.

— William J. Dubin, PhD

I must say it was exciting to finally have my own place. Yes, it was small with a shared bathroom and no cooking facilities, but I began to learn the art of improvisation. The first weekend I was there I felt at home in that little furnished efficiency apartment. It had a main living room with a lovely three-sided window overlooking the HandiCraft Furniture Store, a tiny bedroom off to the left that was completely filled with a three-quarter-size bed, dresser and nightstand, and a huge walk-in closet off to the right. I searched the newspapers and found a tremendous bargain on a used refrigerator so I wouldn't have to share with the other four ladies in the house. I became rather ingenious about heating up frozen dinners by placing them in the electric frying pan partially filled with boiling water. In addition, I quickly found an excellent deal on a black and white television set with stand – my very first TV set! To make the little place my sanctuary, I also purchased a good quality stereo system at a moderate price. By this point, I had only one day left before I would start working at my first full-time job. I didn't know which was more engulfing: fear or excitement because both were intensely present.

My employment at the University of Michigan was within walking distance of the apartment – approximately ten blocks. I was hired to fill a dual role: receptionist and transcript file clerk. Within the first few weeks, my first severe panic attacks since the 4-H camp episode began. I did not know how to answer the callers' questions nor did I know whom to refer them to. My supervisor was inept at training me, and she had an abrupt personality that intimidated me. I found it stressful to perform both functions – trying to be back in the transcript room filing transcripts and dashing out to answer the phones as they rang at the same time. It was not long before the crying jags began much to my total chagrin and embarrassment.

After about two months, from May through July 1967, I began seeking other employment and found a position in a typing pool at the Commission on Professional and Hospital Activities (CPHA). All I had to do all day long was use a dictaphone to transcribe tapes. I enjoyed this work because it was self-contained, and it was more challenging to try to increase my typing speed so I could type as fast as people talked. While I still had a panic attack every morning, the walk to this job was shorter than to U of M, and I made friends with one of the girls in the typing pool who graciously showed me the routines and was kind to me.

However, the panic attacks intensified and even though I didn't have the out-of-the-blue crying jags at work, they often consumed me in the evenings. I soon found a general practitioner and told him of my symptoms. He gave me Stelazine for the anxiety and Seconal to help me sleep. I found both to be somewhat helpful. But it wasn't long before I realized "something" was still seriously wrong. I decided I would somehow find a way to seek Dr. Roger Callahan, the Objectivist psychotherapist whom I had met while attending some of the Nathaniel Branden lecture series in Detroit. My extemporaneous speaking friend whom I met at Eastern Michigan University had a roommate named Bob who took an interest in me. It was merely a distant friendship, but for some reason Bob acted rather protective of me and when I asked him if he would drive me the 45-minute trip from Ann Arbor to Southfield, he agreed to do so. I contacted Dr. Callahan's office and made an appointment after which I was scared to death because I didn't know what to say to him.

I don't remember that first visit with Dr. Callahan other than feeling an immense sense of relief that I was suddenly in a situation whereby I could pour out all of the confusion, fear and frustration, and not be afraid of consequences. He invited me to attend his Saturday morning group therapy and I remember sharing some of Mother's behavior with the group and one gentleman said to me, "Did you ever belt her one?"

After about three weeks of therapy, during a group session, Dr. Callahan announced he was moving to New York City and that Dr. William C. Lawrence bought his practice. Dr. Lawrence was the former dean of student affairs at Eastern Michigan University who recommended I be dismissed! I began to scream hysterically and was told to stop and control myself. I felt betrayed and abandoned. I told Dr. Callahan that Dr. Lawrence asked that I be dismissed from EMU and that I was terrified of Dr. Lawrence, and Dr. Callahan indicated he would apprise Dr. Lawrence of our brief therapeutic involvement, telling me he thought I would be comfortable with him.

That weekend, Bob, who had been taking me to therapy, had a party at which I consumed almost a fifth of Sloe Gin and had to be carried out to the car and taken home. I spent the entire night in the bathtub heaving my insides out and screaming so loudly that the police came to determine if I was all right. One of the ladies in the house said I was "just scared."

The next night, Dr. Callahan made arrangements for Dr. Lawrence to drive me to the final group therapy session. It was July 20, 1967, the night after the severe race riots occurred in Detroit and there was a 10 p.m. curfew. While I was still so sick and hung over beyond reason, I did feel comfortable with Dr. Lawrence during the commute to and from Dr. Callahan's office, and I decided it would be acceptable to try pursuing my psychotherapy with him. Because he lived in Ypsilanti, which was much closer than the Southfield office, I could take a bus to my sessions with him and not have to impose any further on Bob, who was rather put out with me over my drunken behavior at his party.

In the midst of all of this, shortly after starting the job in the CPHA typing pool, I discovered a Saturday afternoon diversion. On HBO was a folk guitar course series – the Laura Webber Folk Guitar Essentials. I immediately bought a guitar and enrolled in the lessons, purchasing all three of the instruction books that accompanied the course which included a series of three six-week lessons. Every Saturday afternoon at 3, I would park myself in front of the TV and watch the lesson, and I'd practice faithfully for the rest of the week. This involvement was my therapy; it captured my very soul, giving me a sense of identity and a disciplined, focused structure. I was rather sad when the sessions were completed. However, I began to play records and listen to the radio practically non-stop because the music provided some degree of peace and something to absorb myself with.

Within two months of beginning my employment in the typing pool, I applied for and received a promotion to branch secretary for the medical records department. There was more stress in this position because I had to answer to about five people and perform all their statistical typing. However, the personnel in this department were all fascinating individuals to observe and get to know. I made friends with the lady who sat next to me, and had several pleasant outings with her and her husband who was completing his internship to be a medical doctor. They had motorcycles which inspired me to purchase my first motorcycle – a 90 cc Honda "step-through" bike. At last, I had "wheels!" This was achieved by my first bank loan making me proud I earned the right to have credit. Now I no longer had to ride my bicycle everywhere I went that was too far to walk. I was in heaven as Don and Judy and I would go biking out to the country on the weekends. I discovered a sense of freedom and "one-with-nature" on the motorcycle that I found exhilarating.

On Sunday nights all during the first two years of living on my own, my parents and little sister Heidi came to pick me up and take me to McDonald's for hamburgers. This was a long-standing routine in our family that we all thoroughly enjoyed. One Sunday night, my father came over by himself and told me he owed me an apology. He said, "I know your mother was way too severe in her methods of dealing with you, and I know she was causing you harm. However, I also knew you eventually had the option of leaving and finding your own way. I couldn't leave – I had to live with her so I elected not to try to intervene and encounter her criticism of me. I'm sorry I didn't do more to stand up for you. I will contribute $50 a month toward your therapy."

While I thought it was honorable of him to admit his shortcomings and I respected his humility, I also felt a sense of annoyance he had been so "spineless" as to not help me when he knew I needed his intervention. However, I was deeply appreciative of his willingness to assist in some small way financially, feeling he was at least trying to accept me and offer the best he was able to.

I continued my therapy with Dr. Lawrence on a weekly basis, and also attending a couple of group sessions during the week which I generally did not like. One of the things Dr. Lawrence stressed was, "**Words have meaning.**" I used to accuse him of "yelling at me," when in fact, he was merely pointing out errors in my thinking. He was quick to help me realize that any time I experienced the sense he was criticizing me, I would retort he was "yelling at me." And he would remind me that "words have meaning," and ask me to consider my use of the term "yelling." This began to help me become aware of my sensitivity to any form of confrontation.

Also, I had an inordinately difficult time making decisions about anything. He pointed out that often, in the decision process, one choice or another would be "**Just noticeable difference**," that either way the decision might go, the consequences would be minimal. This was somewhat helpful as I was faced with future decisions.

One such decision occurred during the spring of 1968 when I decided to go back to college at EMU and enrolled in two night school classes, advanced public speaking and algebra, both of which I completed with a 4.0 grade point average. I found it quite difficult to work and attend night school, but was pleased I added six more credit hours to my transcript.

Another decision could have produced disastrous results. I kept telling Dr. Lawrence I hated men and never wanted to be involved sexually; I thought sex was highly overrated and I never wanted to indulge with a man. My Sierra Leone friend began visiting with me Sunday evenings. Although I was brought up not to be prejudiced and to be "color-blind," I found it very strange when my parents would drop me off on Sunday nights from our jaunts to McDonald's, if Adams were sitting on my doorstep waiting for me, they'd drop me off up the street or around the corner from my house as if to say, *"No daughter of ours is going to date a BLACK man!"*

One Sunday, Adams appeared in the middle of the afternoon and sat in my large, overstuffed chair and asked me to come over and sit on his lap. I made a flippant and rather dangerous decision to allow his advances. He was hugging me, which I thought was all right, but then he carried me over to the bed and removed my clothes and before I knew it, was on top of me and penetrated—no foreplay, nothing. I was totally indignant, felt raped, and didn't know what to do. Suddenly he reached his ejaculation and shuddered and fell limp across me. I was terrified because, being totally naïve as to what happens during sexual intercourse, I didn't know what happened to him and I was convinced he had a heart attack! Right then I knew I hated sex and never wanted to engage in that "creepy activity" again.

Dr. Lawrence turned rather white when I told him what happened because no precautions were used and he could just see me ending up pregnant with a little black baby. After about three weeks, when my period started, he was relieved and so was I. I insisted to Dr. Lawrence that I now knew I could and should do without men, that they were worthless and I neither needed nor wanted anything further to do with them. Dr. Lawrence suggested I purchase a Swedish massager because he knew I never really experienced any form of sexual arousal. Because I trusted him and was curious as to why he would want me to pursue this suggestion, I went to Sears & Roebuck and acquired a hand-held, strap-on massaging unit. I went home and began to experiment--and I climaxed seven times! However, I became ragingly angry at Dr. Lawrence because I felt he had tricked me! He made me desire sex, which I didn't want to have any interest in.

A few weeks later, in the fall on a lonely Saturday, I again became deeply despondent. I could not effectively tolerate the rampant panic that continued to attack my body, and I took three Stelazine. After a while, I took about five more. And then the effect of the overdose engulfed me. My entire body went into a severe, terrifying spasm as my neck and back arched and seized up so I could neither sit nor lie down as the spasms intensified. I called my doctor who was at a football game and the answering service paged him. He returned my call and told me to immediately call an ambulance. They took me to the emergency room where I was promptly given a shot of Benadryl and they pumped my stomach. I must say, the grotesque unpleasantness of that experience made me vow to never "botch it" again and if I ever decided to overdose, I would make **certain** I took enough to end my life.

The hospital called my parents who came to get me and took me back to their house and put me to bed in my old upstairs bedroom. I don't know what they told Heidi, but they acted like they simply did not know how to respond. The following day, they took me to an RV and motor home show at a huge arena and expected me to walk around when all I wanted to do was sleep. They tried to engage me in a "family thing" and to show they loved me. That night they returned me to my apartment, never saying a word about what I had done or why had I done it.

Somehow, I recovered from that extreme level of despondency, became bored with my position at CPHA and began to look in the paper for a more interesting type of employment. An ad caught my eye: **Fore Title Company**. A law firm was seeking a legal secretary who would eventually manage the title insurance company owned by the four partners in the firm. I decided, *"What the heck? This sounds interesting ... why not apply?"* I don't know how I did it, but I seriously impacted one of the law firm's partners who was the title company CEO, and I was hired at $400 a month, $50 more than I was making at CPHA.

I took a keen interest in performing legal secretarial duties – preparing wills and trusts on an old-fashioned (by today's standards) IBM Selectric typewriter in triplicate with carbon copies; preparing articles of incorporation, managing petty cash, while at the same time learning the title insurance business. So rapid was my mind in grasping the concepts of land transfers and the requirements for title insurance issuance that I was soon made the manager of Fore Title Company. I wrote an in-depth document called *"How to Issue a Title Policy"* that outlined each step in researching a chain of title (the warranty and quit-claim deed process); verifying prior mortgages and their releases; checking for any tax, mechanic's or other liens on the property; and validating the legal descriptions of the property. Suddenly, my productivity and creativity soared.

Soon, at 21 years old (1969), I was supervising three law clerks hired as summer interns and teaching them how to verify clear title to both commercial and residential properties. I was soaring with confidence; my panic attacks disappeared; the lawyers highly valued my skill and competence and provided me with season tickets to the University of Michigan Wolverines' football games so I could wine and dine the real estate agent clients of the title company. I became engulfed in and completely identified with my career. The only drawback was the lawyers kept telling me I was worth $800 a month, but they could only pay me $440 because the income from the title insurance business could not support a higher salary. There was keen competition from other title companies in the county, and we were only a fledgling agency of the mother company, Chicago Title Insurance Company.

One of the most difficult things I had to do in my young life thus far was to make a recommendation to the law firm's partners that one of the law students be dismissed for insubordination. He was a third-year student, arrogant, pompous and not overly enthusiastic about being supervised by a young lady not possessing a degree, and he insisted upon shortcuts in his title research verification. He returned one day from a neighboring county's Register of Deeds' office with a gap – a missing link – in a chain of title, and refused to go back to that county to verify the property's owner of record, claiming "It's only a $30,000 piece of property and if anything comes of it, Chicago Title Insurance is wealthy enough to cover it." I must say I was rather impressed with the maturity I demonstrated at the young age of 21 when I requested a meeting with the overseer of Fore Title Company and simply told him I could not tolerate the law student's arrogant, obnoxious attitude, and I could not trust him to accurately validate a chain of title. He was promptly terminated.

I was beginning to find myself and to realize I possessed a keenly intelligent mind, was a problem solver, knew how to assert myself, knew who to trust, and I discovered I was indeed a valuable human being with worthwhile talent and skills to offer. My work became my salvation as I received constant praise and validation from Mr. Fichera and our customers. I was respected and trusted and my spirits soared for a while.

Chapter 6: Keep The Beat

The task is not to try to figure them out – the causes of a particular emotional experience [primary symptom], but to navigate your way through it.

– William J. Dubin, PhD

Throughout the uplifting turn in my career life, I maintained my weekly psychotherapy appointments with Dr. Lawrence and continued to attend one group therapy session each week. Attending this group was a couple who were beginning the divorce process. They had four young children, and the divorce was relatively amicable. Ironically, Wes knew who I was because he attended my father's Nathaniel Branden Institute lecture series out at our dance hall several years previously, and saw me riding my horse Suzie-Q around the dance hall during some of the daytime, weekend makeup lecture sessions.

Soon, Carol, his about-to-be ex-wife, terminated her attendance at the group sessions and I began to feel an attraction for Wes. I was not in the least shy about expressing my attraction. One evening I asked Wes if he would consider going on a date to a Laura Niro concert, to which he willingly agreed. We instantly hit it off, and he was uplifted and entertained by my energy and intellect. He made no sexual overtures and was content just talking until the wee hours of the morning that first night. We had a common bond: psychotherapy through which we were both trying to understand and better ourselves, plus we were both students of Nathaniel Branden and Ayn Rand and their philosophy of Objectivism.

We continued dating during the fall of 1969, and one night I made reservations at a rather exclusive motel for us to spend the night. Yet again, Wes did not pursue sexual advances. He was satisfied just with my presence, and we delighted in talking for many hours, going to bed and cuddling and waking up to the luxury of room service for breakfast.

One of the first things I discovered about Wes was he had financial difficulties, and he was always pursuing a "pie-in-the-sky, get-rich-quick" scheme of one kind or another. However, I was making a good living, supporting myself, and was not concerned about his monetary difficulties. Soon after I knew I was falling in love with him, I went to Beneficial Finance and borrowed enough money to help him make two mortgage payments so his home wouldn't be foreclosed upon and his four children wouldn't end up on the streets.

By New Year's Eve of 1970, he and I decided to move in together at in Belleville, Michigan. One night we walked down to the small lake by the apartment complex where we had a discussion in which I defined my expectations of the relationship, telling Wes I expected him to be faithful to me. I informed him that should he see fit to pursue intimate encounters with any other lady, I would not become enraged or hostile to him but I would merely consider his actions as grounds for me to take the same liberties should the opportunity present itself.

Shortly after we moved in together, my depression returned. We both terminated our therapy with Dr. Lawrence and began seeing Dr.Shulman. He and his associate, Dr. Handlesman, diagnosed me as having severe depression with anxiety disorder, and they tried to assist me with much of the anger and hostility I felt toward my mother. I was terrified of the intense emotions I bottled up during my youth, and the therapists believed I needed to get in touch with those feelings, express them and let them go.

In spite of their help, however, the suicidal thoughts were ever-present.

During that time, I was still taking the barbiturate Seconal, at 50 to 100 milligrams per night to help calm me down and sleep. I liked that medication so much that I was seeing two medical doctors and receiving two prescriptions, filling them at different pharmacies, so I was stockpiling them, just in case I might want to commit suicide. At Dr. Shulman's encouragement, I began to write volumes to him, trying to explain what I was feeling and experiencing.

When I contacted my mother to inform her of my relationship with Wes and that I had moved in with him, she curtly told me I should be careful because he was "a financial disaster," and that anyone with four children and his financial instability would surely be a burden to me. She informed me Wes failed to pay $80 for one of his lecture series fees and my father had to pay it for him and they wanted no further dealings with Wes.

A short while later, I purchased a new American Motors Javelin – my first new car – at a remarkable discount because Wes had a life insurance client who worked for American Motors, allowing us to purchase their cars utilizing the employee discount. Wes and I went out to my parents' farm to show them and my little sister Heidi my new car. When we arrived in the driveway, my mother came stalking down the hill, screaming at me, "Get off this property NOW. You are NOT welcome around here, and don't come back." This rejection sent me into a much deeper depression.

As I sank into a black, troubled despondency, I tried to tell Dr. Shulman how I felt. One day I left a session, sat down in the waiting room and gashed the top side of my hand with a razor blade. Feeling the self-inflicted pain and watching myself bleed helped divert myself from the excruciating internal pain of rejection, confusion and self-hatred, and the tearful emotions that would not stop. Cutting on oneself is a classic bipolar trait while in a depressive episode.

Wes was graciously accepting of me and my difficulties and tried his best to be nurturing and encouraging. He was empathetic regarding my family's treatment of me, and was most appreciative of my native intelligence and diligence at my career in spite of my turbulent emotional state. As our first year together was nearing its conclusion, he convinced me I could make more money selling life insurance with him than I was making as manager of Fore Title Insurance Company. I quit that job, became licensed to sell insurance for United Life and Accident Insurance Company and became not only Wes's lover but business partner as well as instant stepmother of four young children.

I soon discovered my rejection complex proved to be a major hindrance in my effectiveness as a life insurance sales agent. Since we lived in the suburbs of "the motor city" of Detroit, many people already had adequate life insurance provided by the automotive employers. Finding potential customers was difficult; numerous phone calls produced only a handful of promising leads. It seemed as though everyone to whom I sold a policy had serious medical problems which resulted in their policies being issued at much higher premiums and reduced coverage. I found myself lying to place the policies in force just so I could sustain my weekly draw against commissions earned. Major panic attacks over finances and being told "no" by potential customers kept me in an almost constant state of agitation.

Soon the agency for which we worked embarked on a unique program of offering group health, life and disability income insurance to small businesses with too few employees to purchase coverage with group Blue Cross Blue Shield. This package, called the United Chambers Insurance Trust, was offered to participating Chamber of Commerce members. Wes and I would travel to various cities across the state of Michigan and I would go to the local Chamber of Commerce office and make the phone calls to their members, setting up appointments for Wes to present the program to the business owners. We became quite a dynamic team. This togetherness and productive focus served to alleviate the depression somewhat.

During the summer of 1970, we visited the town of Port Huron, located across the Blue Water Bridge from Sarnia, Ontario, Canada. An interesting series of foreshadowing took place, a pattern I noticed evolving throughout my life, such as Wes's knowing who I was before I met him; and Dr. Lawrence becoming my therapist after dismissing me from college. We stayed at a Holiday Inn where, one night Wes wanted to go down to the bar, but I wanted to go to bed. He came back a while later telling me about the funniest, personable and fascinating bartender he met. Little did I know that in only six years, I would meet Danny Smith under quite different circumstances.

The next day we ate lunch at the Fogcutter Restaurant where we were seated by a lovely hostess. Years later, I would learn Linda had been Danny's partner. Wes sold a policy to the owner of the Reef Restaurant. When we returned later in the fall of 1970 around Thanksgiving to issue the policy to the employees of The Reef, we learned Mr. Kessler had been stabbed to death the night before, and I noticed everywhere we went in Port Huron that night, the entire mood of the town changed – a morose, almost ominous cloud hung all over that town which had been so delightful during our summer visit. I found myself to be most sensitive to the overall character or mood of my surroundings, and I knew something was terribly wrong as it seemed to permeate my soul. Wes and I would learn four years later through another interesting turn of events just what happened.

I struggled day and night in the life insurance business throughout the next year, finding the stress of making money and being fiscally responsible to be a major component of my sense of ongoing panic and despondency. Wes and I embarked on numerous weekend group therapy sessions whereby we'd meet on Saturday mornings, spend the night in Dr. Shulman's huge therapy room on sleeping bags and swim in his Olympic-sized indoor pool, and conclude the sessions by early Sunday evening.

One of these weekend group sessions was even conducted by Dr. Nathaniel Branden himself which we found to be enlightening. Sunday morning, Dr. Branden's mother passed away and I recall being so awed when he calmly told us; we had a moment of silence and then he brilliantly helped each member of the group for the rest of the day. My own interaction with Dr. Branden was particularly moving because he tried to help me symbolically "get my mother out of my head." It must have been rather difficult for him to deal with my intense feelings about my mother when he just lost his.

During this therapy with Drs. Shulman and Handlesman, they introduced an interesting anger management technique whereby they had a set of props called batakas which were canvas-covered bats about 15 inches long and 4 inches in diameter with a rubber handle covered by a foam shield. We could hit each other with them and not hurt ourselves, but the batakas were an excellent tool for the release of aggression and hostility. One rather revealing exercise involved us mutually hitting our partners while yelling, "*I wanna be number one!*" It seems as though many patients grew up feeling like lesser members of their families.

Often we would pair off and visualize our partner as someone whom we felt hurt us, angered us or otherwise did us wrong, and we would hit each other with the batakas in an effort to express our pent-up emotions. Ironically, nobody wanted to be my partner because I hit relentlessly with a vengeance and once I got going, I could not stop. Sometimes we would imagine the face of someone who wronged us on a beanbag chair and we would beat the chair. These exercises served to dissipate most of my intense anger toward Mother. The release provided by this technique provided significant and lasting healing. I no longer became easily roused to anger; however, the sadness was haunting.

About a year later, during the summer of 1972, I decided I could no longer withstand the duress of the instability of income as a life insurance sales agent. I studied to acquire my Securities and Exchange license and was prepared to take the state exam so I might also sell mutual funds; however, I could not afford the $100 fee required to sit for the exam. I pursued full-time employment and found a position in downtown Detroit at Coopers & Lybrand as their temporary personnel secretary while the full-time employee was off on an extended maternity leave. I worked as secretary to the senior banking partner and the personnel recruiter.

This job was extremely multi-faceted, highly demanding and required that I learn the art of confidentiality. I quickly discovered in spite of inner turmoil and depression, my external rather light-hearted, outgoing personality did not match the somber stuffiness of the CPAs' overall mentality. I tried diligently to stifle my frequent outbreaks of laughter and my tendency to be too talkative. My naïve and outspoken nature was often met with stern criticism and reprimands by the office manager. I tended to become easily overwhelmed by the daunting number of details and the precision they required for each of the functions I had to execute.

I would often come home to Wes, crying that I felt completely out of place and that I could not handle the oppressive atmosphere. During this time, Wes and I discovered Neil Diamond as we were both music lovers with Wes being an accomplished trumpet player. He would point out to me the sophisticated arrangement of "*Sweet Caroline*" every time we heard it on the radio. It was not long before we acquired Neil's album entitled "*Gold*," his live concert performance at the Troubadour Auditorium, and I first heard "*Holly Holy.*" I became enraptured with the talent of this writer and performer. I believed the song glorified me.

On Aug. 4, 1972, we attended my first Neil Diamond concert at Pine Knob open-air theater having seats in the 14th row along with a couple of friends of ours from group therapy. At the end of the show, when Neil performed "*I Am, I Said*" followed by "*Holly Holy,*" I became consumed by a sense of "spirit" and was so touched, I fell to my knees weeping uncontrollably. I had never before been so intensely moved by any musical performance and

I felt a connection with Neil Diamond that engulfed and mystified my entire being.

A few months after that concert, Coopers & Lybrand fired me citing as their reason that I was "not dignified enough for their office and I laughed too loudly." They paid me three months of severance pay and I was, for the first time since I'd left home, unemployed. This action on their part precipitated a sense of ultimate rejection – I felt completely worthless and cursed because of my very nature. My reward for trying so hard to fit in and perform well was to be outcast, dismissed, and my livelihood snatched out from under me.

A few days later, I was intent on suicide once again. I had a bottle of approximately 60 100 milligram Seconal barbiturates and I poured a thermos full of warm milk that I felt would coat my stomach and prevent me from getting sick before the pills killed me. I took off on a long drive until the road ended far out in the country where I parked the car and wrote a suicide note stating I did not belong in this world; I was not acceptable; I was worthless and unable to continue trying to make it.

I poured the pills out in my hand and uncorked the thermos when suddenly, "something bigger than I was" told me to start the car and insert my 8-track cassette of Neil Diamond's "*Stones*" album into the car's eight-track player. As fate would have it, the track containing "*I Am, I Said*" was the first to play. Neil's beautiful voice poured his heart out in the lyrics, "*I am, I said, ... and no one heard at all, ... 'I am,' I cried; '...* and I started to cry, sob and scream; I pounded the steering wheel and cried and screamed even more intensely, and suddenly I found myself thinking, "*Wait a minute! Neil has surely felt exactly what I am feeling right now; he has to have felt this way or he couldn't have written such a compelling song that expresses these emotions so purely; and **Neil is still alive singing about it**, so what am I doing?*"

I threw the pills out the window and tried to turn my car around to go home. However, it was stuck in the mud and I had to walk to the nearest farmhouse to ask for help. The farmer charged me $25 to pull my car out and I went home, amazed that Neil Diamond and his inspiring song saved my life. I have never again attempted suicide, although the thoughts of it sometimes come with alarming frequency and intensity.

The following week I placed an application for a secretarial position with Ford Motor Company and was almost immediately contacted for an interview and testing. I passed the typing test at 93 words per minute; however, since I had never taken shorthand and relied only upon a self-devised form of speed writing, I failed the shorthand test. Normally the personnel interviewers made potential candidates wait six weeks to return for a second testing. But because I amazed them with my typing speed and accuracy, they allowed me to schedule my retest in three weeks.

I desperately consulted with Dr. Handlesman, my current therapist, telling him I needed some kind of assistance to pass that shorthand test. He and I worked together with hypnotherapy and he hypnotized me, telling me while I was in trance that my right hand and arm had the strength of a steel bar. He had me elevate my right hand and had me visualize being able to conquer the world with confidence and determination, and that I could count on my right hand to achieve whatever objective I set out to accomplish.

I was quite anxious when I arrived at the Ford Motor Company testing center, but I recalled my deep breathing ability that permitted the trance state, and when they began the test, I was instantly relieved it was the same script from the previous test, and, if you will recall, I have stated my uncanny memory had become one of my dominant strengths. Because I remembered the entire test, I was able to not only trust my right hand would perform capably, but also all I had to do was fill in the blanks from what I missed the first time.

I passed the shorthand test at the required 60 words per minute, and on Nov. 16, 1972 embarked on my career at Ford Motor Company working for approximately 25 mechanical engineers. I secured the job exactly one month before my severance pay ran out from the CPA firm and thus made double pay for an entire month. I began to see a pattern emerging that no matter what my difficulties and obstacles, I always got what I wanted, and came out "making lemonade from lemons."

The job at Ford Motor Company was challenging and fun because I discovered the overall character of mechanical engineers as well as the secretaries brought out the best in me. This engineering department engaged in the design of light trucks approximately eight years ahead of their planned introduction to the market. It was exciting to see the prototype vehicles being designed and learning what was being planned for future vehicles. For once, I felt totally in my element, and the salary was excellent.

In the meantime Wes was encountering one financial disaster after another. He needed money so desperately to avoid being thrown in jail for nonpayment of child support that he obtained a loan using his mother's last remaining life insurance funds from the death of his father as collateral. Ultimately he defaulted on the loan and his mother's savings disappeared. She was an alcoholic and began calling me, drunk, insisting that because I was Wes's wife I should repay the loan for him. I found this to be stressful as I had compassion for her plight, but I also informed her I never commingled my funds with Wes and I was totally supporting myself.

Our sex life was less than fulfilling as Wes treated me more like a plaything than as a lady. I never really enjoyed sex with him and began refusing his advances, preferring to sleep and try to escape my ongoing depression. He wanted to try rather perverted experiments using hot dogs and other objects to please me, which I found disgusting.

Shortly after starting the Ford Motor Company job, I felt I needed some form of diversion so I embarked on guitar lessons with an extremely handsome gentleman. I learned he played guitar with another musician at a little hole-in-the-wall bar called

The Nitelight Lounge and I began going up to the bar to hear him play. Shortly after my lessons started, they ended abruptly because Scott contracted mononucleosis due to overextending himself attending journalism school full-time, modeling, teaching guitar and playing in the bar. He had to give something up and the guitar lessons fell by the wayside much to my dismay.

One night Wes and I went to the Nitelight and were delighted to find Scott and Dave had hired a drummer who was one of the most innovative drummers we'd ever heard, and who had a voice that rivaled Paul McCartney's. Wes and I became fabulous dance partners which brought us together and bridged the gap in the unsatisfactory sex life.

In the spring of that year, because I was making such good money at Ford, I purchased a young, spirited horse. One day, after having ridden him only in the indoor ring for a few times, I saddled him and rode him out of the barn, breaking one of the cardinal rules of horsemanship which is to LEAD the horse out of the barn. The horse's eyes take time to adjust to the bright light, and as he trotted past a huge pile of straw and manure, which he must have thought was a buffalo or something, he jumped and shied. His abrupt bucking threw me into a somersault where I landed squarely on my lower back on a large chunk of concrete, knocking the wind out of me. When I came to, I saw stars and could barely stand up.

I was finally able to get up and walk over to the horse that stood there, looking back at me with a questioning look as if to say, *"What happened to you?"* I led him back to the barn, unsaddled and groomed him, and the next day, promptly sold him. I was sore and could hardly walk for several days, but I guess I thought I was the bionic woman because I never went to a doctor to determine if I had been injured, which would come back to haunt me a few years later.

Several weeks after that incident, I had surgery scheduled for a tubal ligation on April Fools' Day. I was tired of taking birth control pills and decided I didn't want children. However, the gynecologist I was seeing at the time did not want to perform such irreversible surgery on a young woman of 25 who had no children. I presented him with four reasons for why I wanted to proceed in this manner: (1) I was terrified of the pain of childbirth; (2) I was afraid I would psychologically mess up a child's mind in the same manner my mother had done to me; (3) being naïve and romantic, I thought Wes's and my marriage would last forever. Since he already had four children whom he could barely manage to support, having more would make it that much more difficult for him; and (4) the psychotherapists believed if I did have a child, I would probably pass on my genetic propensity for mental illness and would have "a monster."

In order for the gynecologist to agree to performing the surgery, the psychologist had to write a note stating I would be unable to handle the stress of pregnancy and motherhood. Thus, I rendered myself permanently incapable of bearing children.

The following month, Wes's oldest child wanted to come and live with us because she found her stepfather intolerable. He didn't want her to do so, stating Wes and I were living together and he would not permit this arrangement unless we were married. Getting married also had the advantage of making Wes my dependent so he could enroll in my excellent health insurance with Ford Motor Company. So on June 30, 1973, we got married in a rather unique ceremony for which we wrote our own vows. Planning the wedding was exciting and it alleviated my depression, all except one critical element: My parents refused to come so my Uncle Leo performed the role of giving me away. We walked down the aisle to *"Holly Holy,"* and our wedding dance was Neil Diamond's *"The Grass Won't Pay No Mind."* The final irony here was after our marriage, Wes's daughter decided she didn't want to live with us after all.

During the time of planning and carrying off the wedding a group of us fell in love with the movie and soundtrack to *"Jonathan Livingston Seagull."* Jeri, the manager's secretary who was my maid of honor, and all of the engineers at Ford were fascinated by my infatuation for Neil Diamond, although none of them knew how he saved my life by his song, "*I Am, I Said.*" It was life in the fast lane with happy hours and going to the bar and lots of rewarding socializing.

Shortly after our wedding, I became motivated to write a letter to Neil Diamond through the Friends of Neil Diamond Fan Club (FOND) in which I thanked him for his song having saved my life, and indicated my husband Wesley and I admired his music so much that we used his music exclusively during our wedding ceremony. I received a nice acknowledgement letter in return along with an invitation to join the fan club, which I did. However, I never had the sense that Neil, himself, actually received my letter of gratitude, which would come back to haunt me in the years to come. I always had a need to pay my debts.

Not long after the wedding I met Joan Boyer, drummer Jimmy Boyer's wife, in whom I found a friend for life. Joan was so mellow and laid-back, I soon found I could talk to her about anything. Wes and I became close to Jimmy and Joan which served to strengthen our bond as we continued to go to the bar and dance to Jimmy's drumming.

I also became close to Debbie, wife of one of the engineers at Ford, and one night the four of us – Wes and I, Tom and Debbie –saw the movie "*The Exorcist.*" I left in the middle of it and could not return. When we arrived home to our townhouse in Dearborn, the shade on one of the windows spontaneously flew up making a horrible snapping sound which scared Debbie and me out of our wits.

She and I began going down to the bar to hear Scott and Dave and Jimmy play, and both of us had an intense crush on Scott. I'll never forget the night Wes joined us after one of his insurance client appointments, and I streaked the bar, having left my clothes in the ladies' room and pranced down the entire length of the bar, strip-stark-naked, mingled on the dance floor and danced for a few minutes, and then cavorted back down the aisle to the ladies' room to don my clothes!

Shortly after that escapade, Wes held a party to which he invited his brother and his girlfriend who had the largest boobs of anyone I had met. She brought a specially baked batch of brownies laced with marijuana. I experienced my first "high," feeling a state of glee quite unlike anything I ever felt before.

The following fall, after having admired Jimmy Boyer's drumming for several months and having experienced almost continual release and relief in the wonderful self-expression of dancing to his playing, I decided I wanted to take drum lessons. I approached him as to whether or not he would be willing to teach me. He asked me, "What makes you think you can play drums?" to which I replied, "Because I can dance to anything." He and I agreed he would teach me, but if I were to come to one lesson unprepared, he would terminate future lessons. So on Labor Day weekend, I had my first drum lesson and I went out and purchased a set of Slingerland drums. I practiced diligently and began to write out the lessons as Jimmy presented them which resulted in Jimmy learning how to read drum music!

As the weeks progressed and Thanksgiving approached, Wes and I went over to the Boyers' for one of my lessons only to find Joan crying and lamenting. This was the magic moment that pieced together our summer experiences in Port Huron back in 1970. Joan informed us that Jimmy had been playing at a bar called The Satellite Lounge at that time, and that Danny Smith, the bartender whom Wes met while we stayed at the Holiday Inn, was in a terrible car accident the night before we placed the group insurance policy at The Reef restaurant. Linda Butler, Danny's significant other, had been thrown from the car and decapitated and Danny's spinal chord was crushed, leaving him a paraplegic. At the time of the accident, Jimmy and the band were staying at an apartment just up the street from the restaurant, and that particular night Jimmy was supposed to meet Danny at an agreed upon time. When Danny didn't arrive, Jimmy left. He always blamed himself for the accident.

Joan's tears of lament were because they just learned Danny had more than a dozen bedsores all over his body, with two of them being so deep and infected they ate away his entire buttocks preventing him from being able to sit in his wheelchair. Thus, all of the foreshadowing of people and events in Port Huron three years earlier during our insurance sales stint came to be a reality through our friends and my drum teacher. Our motto of "keep the beat" had a deeper meaning.

I continued my drum lessons with Jimmy for another year, all the while becoming closer friends with Debbie as she lived so close to Ford Motor Company that I went over to her house for lunch every day. We both began to talk about how unhappy we were with our husbands. Wes admitted to me that he had had an affair with his brother's girlfriend, Juanita with the big boobs. I began to flirt with a couple of the engineers at Ford's and began going off in the car with one of them for sexual interludes at lunch or after work.

I'll never forget one day at Debbie's house, as I watched her smoke her Doral cigarettes, which she made look like so much fun, asking her if I could have one. I never inhaled a cigarette before, but since I started smoking marijuana I learned how to inhale. I will never forget the instant buzz I felt from the cigarette, and I was immediately hooked.

Around Labor Day of 1975, Jimmy Boyer left the new band he had been playing with called Three Man Army and went on the road playing with Billy Swan who wrote *"Lover Please,"* which Jimmy first recorded before Clyde McPhatter made it a hit. Debbie and I continued to go hear Three Man Army and their new drummer. We talked constantly, and I learned she had a very interesting slant on religion. She told me she heard that some day, Jesus, who would be walking the earth, and many would know him, but would not know it was him, would fall in love with a woman; they would get married; and that union would comprise the Second Coming of Jesus. I was fascinated with this information, and never questioned whether it was biblically sound.

As we would indulge in our groupie admiration and fascination with the Three Man Army, Joe, the guitar player who could sing *"To Be Loved"* and *"Unchained Melody"* with such poignancy that I always cried, began to seek me out as a sex partner. Debbie would allow us to have our sexual interludes in her upstairs bedroom whenever the opportunity presented itself for me to slip away from Wes unnoticed. Wes never did know of my affair with Joe.

However, so fulfilling was the sex that I realized I could no longer stay with Wesley. Yes, he had been a devoted husband and helped me in enumerable ways simply by being emotionally supportive of me; by going along with whatever hair-brained scheme I might pursue at any given time; by teaching me all about the mechanical operation of cars and how to troubleshoot signs of malfunction; by teaching me the importance of preventive maintenance; and by basically being an open-minded, compassionate, funny and generous individual.

I came to the conclusion that his financial difficulties were never going to get any better and that I was too young (eight years his junior) to continue to tie myself down to his shortcomings that I believe stifled my own potential.

In seeking my freedom, I went with Joan Boyer to Chicago to hear Jimmy play with Billy Swan. There, in the middle of a severe winter blizzard, the band members and I were snowbound at the hotel for more than 24 hours. I embarked upon a tryst with one of the band members that provided sexual fulfillment such as I had never experienced. I realized that Wes simply never could be "the man" for me partly due to his ongoing financial instability but also due to his inability to sexually satisfy me.

When I returned from Chicago, I packed up my belongings and moved to my own townhouse. On Mother's Day eve that year, my father came to visit me and on Mother's Day itself, he returned with my mother, which was the first time I had seen my parents together in seven years. We had a pleasant, warm kind interaction which was a reconciliation I never thought would happen.

I was now, once again, on my own; however, this time I had a circle of friends and was thoroughly engrossed in my love and passion for music as I still went out and danced until the wee hours almost every night. The chapter of Wes as my husband was now behind me.

Chapter 7: The Crippled Crab And The Merry Widow

We create subjective realities which then influence objective
reality, which in turn influence subjective reality –
sometimes in an amplifying spiral. Your amplifier is
probably more sensitive [the bipolar biology].
A good goal would be for you to learn to influence
the amplification process.

– William J. Dubin, PhD

The separation from Wes was amicable. While he didn't want me to go, he understood my need to remove myself from his ongoing and chronic financial duress. Since I had been economically self-sufficient during our marriage, I had no problem emerging as a successful, single female of 28. I kept myself on a tight budget, allowing myself only $3 a day for entertainment which meant when I would go to the bars with girlfriend Debbie at night, I could have either one mixed drink or two sodas and chase it with lots of water.

Since my drum teacher Jimmy joined Billy Swan, I resumed drum lessons with the new drummer of Three Man Army, the band Debbie and I used to go hear all the time while Jimmy played with them. Danny often invited me to sit in and play drums for a song or two while he would talk with Debbie.

We also frequently went to hear a band called Styx and Stoned who had a dynamic drummer, Marcus Terry. I will never forget the last night Marcus was with the band before joining Jose Feliciano as his drummer because they asked me to play drums on the final song of the evening, Bachman, Turner, Overdrive's *"Takin' Care of Business."* This allowed Marcus to go out front and sing. I never knew when or how to play the cymbals before so I played a nice straight beat, scared as heck, but feeling elated at being totally in my element. The lead guitarist looked at me to end the song and all of a sudden, CRASH! I hit a cymbal, Bobby's face lit up like a Christmas tree and we went into an encore with my exhilaration as to when and where to play the cymbals. It was a moment of glory and victory.

I started smoking pot after the party when I ate brownies laced with same; however, I found about two hits was all it took to get me sufficiently giggly to totally take my mind off any sense of depression. I never abused marijuana although I smoked my two tokes almost every day. Even though I claimed to be an atheist, I used to think, "*It must be okay with Jesus because they wrote a song about it: 'One toke over the line, Sweet Jesus, one toke over the line ...'!*" It would allow me to dance in oblivion for hours which helped me maintain a sense of balance, carefree abandon and gentle peace.

Debbie and I would go to the bar night after night and she would lust after Danny the drummer while I lusted after Joe, the lead singer and guitar player. I would watch Joe leave the bar countless times with other girls, a different girl each time, and wonder why he terminated his trysts with me that began while I was married to Wes. Later I learned Joe told Debbie he was afraid of falling in love with me and since I was now "single" and available, even though I hadn't yet filed for divorce, he feared involvement because he cared deeply for me.

In my loneliness and despondency that Joe no longer had any interest in me, I began to experiment with harder drugs. One time I did blotter acid which produced an amazing "trip," but while it was gratifying, it was simultaneously terrifying because it seemed as though I was caught in a never-ending unreality. Two days later I encountered the worst case of strep throat I ever had. Even though I claimed to be an atheist, I somehow believed this serious illness was nature's punishment for experimenting with the hard drug. Yet, still another time, I tried chocolate mescaline that induced a horrifying experience in which I became engulfed in paranoia; I sat in to play drums to Procol Harum's *"Whiter Shade of Pale"* and I thought the song would never end because I knew I was playing terribly. A couple of days after this trip I again came down with another severe case of strep throat. That was the last time I imbibed that type of street drug.

However, Debbie introduced me to cocaine – speed – and I found I really liked it. The only problem was it didn't last long enough. I experimented with it a couple of times and found one of the musicians in another band I would go hear with Joan Boyer, usually had a stash of cocaine. I invited him over and we did the speed and then had tremendous sex. I was hooked on both and asked him to come back a few days later. Well, return, he did, along with two of his buddies, and before they would let me have any cocaine, they all had their way with me. That was the last time I ever did any hard drugs. I experienced immense shame that I had reduced myself to such a level of trash just to experience the all-too-brief high induced by the speed.

It was about this time during the summer of 1976 that I met Dolores "Dee" Rice, a good friend of Joan Boyer's who was also recently divorced and had three children. Dee soon became one of my dearest friends as she and Joan became my "adopted sisters." Neither Dee nor Joan cared much for Debbie who always seemed to be in competition with me for the men who were attracted to me. I began going home with numerous men who were delighted to have one-night stands with me, but never came back. I was desperately seeking love and acceptance through sexual interactions, yet the guys were simply using me and my passionate energy and had no interest in repeat performances. Indiscriminate sex is another key signal of the manic slope in the bipolar characteristic.

Near the end of that summer, I decided my 1972 Lincoln Continental was costing too much money to maintain. Joan called me and told me she'd like me to go to Port Huron with her to meet their paralyzed friend Danny Smith because he had his car for sale. He had bed sores so huge and deep on his fanny that he could no longer sit in his wheelchair and was confined to bed, lying on his stomach and "standing" on his elbows. She gave him my phone number and he called me teasing, "I have a nine-pound tongue with a two-and-a-half pound wart on the end of it and I like eating at the 'Y'!" We talked for hours on the phone, as if we'd known each other all our lives. He told me his self-acclaimed nickname was "The Crippled Crab," and I never did know how he came by that name for himself.

On Aug. 9, 1976, I went to Port Huron with Joan to meet Danny. When we walked in, he said, "Pardon me if I don't stand; I just washed my legs and can't do a thing with them." Danny lived with his parents who took constant care of him. At their insistence, I parked my car in their side yard so Danny could see it. He told me I should keep my Lincoln and he didn't want me to buy his Buick because if something should happen that it wasn't a good car for me, he'd feel guilty.

The attraction between Danny and me was like magical dynamite. The man made me laugh. He said to me, "You know, no matter how badly you have it, you can always look over your shoulder and find someone who has it worse." I found this to be surprisingly uplifting coming from someone who used to love to ride motorcycles and dance the night away, who had the energy to hold down three jobs, and who now could no longer even get out of bed. That day, Danny kissed me and passionately held me such that I knew there was intense electricity between us. I could hardly pull myself away from him when it was time to go home. I went back to visit him a week later and knew I had fallen in love, and knew it was mutual.

During that time I began having rather serious health problems in that I hadn't had a period in nine months, was not pregnant, had severe colitis and irritable bowel syndrome along with intense and chronic pain in my lower right groin. I went to numerous doctors who each said my pain was all in my head but gave me codeine to help alleviate it. I had forgotten about being thrown from that horse three years earlier. It wasn't long before the doctors put me on a medical leave from my job at Ford Motor Company because I had a hard time walking, was in constant pain and had chronic diarrhea. I began going to Port Huron every weekend to stay with Danny and his parents.

Soon, I found a job at Morton Salt Company in Marysville, Michigan, a small community just south of Port Huron. I also found an upstairs efficiency apartment in a lovely old house on the opposite side of the street from the St. Claire River. I later learned that house had been owned by a Nazi sympathizer dentist during World War II who harbored Nazi spies on its third floor. I moved to Port Huron to be with Danny, and four years to the day I started my job at Ford Motor Company, I began working at Morton Salt as their inventory control clerk.

Every day after work I would go home and change my clothes and go over to Danny's house while his parents went to a factory to perform after-hours janitorial services to help support their invalid son. We spent our evenings smoking pot and listening to rock and roll on radio station WABX, which had been an underground station and was the first in the country to air the Beatles' *"Double White"* album. When Danny's pain level was somewhat tolerable, as his spinal chord was pinched rather than severed in the accident, he would have me lie on pillows across the red table situated in front of his bed to pleasure me. While this didn't happen very frequently, the pleasure derived was well worth the wait.

I had been in therapy for nine years before meeting Danny, and for the first time in my life I felt fulfilled and happy. While I knew I would outlive him because the odds were highly improbable he would live very long in his fragile condition, I also knew I was doing something important because for the first time in my life, I felt I was bringing significant meaning to another. Danny called me his "ambulatory representative," and I would go shopping for him and purchase record albums to add to his sizable collection. He would call his friends in town when I needed car repairs and say, "My girl needs to have her car looked at," or "My girl is coming to pick up the latest Bob Seger album." He put me on a pedestal, something I never before experienced; I felt important; I felt appreciated, loved, esteemed, needed and wanted. My moods assumed a peaceful balance.

It wasn't long after I began working for Morton Salt that their payroll administrator quit and I applied for the job and got it. This was a prestigious position in that community because I was responsible for the weekly payroll of approximately 200 employees. Danny was impressed with my intelligence and he often bragged to his friends, "My girl is the timekeeper of Morton Salt." He more or less became my ongoing therapist because he used to say, "You worry about stupidity! You need to learn not to take yourself so seriously. Just remember, it all works out in the wash." Danny taught me to laugh at myself and I was forever grateful for his light-hearted and optimistic attitude in spite of his tremendous physical pain and limitations.

A year after I met Danny while Jimmy Boyer was still on the road playing music with Billy Swan, Danny received a postcard from Jimmy of the Armadillo World Headquarters in Austin, Texas. I would later learn of another interesting coincidence as to the origin of that postcard.

By 1978, the pain in my right groin was so severe it began shooting down my leg and often, as I would walk down the stairs to leave the Morton Salt building, my right leg would give out on me as I'd grab the railing for support. I finally went to an orthopedic surgeon who performed back surgery on Danny years earlier due to a motorcycle accident, and he took x-rays of my back. I have never seen a doctor turn as white as his coat, but when he showed me the x-ray of my lower back, suddenly a flash played before my eyes of the fall off the horse in 1973. Dr. Walker tried to sound calm as he said, "How did you do this? Do you realize you are walking around with a broken back?" My L5 and S1 vertebrae were crushed together while the disk between them was smashed against my spine. Not wishing to scare me by appearing "knife happy," Dr. Walker said, "Uh, normally, the only way to fix this is with surgery, but we could possibly try some physical therapy."

When I went to Danny's after this appointment, he said to me, "Well, I guess paralysis is contagious!" Dr. Walker scheduled surgery within three weeks as the physical therapy accomplished nothing. Since Danny had similar surgery before, he was my coach and emotional support throughout the entire process. When I got out of the hospital and had to be in a wheelchair for two weeks, Danny's parents, who were well into their 80s, were so helpful and supportive and jokingly said, "You'd think we were running a home for paralyzed children!"

I healed rapidly and was back to work part-time within six weeks after the surgery and finally, my insides began functioning properly once again. I was forever grateful for Danny's presence and encouragement through this rather difficult ordeal. We were both fulfilling a significant purpose in each others' lives. He often shared that he had a dream of going to California, and said if he ever walked again, he would take a trip to California and then come back and get me to return there.

After two years of this romance, which many people could not understand, Danny forewarned me of his eventual departure. Jimmy and Joan Boyer came up to visit us near the first of the year in 1979 when Danny told Jimmy, "I'll not be seeing you again." He told another lady friend of ours, "I will be gone soon." A few months later, he began to get bed sores on his stomach and was hospitalized for a week to heal them up. While he was in the hospital the doctors discovered a slight spot on his lung they believed was malignant, but Danny wanted no part of treating it and he asked to go home. He made me promise if his health declined, I was not to seek medical intervention because he wanted to die at home and never be in the hospital again.

Over Easter weekend of 1979 I went to Detroit to visit Jimmy and Joan Boyer. When I returned Easter Sunday, Danny insisted I watch "Sergeant York" on TV with him, which was about a man who discovered and accepted Christ. Danny knew I was an atheist and he was a backsliding Catholic. He never before insisted I watch a Sunday afternoon movie because we usually spent that time listening to music. I wondered why he was so intent on my seeing a movie in which someone accepted Christ.

The following day he was not feeling too well as he had begun to run a slight fever. By mid-week, he was so weak he could hardly talk to me, but when his parents came into the room he was able to muster the strength to speak in his typical, robust tone. When I arrived at his home Friday, April 21, a week after Good Friday, he could barely pick his head up. I sat there with him until almost midnight and told him I would be over the following day to watch the Detroit Tigers' baseball game with him. He took my left hand in his right hand and I said, "I hope you feel better." He replied, "I feel better now," and suddenly, I experienced a jolt in my entire body as he laid his head down, facing toward the wall away from me and breathed his last breath.

I sat there stunned for a few minutes, and got up as if nothing happened and walked through the kitchen, telling his parents good night. I couldn't tell them their son just died. As I drove home, something began to happen to me. My world as I knew it would never be the same and I began to enter a twilight zone, a "wilderness of mirrors" that few people ever visit.

The following morning I awoke at 8 a.m., much earlier than I ever had on a Saturday and I methodically went to the laundromat to wash my clothes and sheets. Upon my arrival home, I went downstairs to polish the chrome on my Pontiac Lemans I purchased several months after meeting Danny. Not wanting to accept the reality of what I experienced the night before, I went upstairs to call him and let him know I would be on my way over to watch the baseball game. However, I picked up the phone and "something" made me hang it up and go back down for about 12 more minutes to work on the car. I went back upstairs and dialed Danny's number, but it never rang. Instead, I heard a *click-click-click-click* of a phone being dialed and then silence, and I said, "Hello?" Danny's father was on the line and said to me, "Hang up the phone, Holly; I think Danny's dead." I froze, wondering what the odds were that I would call at exactly the moment Danny's dad found his son dead.

The only thing I could think of doing was to go to Danny's house to console his parents and by the time I arrived, Danny's body had been removed. I retrieved some of my belongings I kept there such as an 8-track tape player, bean bag chair and pillows. I felt very cold as I told his mother, "Danny wants to be buried feet-first and have engraved on his headstone, *I'm on my feet again, so party*! He made me promise to make his wish be known; and he wants to be buried in his motorcycle shirt with his Indian serape over it." Mrs. Smith looked at me like I had lost my mind and said, "He's NOT going to be buried feet-first!"

I returned to my apartment and a little while later, Danny's youngest nephew, Shawn, came over so I wouldn't have to be alone. He said, "Are you going to order flowers?" That was when the reality hit me, *Danny's dead*. I began to cry and said to Shawn, "I have to be like Jacquie Kennedy; I have to pull this off with dignity and grace." So I calmly ordered the flowers to be sent to the funeral home and then we talked for a little while. Shawn informed me he had been out in the country with some friends the night before and he awakened at 8 in the morning (when I awoke and did my laundry, obsessed by Danny's saying, "*It will all work out in the wash*") and wandered outside in the fog, and was thinking to himself, *I wonder what Holly will do if Danny dies*. He did not know Danny's health had been failing.

After Shawn left, my phone rang. It was my ex-husband Wes asking me if I was okay. I hadn't heard from him in many weeks. He said to me, "At 8 this morning, I was sitting in my restaurant drinking coffee and wondering what you would do if Danny died." He hadn't even known Danny had come down with the flu. I barely hung up with him when Carol Middleton, my beautician who used to trim Danny's hair, called and asked me how I was, saying to me, "This morning at 8, I got up earlier than usual and found myself wondering as I drank my morning coffee, *What will Holly do if Danny dies?*"

Later that evening Joan Boyer called me and said that at 8 that morning she and Jimmy were having coffee and wondering what I would do if Danny died. They hadn't seen him since January, and when I visited them the week before, Danny was doing the same as he always had. By this time my mind was spinning again, wondering, *what are the odds four people, all over the state, who knew nothing of Danny's catching the flu, would be wondering the same thing at precisely 8 in the morning after he died?* I began to float into a dream-like reality thinking, *"There's a reason for everything; and if you're smart enough, you can know those reasons for everything. There's something happening here."*

On the day of the funeral I drove around all day listening to the Beatles sing, *"Here Comes the Sun"* and *"Let It Be."* The odometer on my car turned over to "000000," which took on the special meaning to me of starting over. That night, I played pool for the first time in my life with friends of Danny's. He had been a pool-playing wizard, and I made almost every shot. At that point I firmly believed Danny's spirit had taken over me and he was still alive and well through my soul – that I had truly become his "ambulatory representative." I began to believe that somehow I owed Danny something and I would do something profound for him.

As the summer months came, I purchased a motorcycle and began riding all over the countryside Danny loved so much. The freedom I felt as the wind rushed by me began to push me into a daredevil frame of mind and I would ride one-handed as fast as I could around the curves. I felt immortal as if I already died along with Danny and "together," we were reliving his ambulatory days. Little did I know that mania was creeping in.

I made it a point to go to the county clerk's office and look up the cause of death on Danny's death certificate. I don't remember the exact terminology, but when I looked it up, it said something about his heart and some wording that implied "straight up." I believed Danny had gone straight to Heaven. And I also believed his spirit had gone far and wide, alerting all of those people at 8 the following Saturday morning he died. I was convinced there was a God and "something much bigger than I am" had taken over me and was telling me what to do. No longer did I doubt the existence of a Supreme Being.

I continued to smoke a couple of tokes of pot every day after work and listen to music. Danny's nephew Shawn painted a unique and remarkable painting of Jimi Hendrix on a piece of plywood with a purple moon painted over one of the knots in the wood, symbolizing Jimi's song, "*Purple Haze.*" I placed that painting high on a door frame in my apartment and one day, as I was getting high on the marijuana, I looked at that painting and suddenly began talking to it. *Aha! You're in on it, too. That's right – Danny's now dancing with you and Janis Joplin and Jim Morrison ... NOW I have ALL of your spirits within me ... I'm talking and walking with the Angels!*

As the summer progressed, the Morton Salt Company hourly employees went on strike and the salaried employees were running the plant. I spent the mornings working at processing the group health insurance claims since there was no payroll to do, and then spend the afternoons sitting on the Lite Salt production line as the inspector. I had to weigh every fifth can and watch the labels to make sure the tube winder was cutting the containers at the correct places. Sometimes, a bad batch would come down and I'd have an amazing burst of energy as I threw all the bad products into a large bin across the line from me. We had a radio on to pass the time and one day, the song "*You Needed Me*" came on.

Up to that point I had been highly motivated by the concept presented in the musical piece, "*Merry Widow's Waltz,*" and exerted every effort to live up to that image of being a "merry widow." I thought of myself as a widow even though Danny and I never married, and when the beautiful words to "*You Needed Me*" penetrated the entire salt plant, I lost it in a crying jag so intense I could not stop. Suddenly, the loss of Danny was so overpowering,

I felt knocked off the very stool I was sitting on. I left work and tried to flee the engulfing devastation by riding my motorcycle out to the beach by the St. Clair River. As I sat on the beach, the idea began to take root ... the spark was ignited: *Danny's going to come back. Danny looked like Jesus Christ ... Danny IS JESUS CHRIST. Danny IS the Second Coming ... I am the woman Jesus fell in love with and He's coming BACK for ME! WE are the Second Coming of Jesus...*

I thought of Neil Diamond's song, "*Holly Holy*" where he sings, "*Touch a man who can't walk upright And that lame man, he gonna fly ... and I fly ...*" and in my mind, at that moment, Neil and Danny became one, and I believed Neil had written that song specifically for me ... that he knew he had a "mission" to find his "Holly Holy."

I went to the cemetery every day where I placed a red rose, symbolizing everlasting love, and a yellow rose, symbolizing everlasting peace on Danny's grave. I talked to him and told him that together, we would restore peace to the world. I sang the Beatles' song to him, "*Come Together Over Me*," and envisioned the entire world coming together in peace over Danny's grave.

I began to believe the vision I had when I was seven years old by the spirea bush was finally coming to fruition and this was the "mission" God foretold to me at that time when He said to me, "You will help a large number of people; you will be great some day." I began to feel immensely important and that I was about to do something in special partnership with God, and suddenly, I asked myself: *Who is your 'Creator'?* The answer was simple to me: Neil Diamond because he wrote "*Holly Holy*" and I **was** Neil's "*Holly Holy*." I adopted the mindset that inspiration comes from God and therefore God is the author of musical inspiration. I remembered my favorite Lennon Sisters' song, "*He*" and the words that went, "*He can turn the tide and calm the angry sea; He alone decides who writes a symphony ...*" and I realized God empowered me with special vision and gifts of understanding no one else was privy to know, and God and I had a unique and privileged "pipeline of communication" with each other.

Immediately I knew that to continue receiving these special insights God had to offer me, I had to become "Holy" and I embarked on an attempt to quit smoking cigarettes, believing if I could rid myself of that sin, God would bring Danny back to me one way or another. In order to stave off the cigarettes, I began dancing in my apartment to the rock and roll played by WABX. I would choreograph a modern dance sort of ballet to all of the new songs that seemed to be coming out in a flood of romantic and powerful majesty. I would stand straddling the arms of my overstuffed chair and dance, tipping the chair on two legs in perfect balance, being able to then set it back down in utmost quiet so I wouldn't bother the landlord who lived below. I possessed a remarkable and endless energy and knew it came from all of the "angels" who were now residing within me.

Over Labor Day weekend I contracted mononucleosis for the second time and had such a severe case that my throat was so swollen I could barely swallow. All I could get down were nutritious drinks made of papaya juice, carrots, strawberries, bananas, sherbet and yogurt in the blender, but my throat became so sore and almost swollen shut that even swallowing those concoctions was next to impossible. I was terrified because I was running an extremely high fever of 104 and 105 degrees.

On Labor Day, I ran the bathtub full of warm water in an attempt to sponge myself and bring the fever down as I was listening to the *"Lunch with Jim Saute"* program on WABX where they were featuring music by the Who. As they started playing the song, *"See me, feel me, touch me, heal me ... I get the glory from you ... right behind you, I see the millions on you ..."* and "something" jerked me out of the tub, strip-stark naked, and drew me in front of the picture of Danny hanging over the radiator. As I looked at his picture, that same "something" pushed me down to my knees and I prayed, *"Jesus, I am sorry I ever doubted You;*

I KNOW You are real; I KNOW You are the ultimate Healer; I accept You as my Lord and Savior!"

At that moment I was "pulled" to my feet with my arms outstretched in a spread-eagle fashion, like Jesus on the Cross, and my entire body went into a spasm, a jolt, and in one fell swoop, my fever was gone; the sore and swollen throat was back to normal; and I was instantaneously healed of the dreaded mononucleosis!

Later that fall Morton Salt Company held a going-away party for one of the employees who was relocating to another Morton Salt facility. It was an elaborate affair at an exquisite restaurant and I had four glasses of Southern Comfort. I won the door prize of a Polaroid camera and even though I was intensely drunk, I tried to converse with my coworkers. Someone said something to me that made me highly angry and I left the party and drove like a wild woman at breakneck speed back down toward Morton Salt and raced into the plant, tearing up and down the parking lot, doing figure eights as if I were performing stunts for a high-action movie. The guard in the guard shack was terrified and didn't know what to do as I peeled out of the driveway and headed straight up to Danny's parents' house, walked in and boldly announced, "Danny's coming back. He will return." They became furious with me and practically threw me out.

As I was incensed with anger and fury, I raced around the curve on a narrow, winding road where I crashed into an oncoming vehicle almost head-on. The entire left side of my car was smashed; the driver's door wouldn't open; the frame was bent; and I hit my head on the windshield so hard it cracked into a large spider web of fine cracks across the entire driver's side, although it didn't shatter. My mouth hit the steering wheel and severely loosened my two lower front teeth as I bit the inside of my lip in a large gash.

The people in the other car got out and screamed at me, "You could have killed us both!" When the police came, God must have been on my side because I did not get a ticket for driving while intoxicated, but merely a speeding ticket. My car was drivable, and I was able to make it home.

The following morning I got the newspaper which contained an article about "Danny the Sandman," and at that point I was firmly entrenched in the twilight zone of mania complete with a complex and radical thought disorder. Reality ceased to exist for me. Since I was terrified to try to drive my rather totaled car, I walked all the way to the cemetery the next day where I was greeted with an green-glowing vision of the Virgin Mary over Danny's grave. At that point, I knew God had connected me with "the Mother Church."

I began to read *The Good News Edition* of the New Testament, and began to believe my job in this world was to rectify all of the curses of humankind. I got out another version of the Bible and poured through it, gleaning a distorted understanding about Cain and Abel and that Cain killed Abel and his descendants through Jubel were cursed to be the musicians and artists and would wander and die young – thus all of the "angels" I was talking to such as Jimi Hendrix, Janis Joplin and Jim Morrison would one day walk again on the earth to avenge the curse of brother killing brother.

I began what I called "soul travel," and literally became, one-by-one, the people from Biblical times. I read the story of Nimrod who, in vanity, shot the eye of the Lord with an arrow after the people of Babylon (now Iraq) built a temple in his honor, and the Lord hit them with a bolt of lightning and scattered them to all parts of the world giving them different languages and they could no longer communicate, hence the term I coined, "babble on." I was determined to somehow define and refine a universal language through the use of radio station call signs and abbreviations and symbols so the world could unite and communicate through my divinely appropriated language.

I also became convinced I could find a cure for cancer and it was as simple as taking mega doses of vitamin C – "C" to cure "the big 'C'!" I firmly believed I had the answers to all of the world's ills and all I had to do was keep putting everything I knew together in a string of believable arguments since I was convinced each experience in my life had special and significant meaning.

Everything I thought took on this special meaning, and as I began to study dates of events I saw interesting parallels, such as my being born on my Grandma Davis' birthday and little sister Heidi being born on our great grandmother's birthday. My father was born on inauguration day; and the hostages in Iran were taken on my older sister's birthday. I was convinced our family was special and God was using us in His plan to bring His Son back to create, once and for all, peace and good will for all on earth.

My friends were growing deeply concerned because the Holly whom they knew no longer existed. Somehow, someone convinced me to go to Port Huron Hospital for help, but I was only there for five days and I refused to participate in their stupid therapy of making baskets and other such arts and crafts. I had to get out in time to pay my ticket for the speeding accident while drunk, which I did.

Upon arriving home from the hospital and not wanting anything to deter me from my "mission," I cut my phone cord so no one could call me and distract me from all the "discoveries" I was making, and I simply quit going to work. I began to pour through the book of Revelations and to believe I understood all the symbolism represented there. I kept thinking, *"What will I do when Danny comes back, all healed and whole? They have frozen his body in cryogenics and they will fix him all up and we will be lovers throughout eternity and we will live forever."* Suddenly the thought of NOT dying became grippingly terrifying, much more horrible than the thought of eventually dying.

The people from Morton Salt gave me a fruit basket and flowers because I'd been in the hospital and I gave it all away to the landlord downstairs except for a large jar of strawberry preserves. I went on a fast for 12 days, eating nothing but the jelly, thinking of myself as "queen bee eating royal jelly," and drinking lots of water. I lost so much weight I was a mere wisp of a lady at 5 feet 9 inches and only 105 pounds.

Christmas time was approaching and I became aware that many of the songs played on WABX had a glory and majesty to them such as none had before. Tom Petty's *"Here Comes My Girl"* was like an anthem to me and I believed Danny was inspiring musicians to write songs specifically for me to communicate his love for me from heaven. Jefferson Starship's album, *"Freedom at Point Zero"* produced powerful ideas, while Bob Dylan's album, *"Slow Train Coming"* with the song, *"You've Gotta Serve Somebody"* told me all musicians, both dead and alive, had united toward the cause of bringing Jesus back for His Second Coming, and the disc jockeys at the radio stations were duly informed to play those songs from heaven to tell me what to do. I believed I was solely responsible for the salvation of the world and I would be the answer for the Jewish people since they never believed Jesus' First Coming was the Messiah and were still awaiting their Messiah. I believed I was "IT"!

Ted Nugent's song, *"Queen of the Forest"* ignited a glorious sense of majesty in me for I was convinced I was queen of the Universe and God's very own special "little darling." All of the songs spoke "the language of God" to me such as "Don't you know you are a shooting star?" And I realized I alone knew exactly what infinity was and I reached and defined infinity. I based this belief upon the infinity symbol (∞) which to me represented a "lying-down figure eight. However, Danny, who wanted to be buried feet-first and who always used to say to me, "Turn it around," in an attempt to get me to look at things from a different perspective, represented infinity, "standing up" or a regular "8" symbol. I would spend hours, drawing various symbols and superimposing the infinity symbol upon the number eight, which looked both like an embellished cross and a flower combined.

And since Danny's nickname was "The Crippled Crab," I called it "CC" for short and since Christ was represented by "C," I "saw" "CC" as double, or the Second Coming. A song even came out around that time called "*Double Vision,*" and I knew I had an "understanding" and comprehension of reality no one else was privileged to have ... I believed since we are created in God's image, and since God is all-powerful and all-knowledgeable, then we, too, could be God and attain His omnipotence and omniscience.

I began to play with every concept I knew such as Einstein's Theory of Relativity and reworked that theory saying "E" (eternal "E"nergy) = "M"ass (Masses of people; Roman Catholic Mass) times "C" (Communication, from "*Jesus Christ, Superstar*" where they sang, "*Why did you have to come in such a backward nation ... where there was no mass communication?*") And suddenly, Neil Diamond's "*Brother Love's Salvation Show*" took on a new reality and meaning for me. I was told by a nutritionist friend that "Jesus would walk the earth and many millions would know Him, but they wouldn't know it was Him." That's when I realized Neil Diamond WAS Jesus and Neil was really in love with me for my devotion to Danny and belief that Danny would come back. I believed God really meant for me to "have" Neil Diamond as Danny's replacement, especially since God used Neil's song, "*I Am, I Said*" to prevent me from suicide back in 1972. And since Neil is Jewish, I became convinced our marriage would, in fact, be the Second Coming of Christ – the ultimate Messiah the Jewish nation would accept and embrace, and peace would finally descend upon the world. And I was Eve, and prepared to rectify the curse of Original Sin whereby Eve listened to the Serpent in the Garden and then blamed Adam. I was the "woman of all humankind" who would turn around the "curse" of Eve's transgressions.

So I began listening to the "Jonathon Livingston Seagull" medley from Neil's "*Love at the Greek*" concert album (interpreting it as "John" – the Baptist, "Living Stone" (the dead shall arise first), "See Gall" or the term, "holy boldness"). I would lie on the couch with headphones on and listen to the intricate cymbal work in that medley, and I taught myself how to levitate my hands to the music ... it was hypnotic; I developed a mind-over-matter skill that, little did I know, would serve to protect me during the next phase of this manic episode. I practiced over and over again, allowing my hands to levitate to that captivating, majestic music.

With the coming of Christmas, I noticed the big ships coming down the St. Clair River across from my house were ornately decorated with Christmas lights on their masts. Believing I was the new birth of the Israeli nation, the promised Messiah to the Jewish people, I meticulously crafted three stars of David on my bay windows in Christmas lights, and I would flash the lights to the ships as they passed by the house. I was also extremely into Jimi Hendrix and his song, *"Electric Lady Land,"* since Port Huron was the birthplace of Thomas Edison, and I believed I was the ultimate lady of the universe, capable of sexual expression quite unlike anything any man ever experienced.

I began to have complete disregard for the value of life because I felt as though I was with the angels and the spirits and no longer was living a carnal life as a human being. One time in mid-winter it was extremely cold, and I tied a scarf over each breast and had on a pair of underwear and rode up to the post office on my motorcycle in the middle of the night to mail a letter to Neil Diamond. Hypothermia could have set in, and I told my friends I didn't care if I died because then I'd be with Danny anyway.

As I'd read about some woman in Revelations who had a significant amount of jewelry, I realized I had to rid myself of all of my worldly possessions in order to be truly "of the Spirit." I began to throw out all of my jewelry and possessions that meant anything to me by placing much of what I owned into garbage bags and taking them to the trash. I became obsessed with order and cleanliness, believing in the saying, "Cleanliness is next to Godliness." I would look to the house up the street from me and see a gentleman washing the interior window surfaces who looked just like Neil Diamond from the *"You Don't Bring Me Flowers"* album jacket. I believed Neil came to Port Huron and moved into that house to let me know he was near me and allowing me a tangible evidence of his presence in my life. Every time I saw that man washing the windows in his house, I became obsessed with cleanliness and discarding extraneous belongings I believed were sinful to own.

Just before the holidays, the Assistant Plant Manager at Morton Salt came to my house and asked me if I would ride with him to Ann Arbor to be evaluated at the University of Michigan Hospital, to which I agreed. I took all of my "supporting documents," volumes of "concepts" I had written, believing I now finally had an opportunity to convince the medical community of my special talents, insights and mission. I talked to one doctor who wanted to commit me and I refused, stating I simply could not be in a hospital over the Christmas holidays, so the Morton Salt official brought me back home.

Upon my arrival home, I spliced my phone cord back together so I could make phone calls, and I arranged to spend Christmas with my ex-husband Wes and his family. I gave everyone record albums as Christmas gifts. After that visit, I realized I had one more thing to do: I had to fulfill Danny's life-long desire and be his "ambulatory representative" and go to Los Angeles, California in search of Neil Diamond. I had to "walk for Danny" to prove the words, **"Holly Holy Love"** for Neil so he would be inspired to marry me and we could together save the world in Neil's *"Brother Love's Traveling Salvation Show."* The wildest trip of my life was about to begin.

Chapter 8: The Bird Has Left The Cage

The goal of our work is for you to develop the capability to use your own resources, to influence your state of mind, your mood so you can to remain strong, vital and calm even when exposed to environmental stressors or primary symptoms.

–William J. Dubin, PhD

I set in motion the boldest plan of my life between Christmas 1979 and New Year's Day 1980. In my mind, Neil Diamond sent for me and would have a plane waiting for me at Detroit Metropolitan Airport on New Year's Day for my departure to Los Angeles. I had much preparation to do such as paying my rent and all of my other bills for three months, selling my wrecked car to my ex-husband, Wesley, and getting $350 worth of traveler's checks. I considered these actions, which completely depleted my savings account, to be those of someone who is fiscally responsible, and I "knew" after three months, the whole world would be supporting Neil and me because we would be the Messiah and our marriage would bring about the ultimate peace the world has been waiting for since the Crucifixion of Jesus Christ. Everyone would bow down to us and all of the resources of the world spent on wars would be diverted to making Neil and me happy for the gift we would give.

The year 1980 had special meaning to me because of the complex belief system I developed based on the number "eight" and the infinity sign, and I knew I was the epitome of infinity; I was living infinity; I was both dead and alive; I had the soul and spirit of Danny Smith residing within me and was therefore no longer just a woman, but I was the embodiment of humankind. I believed I acquired something miraculous both in the jolt I experienced as Danny and I held hands and he died, and in the instantaneous healing from mononucleosis.

On New Year's Eve, I paid particular attention to arranging my apartment to send a message to anyone who would discover it. In the center of the room, I stacked my belongings in a symbolic way as to represent a pyramid – I saw and manufactured reality in symbols and multiple meanings. At the very top of the stack was a small, two-ounce Tupperware container inside of which were three gold pieces my father sent me. He made a most brilliant investment back in the early 70s and purchased thousands of dollars of gold when it was selling for about $30 an ounce. My instructions to my father were if I needed money after my traveler's checks funds were exhausted, he was to sell the gold and wire me the proceeds. Everything in the apartment was arranged to convey "balance." To this day my ex-husband wishes he had taken pictures because he had never seen anything like it – it was a meticulous external expression of the inner workings of where my mind had taken me that was clearly a departure from the real world.

On New Year's Day Wesley came to pick me up and deliver me to the airport. All I took were the clothes on my back, a fuzzy winter coat, my purse, and an FM radio-cassette player. Neil would provide me with my every need. Upon our arrival at the airport, to my amazement and shock, the plane I was about to board was not painted in the typical silver tone embellished with red, white and blue trim. This plane was painted a "frog-green!" Neither Wes nor I had seen a plane painted that color before, which was most comforting to me because I was more convinced than ever that this was, indeed, the plane that Neil, who sang, *"Did you ever read about the frog who dreamed of being a king and then became one?"* had sent for me, especially since those words came from his song, "I Am, I Said" that prevented me from suicide back in 1972. I "knew" Neil Diamond was going to meet me, his "little darling," at LA International Airport some four hours later.

During the long, non-stop flight to LA, I was unduly excited and restless. The mania began to take its toll on my sleep pattern as I was only able to get about four hours of sleep or less each night. This pattern would worsen in the coming weeks as the energy within my body continued to churn and intensify. I no longer felt carnal, but rather like a visible spirit.

When I landed at the airport and exited the plane, I didn't quite know what to do because I didn't know how Neil Diamond would meet me. *Will he have a limousine waiting for me? Will he send a representative because he likes to remain private? How will I know what I'm supposed to do?* So I sauntered into the airport and the first thing I saw were a couple of Roman Catholic nuns who were complaining they were cold, so I gave them my fuzzy winter coat. I figured Neil would soon meet me and he would give me whatever coat I wanted.

I began wandering around the airport and then decided I needed to find a motel so I checked the yellow pages at a phone booth, seeking the "perfect" motel whereby Neil could find me. I selected the Walker-Caravan motel because of Dr. Sidney Walker who performed my back surgery, and because of "caravan" reminding me of Neil's *"Brother Love's Traveling Salvation Show"* song, so I took a taxi there and checked in that Tuesday night.

The following day I listened to my FM radio and found the rock and roll stations in the area so I could begin listening to the music for it to tell me what to do. I knew that through this trip to LA, I was still "walking for Danny" since he said he always wanted to go there, and I knew all the disc jockeys were "in on" Christ's eminent return. I knew they would be inspired to play the music that would continue to communicate Danny's love for me from heaven, which would give me direction as to what I was "supposed" to do next.

I spent most of the day dancing in my room and on the balcony. As evening approached, I decided I should go to the nearby strip mall and get a hairbrush, toothbrush and toothpaste, and a nightgown. I also had brought my mother's cultured pearls with me as a token of Janis Joplin's spirit, which communicated with me through her album called "*Pearl*." In addition, the pearls were an inspiration from my father who only told me one time that he loved me in an autograph by saying, "*The world is an oyster and you are its pearl; and I love you because you're my little girl.*"

As I walked toward the small strip mall, two guys in business suits pulled up beside me and asked me where I was going, and I said I needed to do some shopping. They said, "Well, get in and we'll take you to the mall where you can get something really nice." At that point, I was trusting of everyone and I was lonely, and they seemed harmless enough so I got in and we all went to the mall where I made my purchases. I found them to be entertaining and I think the sentiments were mutual, so I allowed them to take me back to my room at the Walker-Caravan Motel. There, I danced for them on top of the bed, and I told them who I was, that I was one-half of the Messiah, the bride of Jesus Christ and that Neil and I were going to save the world.

I went into the bathroom and one of them followed me, shoved me into the shower, turned it on and held my head under the water saying to me, "Have you ever heard of the hydra?" And he made another Biblical reference and suddenly was gone. I wrapped a towel around myself and went back to my room only to find them both gone ... along with my travelers' checks, my mother's pearls, all of my cash except for about a dollar in quarters and the shopping items I purchased. "*Well?*" I thought, "What are you going to do now? *Listen to the music; it will tell you what to do.*"

The next morning I heard the song by The Who called "*Magic Bus*" and I decided to take advantage of the "ride-all-day-on-a-quarter" the transit company offered. I rode around the city of Los Angeles all day long, transferring to various buses, listening to my radio and trying to figure out why Neil hadn't found me yet. I determined the time wasn't right and it would happen in God's Perfect Plan. My job was to spread the word to as many people as I could that the Messiah was coming, which I did. I stopped at a phone booth long enough to call Morton Salt Company in Michigan telling them I was terminating my employment and would not be coming back to work.

Shortly after I arrived back at the motel, my room phone rang and it was the manager asking me to pay Wednesday's rent. Of course, I had no money, so I told him to come by a little later and I'd pay him. I began to try and figure out how I could find Neil Diamond because by this time, I knew I needed his help to bail me out of the mess I was in. I barricaded the motel room door with the dresser and the bed and began to make phone calls from the Yellow Pages.

At about 9 that night, I heard a knock on my door. "Who is it?" I asked, and a gruff voice said, "The manager. You need to pay your rent." I started to cry saying I'd been robbed the night before and I didn't have it. He replied, "Well then, you'll have to get out because I can't allow you to stay here without paying." After I yelled, "I'm not leaving here until Neil Diamond comes to get me," I heard his footsteps walk away and all was silent ... for a short while.

About an hour later, I heard several male voices outside my door and they began pounding, pounding, pounding on it, insisting I come out. "NO!" I yelled. "Not until Neil Diamond comes here to get me." Then the manager and two policemen knocked in the door through my barricade and bodily removed me from the room. The two cops shoved me in their car and drove me about five blocks and told me to get out, and left me stranded on the side of the road headed toward LA International Airport. I had no money, no food, no cigarettes and no place to stay, so I walked to the airport and proceeded to make that my home.

I wandered around the airport the rest of the night, and the next morning I saw a seagull outside the terminal window. I walked down the terminal and the seagull followed me. *"Aha!" I thought. Neil has come to me in the form of Jonathon Livingston Seagull! This is the sign I've been waiting for ... the seagull will tell me what to do."* Everywhere I went, the seagull followed me ... I went outside and walked up and down the boulevard by the airport, and the seagull followed ... I felt so comforted that Neil was really with me. I told several people I had not eaten in 24 hours and I really needed a cigarette and many of them gave me cigarettes. One gave me $5 so I walked to a nearby restaurant and ate breakfast.

The next night was a Friday night and I was exhausted, scared, cold and didn't know what to do, so I walked across the boulevard to the elegant Hyatt Regency Hotel and wandered into the ladies' room where there was a couch. The lights were so bright I couldn't sleep, but it was finally warm in there and I curled up on the couch for a while until the cleaning lady came in and told me I had to leave. I walked back across the street to the airport and spent the rest of the night there, wandering around and playing at unoccupied computer terminals, trying to connect somehow with Neil.

On Saturday, I finally got the bright idea I should do something about trying to retrieve my lost travelers' checks, but the bank told me it would take more than a week for them to get my money to me and only if I had a permanent address. So much for that plan. I called Beneficial Finance with whom I had a perfect credit rating to try to borrow some money, but they wouldn't loan me any because I was not working.

Saturday night I curled up on one of the benches in the airport terminal and tried to sleep, but could not. When Sunday morning came, another kind traveler gave me $5 so I could again eat breakfast. That's where I had my inspiration because someone played Neil Diamond's *"September Morn"* on the jukebox from his newly released album. Someone at the restaurant told me he was back in Los Angeles from New York where he had been filming "*The Jazz Singer*" under Jerry Leider Productions. And then I knew what I had to do next: I had to walk to the Greek Theater since I had no money for bus fare, and in keeping with his concert album, "*Love at the Greek*," he would meet me there anonymously and it would be our own private moment. I would be able to dance my choreographed "ballet" to the "*Jonathon Livingston Seagull*" medley and he would fall in love with me.

After fortifying myself with a rather large breakfast, I set out upon the lengthy journey on foot to the Greek Theater. When I finally arrived, it felt like I had died and gone to heaven. I took my FM radio-cassette player out onto the stage and turned on my tape of "*Love at the Greek*" and danced my "ballet." I danced with all of the passion and sense of romance I had within me to an imaginary crowd of people. I thought my exertion and expression of energy would somehow reach Neil and let him know where I was. I kept waiting for Neil to arrive. Soon, a helicopter flew overhead and I "knew" it was Neil, watching me, and letting me know the time was not yet right for our union. The afternoon progressed and it began to get rather cool and cloudy, and a combination of panic and devastation swelled up and engulfed my body.

I decided the only thing left to do was to walk back to the airport. I was cold and hungry and had a mere 25 cents in my wallet. I kept trying to catch a bus, but continually missed them and I began to have serious suicidal thoughts. I wanted to simply run out in front of a truck and be run over and once and for all stop this Messiah thing because I did not feel up to the enormous responsibility of saving the world.

Finally I managed to be at a bus stop when the bus arrived and was able to ride the rest of the way to the airport. When I got there, I began talking to someone and told them what happened regarding my robbery and they suggested I try to locate travelers' aid for some assistance. However, because it was Sunday, no one was available to offer help so I was destined to spend one more night wandering around the airport.

When Monday morning dawned, I went straight to travelers' aid and started making some phone calls. They arranged for me to be taken by bus to the YM-YWCA off Hollywood Boulevard where they would provide me with shelter until my travelers' checks were reimbursed and I could pay them back.

I checked in to the extremely small room at the "Y" and used the community shower to finally get cleaned up. One would think after having gone for so many days with essentially no sleep, I would have crashed into the comfortable bed and gotten some rest. But no, I was so energized, I had to go downstairs and check out my surroundings because now I was in Hollywood! A young man who looked a lot like Neil Diamond was nervously waiting at the desk, and I introduced myself to him and he told me he was Kenny Christopher from New York City and had been visiting his uncle in San Diego. He came to Los Angeles to find work and rented the last available room at the Y.

After Kenny checked into his room, he asked me if I wanted to go out for a ride up and down Hollywood and Sunset boulevards to see the lights of the city and have dinner. We got along very well and spent the entire next week together, doing sightseeing and eating together. I told him I was keeping a tab of all of the meals he was purchasing for me and would pay him back when my travelers' checks funds were returned to me the following day, which I did. I paid up my bill at the Y and now had some money in my pocket.

We drove up to a hamburger stand that day to grab some lunch before doing more sightseeing and something happened to Kenny's car where the transmission got stuck and would not go into reverse. He was quite annoyed and went in to call a wrecker. While he was making that call, I got out, lifted the hood and looked at the engine compartment. I waved my highly energized hands over the entire engine, and Kenny came out and asked me what I was doing. "Oh, I think I just fixed your car. Try it now." He started it up and the car's transmission worked just fine. He turned white and said, "What did you do?" I replied, "I just prayed

God would fix your car, and with my magic hands, I transmitted that eternal energy of all energy into your ailing vehicle and it got fixed!"

That incident rather gravely spooked Kenny. However, that night we had scheduled to attend a concert at the Troubadour Auditorium where Neil Diamond performed his concert that became his "*Gold*" album. I was sure Neil would meet me there. When he didn't, after the concert Kenny and I checked into the Riviera Motel and went to a disco bar that turned out to be a gay bar, an entirely new experience for me. I danced the night away and suddenly realized Kenny disappeared so I took a cab back to the Riviera Motel only to find he had not returned. I was abandoned.

The next morning I boarded a bus to Hollywood to find another motel closer to town and to the restaurant next to the Y where I had made some friends. An older gentleman who was a disabled musician took me under his wing and listened to my story and offered me one bit of advice: "Don't spook the natives." While on the bus, someone became ill and I walked toward him to see if I could help. When I returned to my seat, my wallet was gone! I went to the bus driver and told him, "This bus is not going to move until you find out who stole my wallet and get it returned to me." The driver found the culprit and returned my wallet and funds to me. I sat down next to a clean-cut, nicely dressed man named Tommy, and we talked. We both got off the bus together and he walked me to the next motel I would stay at, a roach-infested, cheesy place that didn't even have a blanket on the bed. He wanted to come in but I wouldn't let him.

There were so many roaches in that motel I used almost a whole roll of toilet paper squashing them. In a frenzy to rid the world of all of those evil "spirits," I believed that in order for Neil to come to me there had to be a balance in the number of souls who died and the number left, and the more roaches I killed, the less time it would be before the "life-death" balance would be achieved and I would be Neil's bride.

To stay warm that night, I took down the draperies and used them as a blanket and since I couldn't sleep, I listened to Jim Ladd, the radio station disc jockey who seemed to be the most tuned in to the master plan I believed I was on. Soon I heard a lot of yelling and scuffling outside my door, and suddenly someone started beating and pounding upon my door. "Let me in, please, Holly; it's Tommy; I'm hurt, hurt bad; I need help." The radio station was playing Led Zepplen's *"Stairway to Heaven,"* and the words, *"There's still time to change the road you're on ..."* pierced my soul in my terror as to what I should do. I refused to allow Tommy entry, as I allowed the song to devour my soul, and eventually, he went away. I finally learned I didn't have to help everybody, especially if it meant putting myself in danger.

The next morning was cool and sunny and when I went outside, there was blood all over the sidewalk from the fight the night before. I almost fainted when I realized I could have been implicated or hurt had I not followed the words to that song and attempted to "change the road I was on" by trusting everyone. That day I threw away my identification, cut up and destroyed my drivers' license and Social Security card because in my mind, no longer was I Holly Ralph, but Mrs. Neil Diamond. I went to the Social Security office and somehow they issued me a Social Security card in the name of "Holly Diamond."

It was Super Bowl weekend and I made the mistake of checking out of that horrible motel in an attempt to find another that at least had a blanket and fewer roaches. I walked all over, trying to find a vacancy, which was next to impossible. I remember calling my sister Heidi, crying that I witnessed a man getting stabbed, Neil had not yet come to get me and I didn't know what to do next. She said she had been on her knees in prayer because her own marriage was falling apart and her life had turned into a living hell. I felt responsible for her duress and I told her Jesus Christ's return was eminent and she had nothing to fear.

I walked and walked, and finally, at a street corner, a well-dressed man stopped and asked me if he could help me. I told him I was waiting for Neil Diamond to find me because together we were going to get married, Neil was really Jesus Christ and I was his bride. The man said, "Well, I'm Neil Diamond's alter-ego and I can take you to him." We went on a long drive out along the coast and toward West Palm Beach. He took me to a huge home with a wrought iron fence, telling me it was Frank Sinatra's house, and then drove several more miles out to an abandoned motel in the middle of the desert.

When we got there he pushed me through the door of one of the rooms and shoved me down onto the couch saying, "Stay there if you know what's good for you," as he undressed. Then, using all of the crude words he knew, he said, "Well, are you going to give it up to me or do I have to use this?" as he whipped out a switchblade knife. Terrified, I let him rape me and he disappeared, leaving me stranded, after which a violent thunderstorm dumped a huge amount of rain in a short time, flooding the motel and knocking the power out. I was thankful my little radio ran on batteries because the music was the only thing that soothed my tortured soul.

The next morning, I set out walking and didn't even know which direction I should go. I never hitchhiked in my life, but I knew I needed help, and an elderly, dirty, grungy truck-driver type of guy picked me up and took me back to his trailer. He also wanted to have his way with me, but I told him no one could ever have me again except for Neil Diamond and he begrudgingly took me to the bus station where I made my way back to Hollywood.

When I arrived, I went to a pay phone, called my father and asked him to send me the money for my three gold pieces as the price of gold had risen to just over $900 an ounce. I also called my former boss Marion Evans at Morton Salt Company and asked her to sell my furniture and stereo and wire me the money. Later, I went to Western Union and acquired my funds and then to a bank to open an account. I learned they wouldn't let me have my own money for 10 days! I still had enough funds for a couple of nights at a hotel and I stumbled on the Roosevelt Hotel on Hollywood Boulevard where I made a reservation for a room on one of the upper floors. I pulled the paper drawer lining out of the dressers and began writing in the code I was developing in my effort to define a universal language. I couldn't stop writing, as I would listen to songs and try to decipher what the music was telling me to do. The only choice I had was to walk.

So I went downstairs and began walking again, and soon came upon a happy looking, hippie-type man, playing drums on the sidewalk. He told me his name was Jimi Hendrix, and I told him I was a drummer, too. He asked me to come back to his place where we could "share some licks." Still being way too trusting of people, I accompanied him to his apartment where I saw an alarming drafting board with drawings similar to my own. Suddenly, he forcibly grabbed my upper left bicep and tried to push me toward his bed. In my terror at the thought of being raped again, I began to "think" the cymbal work to Neil's "Jonathon Livingston Seagull," and as I heard those angelic notes flowing through my head, both of my hands and arms began to levitate high above my head and "dance" to the imagined music. Jimi's eyes turned wide and white in fear as he yelled, "Holy Christ, the law is here," and he ran out the door of his apartment with his pants unzipped and disappeared.

Not knowing what to do next, I walked more, and made my way to the large, neon-lit cross on a hill overlooking the city. I danced for Jesus and I removed the bandana I wore around my forehead, which seemed to provide me with a sense of balance, and used it to tie Neil's picture from the "*September Morn*" cassette case onto the cross, symbolizing that Neil, too, had suffered from his own form of crucifixion or he wouldn't have been able to sing of dire loneliness as he had in "*I Am, I Said.*"

I walked back to the Roosevelt Hotel where I resumed my writing. I finally located the phone number to Neil's record company, Arch Angel Recordings, which I wrote on a tiny slip of paper and placed it on the dresser. I was now excited because I believed that finally I had the ultimate connection to "the arch angel," who was Neil himself. I finally had a phone number that might get me in touch with Neil to let him know I was there, waiting for him.

I curled up in bed to try to find some peace and relief in sleep that first night in the Roosevelt Hotel, but my weary body was restless and agitated. It was Martin Luther King's birthday, which, in two short years, I would learn of another amazing event that had taken place this very night. I tossed and turned, and opened the curtains so the night lights could shine in and help me to not feel so devastatingly lost and lonely. Then it happened. I heard that familiar "voice" by the spirea bush saying to me, *"Holly, you MUST NOT MOVE ... you MUST lie perfectly still ... on your back ... and DON'T MOVE ..."*

I froze in fear but did what the voice told me to do. Each breath I took sounded almost like a shout, when suddenly I felt an eerie, chilled "presence" come into the room, under the crack in the door, as it slowly circled around the room, then over me, and was gone as quickly as it came. I laid there in stark terror, trembling, for the rest of the night. The next morning the first thing I did was to go to the dresser to retrieve the little scrap of paper with the phone number on it for Arch Angel Recordings, only to find it was gone! I searched every nook and cranny in that entire room, and that piece of paper was nowhere to be found. I concluded that a ghost had come and removed it, trying to impede my progress toward finding Neil.

Thus, my first order of business for the day was to locate the Arch Angel Recordings phone number again, which I did, and I called them and spoke with a young lady named Allison who told me Neil was married and I was among countless thousands of women who were in love with Neil. I thought of one of the new songs that had come out and the words that went, *"American divorce, you've got to do some drinkin' fast!"* I knew that was what the hold-up was; Neil had to get his divorce before he could legally have me, which meant I probably had a good bit more time to kill.

I don't know how I did it, but somehow I acquired the name and phone number of Neil's attorney, Marsha Gleeman, and contacted her. She confirmed what Allison said and I told her, "Well, you folks just don't know what I know," and hung up. I went back to the Roosevelt Hotel and checked out because I didn't want any more night-time terrors such as I experienced the night before, and I checked in to the Montecito Hotel that had a phone in the room. I also had the phone number for Jerry Leider Productions who were producing "The Jazz Singer" movie scheduled to come out later that year. I called them, but they said Neil was busy and had no time for socializing with fans.

I walked over to the radio station where Jim Ladd was DJ and who should be there but Lauren Bacall to whom I introduced myself, and we shook hands. I was awed by the mighty presence of that woman as she had a charisma about her that completely filled the room.

For the rest of that week, I engaged in "touristy" types of things such as visiting Universal Studios, the wax museum, seeing the movie "1941" because that was the year Neil was born. I also went to a benefit where Charro performed and I met her, but suddenly, I bolted and ran out of there through the fire exit, setting off an alarm, so I ran as fast as I could toward the huge CBS compound on Sunset Boulevard where, to my surprise, I found Kenny Christopher working as a security guard in the guard shack. He was happy to see me and told me he'd found an apartment and would like to take me there when he got off work. He let me into the compound where I proceeded toward one of the doors, only to find Jimmy Stewart exiting, and I met him and shook hands, introducing myself. Again, I had that intense sense of awe come over me as I stared at that massive man and practically got sucked up into his charisma. I guess since I had no identity myself, I was trying to find myself in whomever I met. When I left the CBS compound, I told Kenny I paid a week's rent at the Montecito Hotel and I frequently ate at Love's Restaurant as all I could afford each day was one dollar for a baked potato with the works which filled me up and I felt was nourishing.

One Sunday morning, I wandered into a Catholic Church because I wanted to be closer to God. I made the sign of the cross everywhere I went, but to my embarrassment, the priest, in a charming, fatherly sort of way showed "us" the correct way to make the sign of the cross, as I had been doing it backwards. I felt singled out in my ignorance, but in a way very much loved.

I stayed inside at the Montecito Hotel for several days because torrential rains came for days on end. During that time, I heard the song by ZZ Top where they sang, "*I'm bad, I'm nationwide ...*" and it told me what to do. I went out in the rain to the nearest library and wrote down two radio stations in each state – I did everything in "twos" because it represented the "Second Coming." I sent coded telegrams to each of these radio stations, telling them Neil and I would be getting married, and I charged the telegrams, approximately eleven hundred dollars' worth, to Jerry Leider Productions. I also sent coded telegrams to my friends Joan Boyer, Dolores Rice, and my sister, asking them to please send me some Kool Long Mild cigarettes among other things.

My week's rent at the Montecito was soon to expire and I had no more money. I sold everything I owned, telling people I was living on my assets. One night, I heard a knock at my door and when I opened it, a gentleman introduced himself to me as Marty Drury, a detective for Neil Diamond. "*Oh my gosh,*" I thought; "*now it's really happening. He's going to take me to Neil.*"

I sat cross-legged on the bed, looking as cute and demure as I knew how, and Mr. Drury began asking me what I was all about. I told him my story, that I was waiting for Neil to come get me, or for someone to take me to him. I believe the detective realized I was harmless as far as having any intentions of hurting Neil, but I also think he was concerned I might become suicidal once I realized my "reality" was a total fabrication of my manic mind and not at all real or true. The last thing Neil needed was to have a fan commit suicide over him and the publicity that would raise.

The next morning, I learned "Neil Diamond's people" paid for another weeks' rent at the Montecito Hotel, but the phone service in my room had been cut off. I went walking and exploring more and found the house Sharon Tate had lived in. I fell prostrate on the ground in front of her house, sobbing at her fate that Charles Manson had perpetrated. I told her I would be instrumental in resurrecting her from the dead once the Second Coming of Christ occurred through my marriage to Neil.

Someone told me Neil lived out by Malibu Beach, so I made my way out there, only to discover it was a gated community, and I learned Cher Bono also lived there. I ended up at a house inhabited by a bunch of hippies and stayed at an all-night party, smoking pot and dancing, and keeping the guys from trying to have their way with me. In the morning, one gruff, unkempt, derelict man asked me how I planned to get back to the Montecito Hotel, and I told him I didn't know the way. He told me he'd take me, but only if I stopped at his place first. Being desperate for a ride since I was totally lost, I agreed, which turned out to be another of my many judgment mistakes in my manic stage.

He took me to a run-down trailer park where he had a dilapidated camper trailer with a sleeper over a truck and he pushed me inside and said, "You'll like this. You need this." Being terrified and remembering the switchblade knife from the previous encounter out in the desert, I acquiesced and allowed him to undress me and basically to rape me. Late that afternoon, he did take me back to the Montecito where I took a shower to try and feel "clean" once again. I was so thankful for the tubal ligation I'd had several years before because at least I couldn't get pregnant from the men taking advantage of me.

The following day, I again walked over to the CBS compound to try to find my only friend, Kenny Christopher. He was just getting off work and asked me if I wanted to go to his apartment and drink some vodka. I told him I wanted him to take me by Jerry Leider Productions so I could audition for a part in a movie. Reluctantly, he took me there, and I went in and asked to speak to Mr. Leider while Kenny waited outside in his car. I sat in the waiting room for a while, hoping that the staff was getting hold of Neil when, to my surprise, two police officers, one male and one female, entered the building. Kenny followed them in just as they were saying to me, "You must leave these premises NOW. You are trespassing." I sat down on the floor and screamed, "I AM NOT LEAVING HERE UNTIL NEIL DIAMOND COMES TO GET ME!"

The officers said, "Do we have to physically remove you? We have been instructed to get you out of here; you are trespassing ..." and Kenny interrupted them saying, "Come on, Holly. Come with me. They don't want you here. I'll take you back to my place." I became dizzy and faint, it felt like the walls were closing in on me, but I followed Kenny to his car and we went to his apartment.

Shortly after we got there, Kenny got a phone call, and I only heard bits and pieces as he said, "Yes, I will. I will do the best I can." He was visibly shaken and white when he came back and offered me a shot of vodka which he was gulping down rather heavily. I said, "Kenny, PLEASE, take me to the mountains; I want to go to the mountains ... I NEED to go to the mountains ... PLEASE take me there ... The mountains are the only place I feel FREE ..." and he said, "I've had too much to drink to drive you anywhere right now."

After what seemed an eternity, there was a knock at his door, and Kenny let in the two police officers who requested that I leave Jerry Leider Productions. They said, "Why don't you come with us? We can take you to Neil Diamond." I later learned the phone call Kenny received had come from Marty Drury, Neil's detective who interviewed me at the Montecito, and he told Kenny to keep me at his apartment no matter what he had to do.

I willingly got in the patrol car and asked, "Where are you taking me?" They replied, "we're taking you to Neil; that's what you want, isn't it? What are you going to do with Neil once you meet him?" I said, "Oh, well, I'll probably chase him around the bed and get him to seduce me. But first, would you take me by the Montecito Hotel so I can get my clothes and radio?" They agreed and when we arrived there, they followed me to my room and allowed me to retrieve my belongings.

Then began the scariest ride of my life because they took me to L.A. County General Hospital, and when I arrived, I asked, "Is Neil going to meet me HERE?" They took me to the admissions area and vanished from sight as the orderlies began to check me in. I was ushered to a very small room on a locked ward with two tiny, hard twin beds and told to go to sleep. However, by that time, even lying still was such a joke to me that I proceeded to jog up and down the hallway to try to wear myself out.

An orderly grabbed me and said, "You're supposed to be sleeping. We cannot have you running up and down the halls," and escorted me back to my room where I started screaming, "YOU'RE SUPPOSED TO GET NEIL DIAMOND HERE TO PICK ME UP!" And I started kicking and thrashing about and a very large woman came in to try to restrain me and I kicked her with all of my might in the sternum. Suddenly, I heard "CODE RED" and some kind of alarm went off, and the room was instantly filled with doctors and orderlies who strapped me into a straight jacket and wheeled me into another room under an open window. They gave me a shot of something telling me I had to stay there for the rest of the night since I wouldn't behave. I felt like a caged animal, being punished ... and I laid there wide awake all night in the freezing air coming through the window, singing *"Song sung blue, everybody knows one; song sung blue, every garden grows one ..."*

The next morning they removed the straight jacket and ushered me into the breakfast room where I met some of the other patients. They allowed me to make one phone call, and I called Kenny, asking him to bring me some cigarettes which he did later that day. No one was allowed to have any lighters and we couldn't leave the ward without being accompanied by an escort. I watched as patients would light their cigarettes from each other's lit cigarettes and to this day, I will not allow someone to light their cigarette from mine.

The ward I was on had a tiered plan relating to the severity of the patients' conditions, called "A-plan," "B-plan," and "C-plan." The lower the letter, the more privileges the patients would have. Of course, that first day, I was considered a "C-plan" patient. However, I attended group therapy and later on the first day the doctors started treating me with lithium. They told me I had bipolar disorder and had been experiencing a severe manic episode. That was the first I ever heard of bipolar disorder. I asked them how long I had to stay there and they told me a minimum of 72 hours, so I thought I'd be free fairly soon. I did everything they told me to do but trusted no one.

By the third day they informed me that a judge had committed me for the full 18 days the law would allow someone to be confined without their consent. One of the "A-plan" patients was permitted to have scissors so I had her cut my hair into bangs and trim the ends, which she rather botched as it was all uneven and straggly looking. Since I had so few clothes, another kind lady gave me a pair of her jeans. By the fourth day, because I behaved so well, I was moved up to "B-plan," and was granted a pass to leave the premises accompanied by an "A-plan" patient, and I went for a walk with her to an ice cream place and purchased a milk shake.

I believe the shock of being hospitalized was part of what began to bring me back to reality, and I realized soon that I had literally been out of this world. During the group therapy sessions, I was suddenly able to offer sane, reasonable help to others, which shocked the doctors as I was finally making sense. Of course, I'd had nine years of therapy previously and I knew lots of principles that could help others. It was rather strange to watch how quickly the other patients seemed to recover, almost as if they were motivated at the dramatic change in me. I became a model patient, graduating to "A-plan" by the end of the first week, and I almost felt used because everyone seemed to benefit from my insights and intelligence. Of course, the lithium was probably helping as well.

I celebrated my 32nd birthday in L.A. County General Hospital and Kenny Christopher brought me a small cake. He apologized for my having to be there and emphasized that he had done what he thought was the best thing for me by keeping me at his house so I could be taken to get help. I told him that they would not let me out unless I could be turned over to someone who could take care of me; otherwise, I'd have to go to a half-way house. He agreed to take charge of me and let me stay at his apartment.

So when my 18 days passed, they discharged me to Kenny's care and I went to his place, wondering what I would now do with my life. I decided I needed to somehow get off the streets" and get connected to "real people," so I called Dr. Roger Callahan, the first therapist I had seen in Detroit back in 1967, who moved to New York and later relocated his practice to Los Angeles. I asked him if I could attend a few of his group sessions, and he said, "I'll have to charge you, you know."

I said to him, "Dr. Callahan, have you ever heard of charity? Do you have a charitable bone in your body or are you so steeped in Objectivism that you cannot offer help to someone in dire need? I just got out of L.A. County General Hospital after 18 days and I need your help and I don't have any money." So he agreed to allow me to sit in on a few of his group sessions, but told me that I'd have to let the "paying patients" talk first and if there was any time left, I could talk. I thought, *"How generous of him!"*

The next day Kenny took me to Dr. Callahan's office, and I was amazed at how plush, elite and upper-class the environment was, and I knew that that's what I needed—to be reintroduced to the environment I had once been a part of. I listened to one of the group members whining that her husband wouldn't get her the car she wanted and how could she get him to purchase what she wanted rather than the one he desired to get her. I tentatively asked, "Dr. Callahan, may I please make a comment here?" And he said, "Yes, what do you have to say?"

I said, "Ma'am, do you know what? You should be grateful you even HAVE a car to drive; you should be grateful you have a husband who WANTS to get you a car. Why are you wasting your precious mental energy arguing about such a trivial thing rather than being grateful for what you do have? You know, there are those of us who have NOTHING." There was something about that exchange that set about in me a determination to somehow turn my life around. Interacting with these high-society people made me realize I could come back to reality and start my life over again.

After that group session, I called my parents in North Carolina and asked them if they would allow me to come there and stay with them until I recovered. They indicated that Neil's attorney, Marsha Gleeman, had already contacted them and that there was nothing they could offer me. So, out of desperation, I called my Aunt Janet and Uncle Leo in Michigan and asked them if I could borrow $200 for bus fare to come back to Michigan, and if I could stay with them until I could get back on my feet. They were so happy to learn that I was finally coming back to reality, they were only too willing to help. My family felt so helpless during this entire episode because there was absolutely nothing they could do, and they feared the worst would happen to me. Little did they know what I had experienced.

I stayed with Kenny a few more days until the money was wired to me, and attended a couple more of Dr. Callahan's group sessions, each of which helped me acquire more of a grip on reality. At least I knew I finally made a rational decision to return to Michigan. I thanked Dr. Callahan for his generosity and told him how helpful he had been. Then I made one last phone call before boarding the bus for the long journey back to Michigan. I called Marsha Gleeman and told her I was going home. I told her I was sorry for the trouble I may have caused and she said, "Holly, L.A. is not a good place for someone to regain their stability. I believe you are doing the right thing in going back to Michigan, and I wish you well in your recovery."

That journey seemed to be the longest of my life as it took three days and two nights of constant traveling to make it home to Michigan. We stopped at Las Vegas, Nevada, where the power went out and the bus terminal was totally black; we stopped in Salt Lake City where I bought a car coat because I was so cold. On the way through Wyoming, we were traveling through a snowy mountain pass when the bus started to slide dangerously. The driver asked us all to move to the left side and front of the bus as the rear of the bus actually slid off the road and was hanging over a precipice. He called for help and a huge tow truck came and pulled us back onto the road. When we were once again stable, the driver stood up and said, "That's it. After tonight, I'm retiring!"

The remaining trip home was uneventful and I found I was able to get some sleep as we traveled. When we pulled into the bus depot in Farmington, Michigan April 1, 1980, I was never so glad to see two faces as I was when Aunt Janet and Uncle Leo came to greet me. They said I looked like a waif because I was so skinny, grungy and bedraggled appearing. They took me to the comfort of their home where I immediately took a long, hot shower and put on one of Aunt Janet's nightgowns. I don't believe I've ever been so grateful to two people in my entire life. We talked for a while and I fell into bed getting the best night's sleep I had in months.

The next morning Aunt Janet fed me a perfect breakfast, and we began to discuss how to implement my recovery. I was beginning to feel like I had completely left the cosmos. Coming back to reality had only just begun.

Chapter 9: Return Through The Stratosphere

Self doubt has held you back before, and may hold you
back now. Don't let it! Don't worry about whether or not
you are good enough: Focus on performing the task at hand.

—William J. Dubin, PhD

"Who am I? I have nothing. Nothing but the clothes on
my back and an FM radio-cassette player. Where have I been?
Who have I been? I am nothing. What's going to happen to me
now?" These thoughts churned over and over in my mind as I sat
on the couch in the comfort of Aunt Janet and Uncle Leo's home
in the realization that for the last year I totally departed from the
boundaries of natural reality and gone off far away into the outer
limits of the universe somewhere, maybe even to another galaxy.
In fact, I felt as though I had "visited" some other universe light
years away in space and time. The Talking Heads had sung a song
that went something like, *"...Moving into the universe, and she*
was; ... she was not touching the ground, and she was; she had
a present elevation, and she was; ... in the world as a missing
person, and she was."

That's what I felt like as I sat there wondering what I needed
to do to come down from this intense and lengthy escapade into
a disturbing thought disorder. I felt like a "missing person" as I
pondered, *"How do I get back into the realm of normalcy? What*
is normalcy? What next? Will anybody ever trust me again?
What is the point of anything? I can't sit here and mooch off Aunt

Janet and Uncle Leo forever … I wish I could just wave a magic wand and be back to normal …"

Amazingly, through the patient love of my Aunt Janet and Uncle Leo, I finally felt safe and accepted, at least to them. I realized my thoughts simply must turn to one word: <u>survival</u>. In a way, although I was lost, empty and devastated that the "reality" my brain created was purely a trip into psychosis, I had a drive and motivation to pick up the pieces and do what I could to resume a realistic life style.

We all knew that the first order of business was to get me to a health professional so I could continue receiving the lithium for stability. Other health matters needed attending to as well because my lower front teeth were practically falling out due to the near head-on collision in Port Huron the preceding fall. Also, while in Los Angeles, I had given my glasses away as part of my conviction that I needed to surrender all of my identity in order to become "Mrs. Neil Diamond, the Bride of Christ," and I recalled leaving them in the form of a particular "imagery" around a candle at a restaurant as if to tell someone that I had "seen the light" and to give them the message that they would also soon encounter the same revelation some day.

Since I was an indigent, I could only pursue governmental sector health care providers, and we found an agency that had a psychiatrist on staff. When I went to see him I was frightened because I found he was a foreigner who spoke English in a thick, extremely difficult-to-understand accent. *"How can I possibly communicate with him? How can I understand him when I can barely perceive reality? How is he ever going to understand where I am?"* He talked with me for a while, and I tried to tell him where I'd been – *"basically, lost in space among the angels and the stars,"* I remember saying to him. He was immediately fascinated with my case, and brought in another doctor to talk with me. This was a repeat of several of the scenes in L.A. County General Hospital: all the doctors were extremely curious about me and in no time at all they each developed files on me at least an inch thick!

The doctors had me leave the room and asked Aunt Janet and Uncle Leo to come in for a consultation. When this discussion was completed and we were on our way home, me with a prescription for lithium in hand and an order for laboratory work to obtain a serum lithium blood level, Janet and Leo told me the doctors told them I would never work again. They suggested I apply for Social Security Disability Income (SSDI) because they said my cognitive abilities were all but annihilated. Their cynicism was the motivation I needed to begin to come around because I began to adopt an attitude of, *"Oh yeah? Well, I'll show them who's competent and who's not. They're fixin' to learn a thing or two about Holly Susan Ralph."*

During the first and second weeks that I was "home" at Aunt Janet and Uncle Leo's pleasant surroundings, we continued to pursue getting me put back together. They took me to a dentist and paid for me to get a lower partial denture; they invested in an eye doctor's appointment and new glasses. They graciously ran me around to all the various state service agencies where I applied for and received a monthly assistance check and food stamps. I gave them all the funds I received except enough for my cigarettes.

Our time together was most enjoyable because they knew I was trying to pitch in and help what I knew was an inconvenience to them. I felt I was disrupting their home and retirement by my fears and frustrations, and periods of elation and despondency. I volunteered to do as much as I could to help them and took on the tasks of cleaning up the kitchen after Aunt Janet prepared dinner; washed the dishes; took out the trash twice a week; mowed the lawn for Uncle Leo; and vacuumed and dusted. These tasks began to incorporate a sense of purpose and structure to my life, something highly important to assist in coming down from mania, as well as useful to help divert the intensity of depression that was trying to set in. After one experiences such a high mania, a rebound depression almost consistently follows.

Every night after dinner I'd finish cleaning the kitchen, and we'd settle in to watch some TV with "*M*A*S*H*" being our favorite show. We'd stay up and watch Johnny Carson and then I'd go to my bedroom and listen to the rock and roll on my little radio in an effort to fall asleep. It was the only connection with "my world" that I wasn't quite ready to let go of. The music was healing to me as it allowed me to fantasize and lighten up for a short while regarding the severity of the position I was still in of having basically nothing.

A friend of my drum teacher and his wife had a bicycle he let me borrow and, although it was a man's bike, it allowed me to at least ride around the neighborhood, get some exercise, and see something besides the four walls at my aunt and uncle's home. It provided me with some "wheels" that afforded a tiny degree of freedom. By getting out in that way and communing with nature – the huge trees and lovely flower gardens of the neighborhood – I was able to get into a mental trance whereby ideas came to me that would continue to assist in a return to my former stable, productive self. My "legal mind" was liberated to work on all of the angles that would result in further assistance out of my dilemma of having nothing and having to depend upon Aunt Janet and Uncle Leo.

While on one of these rides, I decided two things: One, to file for bankruptcy and discharge all my debts, including the $1,100 of Western Union telegrams I charged to Jerry Leider Productions just in case they had any ideas of suing me to collect; and two, to find a workers' compensation attorney and sue Morton Salt because the conditions on my job the previous summer and fall "accelerated and aggravated my disorder."

I handled the bankruptcy completely with no legal assistance and Uncle Leo again loaned me money for the filing fees; I represented myself at the court hearing and all of my debts were discharged so I could start anew. The attorney in the Morton Salt lawsuit was exceptionally good, and eventually, about a year later, we won an award of $12,000 dollars of which I received

$8,000. However, that suit would not be of any immediate help because I needed to regain my independence NOW, not a year from now.

I began pouring through the papers, looking for jobs I thought I could perform, which was a motivating and somewhat uplifting exercise because it forced me to look at my strengths and interests, knowledge and abilities. Of course, part of this process dictated the necessity of preparing a resume. Again this sort of stabilizing project requiring mental discipline was a positive and healing challenge. I thought of my determination to show the doctors a thing or two about my nature as a "comeback kid," so I worked diligently to make my mind move in the direction of producing a winning resume that would allow me to reenter the workforce.

The next item needing attention was the acquisition of a starter office-attire wardrobe. Uncle Leo came through for me again and loaned me enough money to get a few outfits that I could mix and match and have something suitable for at least a week. Once I obtained some dresses and got my hair trimmed and styled, I began submitting my resumes to employers having open positions I believed I could handle.

This entire process served as a real-world focusing of my thoughts, geared toward taking responsibility for my well-being both personally and fiscally. However, the lithium made me numb; it made me walk in a subtle, slowed sort of shuffle; it made my hands tremor which I found to be both shameful and embarrassing. It also definitely slowed my mind down, which, of course, was the whole point in taking it – to eliminate the racing, manic thought processes. Yet I felt slowed almost to the point of retardation because I found it hard to think at all as it felt like a tourniquet had been placed around my brain to prevent it from erupting into the devastating thought disorder.

I accepted these limitations and forged ahead with my next challenge: "*How will I be able to pursue potential job interviews without a vehicle?*" This is where networking with people;

establishing close, loving friendships; and endearing myself to others paid off because Jimmy and Joan Boyer had an old, junky Pontiac they were willing to sell me for $100 that I paid for out of my monthly assistance checks. Joan came up to Farmington Hills from the downriver area where they lived and took me back to their place so I could pick up my "wheels." The car certainly was nothing to look at and needed lots of repairs, but it was drivable.

As I left for the first interview, it started to pour down rain, and I discovered to my dismay that the car's windshield leaked at the roofline right on my lap! The rain came down in sheets and I became soaked, but I went to the interview anyway! At least the rain provided some relief from the summer heat since the car's air conditioning had long ago given out.

The job was for a data entry clerk in a rather dingy building with garish blue paint in all the hallways. I was glad I did not get that job because the whole atmosphere was confining and depressing. However, the next day, I got a call from an advertising agency quite close to my aunt and uncle's home. The agency was seeking a receptionist, and I did well at the interview as I was able to hide the tremors in my hands and present myself with enthusiasm, optimism and enough professionalism such that they offered me the position on the spot. I was shocked, delighted and terrified all at once. Immediately, I began to have doubts as to whether I could handle it, but I knew I at least wanted to try.

I started working there the following Monday and right away,I knew something was wrong with this work environment. The chief executive officer of the agency was a bit of a nut case in that I could hear him in the back, yelling at the agency's advertising representatives, graphic artists and the office manager. He cursed incessantly and one time, when I had to walk by his office to use the ladies' room, I saw him standing up on his desk, waving his arms and shaking his fist at one of the other employees. I hadn't seen that kind of overtly aggressive and insane behavior from any of the folks in L.A. County General Hospital!

One of the secretaries immediately befriended me as she had only been on board for a month longer than I had. She lived right around the corner from my aunt and uncle and she stopped by one day after work to tell them what kind of environment we were in. Thank heavens she did because I was beginning to wonder, after two weeks of yelling between the office manager and the CEO, and his completely unprofessional behavior toward his other employees, if Uncle Leo would believe my stories about the agency since I just returned from an out-of-this-world mental adventure into delusions of grandeur myself.

Uncle Leo told Roseanne, "This is the worst possible environment for Holly because she just got out of the hospital a few months ago and is still very fragile. I'm so thankful she has you to confide in about her anxieties about working there." Confiding in her soon proved to be the least of my concerns because the muffler went out in the Pontiac, and I took it in to have it repaired, only to discover the gas tank was leaking. Uncle Leo suggested I junk the car after I determined my secretary friend was more than willing to provide me with transportation to and from work.

It wasn't long that one of the advertising representatives approached me saying he had a Dodge Demon for sale for $1,500 that he had refurbished, and he would accept payments directly from me. Now I had a car that was quite dependable and I could resume a social life of my own. I could drive to Berkley, Michigan and visit with my girlfriend Dee, who was dating Danny's best friend. I could drive down to Jimmy and Joan's and I could go out to the bar once in a while. Life was beginning to normalize and stabilize for me. I was becoming free and responsible.

It wasn't long after acquiring my own car, before I completely paid for it, that my employer's CEO called me into his office and laid me off. For someone like me who lacked confidence, had serious rejection and abandonment issues and was riding a borderline of depression most of the time, this action was devastating. I immediately became both suicidal and hysterical because the next day I drove to the building with a vengeance and contemplated killing myself by driving my car through the glass doors such that I could do damage to his property as well as ridding the world of a loser such as me. I viewed myself as an inveterate failure who couldn't even keep a job because I was certain he laid me off simply because I showed outward fear of him. *"I'll show him who has the power in this world; he only thinks he can push me around; I'll make him sorry he ever hurt me; I'll hurt him a good one and it will be on his conscience."*

However, I went home from my failed mission of demolishing his property, crying and screaming all the way, and disappeared into my room where I buried my head in the pillow and softly cried myself to sleep. Later that afternoon, Aunt Janet and Uncle Leo lovingly told me they thought it was the best thing for me, that I was in no danger, and I would be able to find another job as easily as I found that one, which they admitted had taken them both quite by surprise. Their encouragement and support helped me feel a bit more worthwhile because a tiny bit of optimism crept back into my overall view of life.

Within days, I had a job interview at another advertising agency at which I performed with dignity and expertise. I was intensely excited about this opportunity because, while the position would be responsible for advertising copy typing and receptionist duties, it also afforded a new challenge: producing the final typesetting for the magazine ads in the sheet metal industry using an AM International Varitype computerized typesetting machine. I would be able to learn all about various type fonts and graphic design layout in addition to typing up raw ad copy and the agency billing statements. The job was diversified and complex; I felt up to all of its tasks. Mr. Temple informed me he would make a decision following the Labor Day weekend.

In the meantime, my friend whom I met in Los Angeles, Kenny Christopher, was back in New York and he invited me to go to the "Big Apple" for a visit over the holiday weekend. I paid for the round-trip bus fare myself as I had been given an adequate severance check, and was almost all caught up in paying back my debts to Uncle Leo. As well, I made the final payment for the Dodge Demon.

The Friday before Labor Day, Mr. Temple called my aunt and uncle who gave him the number at Kenny's. Before my weekend had hardly begun, I received a phone call with a job offer and I was to start "as soon after Labor Day as possible." My entire family was amazed at how easily I was able to acquire not only a job, but interesting work that stretched my knowledge, no matter what the labor market and state of the economy may have been at any given time.

The first day of my new job couldn't come fast enough because I noticed during the interview process that everyone at G. Temple Associates seemed happy, upbeat and sure of themselves. And they were delighted with the prospect of incorporating my enthusiasm with their staff. When I walked in, everyone greeted me with such warmth and openness, I felt like I found a new home and family. I dazzled Gerry Temple with how fast I could whip out the ad copy for him to proofread; and I amazed the art director with how quickly I learned the Varitype equipment. The first several months on that job flew by almost like race cars flying in the Indy 500!

I was engaged; I was learning new things; I was impressing people right and left with my mental acuity; my ability to edit and improve the ad copy and news releases; my suggestions as to type specifications, white space and design; and my ever-present enthusiasm and optimism. I was just about as high as I could get while being constrained by the lithium, which I continued to take faithfully.

Soon springtime of 1981 rolled around and I was steadily improving my lot in life, having paid back Uncle Leo for all of the money he loaned me to get back on my feet again. I was paying him rent for my room, buying my own food and continuing to help with the chores around the house. My little sister Heidi, who was living in Orlando, Florida, wanted me to come down during the Easter season for about 10 days, as she was determined that

I acquire a "Florida tan." She wanted to share her church with me as she had become quite involved with the Assembly of God charismatic movement.

Gerry Temple granted me enough vacation time around the holiday such that I could fly down and visit Heidi and meet my little niece Ginger, whom I'd never seen and she was already 2 ½ years old. Uncle Leo and Aunt Janet encouraged me to go since I was debt-free; had won the lawsuit with Morton Salt Company and had more than $8,000 in the bank. They were preparing to have a celebratory mortgage-burning party since my payment of rent to them facilitated their paying off their mortgage almost three months early.

I flew in to Orlando late in the evening, so thrilled to see Heidi since I had not seen her in five years. She picked me up and we went out for coffee where she excitedly told me all about her friend who could lay hands on people and pray for them in Jesus' name and they'd be healed. Heidi desperately wanted Sarah to pray for me and heal me of my bipolar disorder so I wouldn't have to keep taking the lithium and getting blood levels drawn, and so forth. Heidi wanted to share her faith and church with me.

She prepared a pallet for me to sleep on in their living room, so we came in quietly to keep from waking up little Ginger and Heidi's husband. The next morning I awoke to the most darling presence of my baby niece, squatting down with her elbows on her knees, watching me sleep! It was my introduction to what I thought was absolutely the cutest little niece in the world!

The visit with Heidi, Fred and Ginger was packed full of love and adventures in sunbathing as Heidi tended to me with expertise so I wouldn't burn, but rather slowly "brown" because she wanted me to go back to Michigan with an obvious Florida tan! It was a vacation I will always cherish.

By mid-week Heidi introduced me to Sarah, her friend of strong faith and belief in the healing power of God, who prayed for me. As she did, she laid her hands on my head and I felt a sense of magic wash over me – a strange power that I could not describe. Sarah prayed, *"Dear Father, we know Holly is one of your children and you don't want her to be sick. We know she has been anointed with the perfect mind of Jesus Christ and she isn't meant to be ill and having to take drugs. Father, I ask you, in Jesus' name, to permit Holly to be well without having to rely on medication."* This planted the seeds of another manic episode soon to come.

The following day was Good Friday, and I decided to be baptized in the Holy Spirit through a full immersion baptism at the Assembly of God church. To my knowledge, I had never been baptized and since Sarah prayed in faith with me, I believed this to be the correct action to take to help enhance my faith and to channel it in a more definitive direction than the wild, unchurched faith I engaged in during the period after Danny's death when I experienced my first manic episode.

Full immersion meant I had to go into a changing room and don a baptismal robe. My sister Heidi and I were so thrilled that not only were we blood sisters, but now we were finally going to be "double-sisters," as we would be sisters in Christ, both daughters of the King Himself. We squeezed into the tiny changing room, excitement mounting, and I removed all my clothes but my underwear when suddenly the door was pushed open by the pastor himself! What a hysterically funny moment as he turned beet red in embarrassment, saying, "Ooops! Sorry ladies," and hastily shut the door so I could slip into what I felt was the sacred robe. I was nervous and thrilled, and hoped he wouldn't hold me under the water for too long.

Actually, in that spirit-filled, gorgeous house of God, elegantly dressed out in Easter lily splendor, he simply dunked me once and prayed for me while the large congregation also prayed for me. I was now fulfilled as a Christian, a legitimate member of the Body of Christ, part of a royal priesthood, an ambassador of Christ, a messenger of good will, a bearer of light. At that moment, I made the commitment to spend the rest of my life honoring God and striving to be more like Jesus by seeking to understand Holy

Scripture and carrying out what I perceived to be the Will of God for my life. I didn't know exactly what that was, but somewhere in the far reaches of my mind, the vision I had when I was seven years old by the spirea bush began to take shape.

I returned to my aunt and uncle's in Michigan the next day, and as Sarah had prayed over me, in faith I stopped taking the lithium in April 1981. I felt calm, tranquil and fulfilled, and did not believe I really needed to ingest something that reminded me of a battery. I was tired of the tremors, walking with a shuffle and experiencing my creativity as being shackled. I thought I was okay before Danny died and I would be okay now.

Since I had the money from the lawsuit against Morton Salt in my bank account, I purchased a nicer, more reliable car; found an extremely small, furnished, one-bedroom apartment above the living quarters of an elderly couple; purchased another motorcycle; and struck out on my own again. Work was going well; I was challenged daily; and now I was faced with my age-old dilemma: I was lonely again and had too much time on my hands.

Fortunately, my little apartment was within only a few blocks from my good friend Dee, and as the summer progressed, I spent much of my free time with her and her children and went out to the bars with her and Joan Boyer since my friend Deborah moved back to Seattle. I didn't drink very much and tried to consume sodas most of the time in an effort to save money and to not become used to alcohol. On Sundays, I went to a little Assembly of God church for a while, and then to the charismatic Catholic Shrine of the Little Flower right around the corner from me. It began to eat at me that I could not partake in Holy Communion, the Lord's Supper, because I was not Catholic.

I met a couple through one of the news release writers at my job, and she and her husband, the new couple and I went to T.G.I. Fridays for happy hour a few times. The husband seemed quite taken with me, but I vowed I would not be a flirt toward a married man ever again because that was not "Christian;" it violated the Ten Commandments explicitly. One time, Mike called me and asked me to come over to his and Betty's house to have a drink with them and smoke some "excellent **sinsemilla** weed" that Mike just purchased. Since I knew they were friends of Patty's and had been out with them a couple of times, I figured it was a safe social engagement and I rode my motorcycle over to their house.

When I got there, Betty was rushing about the house and I thought, *"There's something wrong with this picture. Why does she appear to be getting ready to go somewhere?"* Mike asked me to come down to the basement with him where they had an exquisite entertainment room complete with wet bar, and he prepared me a Black Russian. Soon, I heard Betty opening the front door saying, "Good-bye, dear. I'll be back in a little while." I realized that I actually did not know this couple too well other than the fact that they were friends with Patty from work.

After she left, I asked, "Mike, where is she going? I thought we were all going to have drinks and try out your stuff?"

He replied, "Oh, she's going to some dumb hen party ... they're fashioning macramé plant hangars and she wanted to hang out with the girls this afternoon. We can still have our fun."

My blood ran cold because I was now in the room alone, getting a bit tipsy with one of the sexiest men I'd ever met. He loaded some of the marijuana into a small pipe and we began to smoke it. I tried to stop after my usual "two-toke-wonder" high, but he encouraged me to have more, after which he said, "Let's go upstairs where it's more comfortable."

"I assume that means the living room?" I asked.

"Yeah, if you're comfortable there – that would be just fine," he replied, and patted my fanny as he mounted the stairs behind me.

I sat in one of their plush chairs and put my feet on the large ottoman, continuing to sip my second Black Russian. Soon he came over and gently pushed my feet to the edge, sat down, and began to caress me. At his first touch, I was "gone" into a state of arousal and sensation beyond anything I ever experienced with a man. This man not only looked sexy, but he had sensuality down to both an art and a science!

It wasn't long before he lowered my jeans and underwear, and I lost all sense of propriety. By that point, the Christian vow that I made to honor the Ten Commandments was obliterated when suddenly, the front door jerked open and Betty came charging in, screaming, "You get the hell outta here ... NOW ... Michael, how many times are you going to do this to me? I can't turn my back on you and there you go again, hustling anything in a skirt ... Get out of my SIGHT you low-down, two-bit *&#%$*!"

As she continued screaming and yelling, I tried to make myself invisible as I fumbled for my zipper and slithered on out of the house. I hopped on the motorcycle, started and revved it up, and practically flew home where I immediately called Dee and told her what happened. "Dee, I feel so badly ... it just happened ... and I couldn't control the situation ... he is so sexy and just took over and seduced me ... and it felt so good ... I feel awful for Betty ...," I stammered. And of course, that had to remain my secret from Patty and others at work who knew Mike and Betty. I didn't realize sexual indiscretion was a preliminary signal to the oncoming mania again.

About a week later, Patty came in to work and I could tell her eyes were all red and puffy from crying. "Patty," I said, "What has gotten in to you? You look so sad." Compassion for others is something I've always had in bountiful measure even though sometimes during mania, I could be irritable, rude and inconsiderate, like calling people at all hours of the night, simply because I never minded if someone needed to reach me at any time.

"Holly, did you read the paper? Do you know what happened?" Patty replied.

"No, I don't bother to read the paper," I responded. "Tell me what's going on."

"Oh, Holly, Mike was killed ... he was driving down to Ohio for his work and an 18-wheeler rear-ended his car, and there were tires in the trunk that could have protected him, but they didn't, and ... oh, Holly, Mike is DEAD! Mike is DEAD! What's Betty going to do?" Patty's tears started all over again as I hugged her partly to support myself as well because my knees had turned to Jell-O.

"Oh my God," I thought. "It's my fault: God has stricken Mike down in His wrath over Mike's infidelity to Betty, but it's my fault. Betty is the one suffering, not me. Oh, God, I'm SORRY! Why didn't you take ME out and not Mike? Oh, dear Father, PLEASE comfort Betty...." At that moment I vowed never again to become involved with a married man; at least I thought I never would because I didn't want to press my luck, nor did I want to cause another woman to become widowed. I believed Mike's accident was fully my fault.

Not long after that most unfortunate incident, I decided I wanted to try to quit smoking again. Somehow I believed that if I could honor God in that way, by giving up that nasty habit, I would find "Mr. Right," or rather, God would send him to me. I had been dating another friend of Patty's who was exceptionally nice looking, dark, swarthy, extremely intelligent and also quite satisfactory in bed. However, Duane had one habit that continuously disappointed me and that is, he'd come to my little apartment, make love to me, and then leave to go home. He never spent the night with me; he never cuddled or talked afterward. It was the proverbial "wham, bam, 'thank you, ma'am'" sort of interaction.

One time, he asked me to make the rather long drive to his house and he cooked me dinner. It was an elegant home, and I welcomed being away from my tiny apartment. The sex that night was better than usual, and I wondered if he was more comfortable on his own turf. He even held me afterward and let me spend the night. However, early in the morning, he wakened me and said, "Holly, there's something I must tell you. You have to leave because my girlfriend might be over at any minute. She's been away all week and was due home last night and said she'd be coming over today. She's married and can only see me at certain times...," but I was no longer hearing him.

Suddenly there was meaning to his apparent coldness. I didn't stand a chance with him. I was "the other woman" and would never be his girlfriend. I went home and never saw him again because it resulted in nothing but anguish.

During this time I embarked upon two ventures: One was attempting to occupy myself by writing a novel and the other was to open a typing service business whereby I solicited college students to type their Masters' theses and dissertations. I only completed about 60 pages of the manuscript when the ideas ran out. I was in the middle of typing a paper for a student one night when there was a loud knocking at my door.

I barely got the door open when "JR" sauntered in and I could tell he'd been drinking. He had been Danny's best friend and fishing buddy during Danny's ambulatory days in Port Huron. He shoved me over to the bed saying crude words to me and demanding that I perform.

I started to tremble as I began to recall the two rapes in Los Angeles, and I said, "Junior, what's wrong with you? I don't want to go to bed with you. Danny will make you rot in hell if you hurt me."

"Danny was my friend," Junior almost chanted, "and you couldn't get any action from him; so now you can do so with me, oh let me have you. Oh, yes, you want me, you like men, you need men, here, take this," and he slapped me on the side of the face as he pushed me down, ripped off my jeans and underwear and forced his way with me. I was petrified and crying as he left. I was shocked because I thought he and Dee were still dating, but she had thrown him out for being a drunk and for behaving rudely toward her three children. I called her, hysterical and shocked and asked if I could come over and have a cigarette. She told me to wait while she made a phone call and she got hold of the couple where "JR" was staying, threatening to call the police for what he had done. When she called back, I told her not to contact the authorities, that I didn't want to get involved in that kind of scene.

A few weeks later I became aware something was happening to me again. I felt as though Neil Diamond was calling to my spirit one more time. He just released his *"On My Way to the Sky"* album, and I felt I may be going there with him. The music somehow talked to my soul and eradicated my humiliation and tension. I could no longer type for my clients because I couldn't concentrate on their material. I had "material" of my own to work on as I began to draw my infinity signs with the number "8" superimposed on them which looked like sinsemilla flowers! *"This time, I'll get it right; this time, he will come; I know what I'm doing now and I know how to get him to come. Because last time, I was destitute and walking the streets; now, God will allow His Bride to come forth as a mature, successful lady who is self-sufficient, has money in the bank and is an example to other women the world over."*

Again, I listened to WABX rock and roll so the music could soothe my soul and inform me what to do next. I managed to go to work but everything looked far away as I was not engaged in the present reality. I practiced drums on my thighs with my sticks which left them bruised.

One September morning, on Dee's birthday, I sat bolt upright in bed as I felt my Grandma Ralph "enter" the room. *"Okay, Grandma,"* I said. *"It's okay ... I'm so glad you're relieved of your suffering. My God, you're 93 years old; it's about time God took you into His arms and rocked you. I'm glad we got to spend what time together that we did; and I'm glad I was able to be your secretary and write letters to your friend that you dictated. Thank you for being such a cool Grandma, even if you did snort when you laughed"*! I knew Grandma Ralph had died.

About 45 minutes later Uncle Leo called me, "Holly ...," he started, and I interrupted him. "Yes, Uncle Leo, I know she's gone. She died about 45 minutes ago."

"How'd you know that?" he asked, stunned and shocked.

"I just knew, Uncle Leo. I know stuff like that. She came to see me," I replied with confidence. Of course, that really rattled him, but for the first time I was able to share with another human being the reality of the "other-world knowledge" I had been privy to glean.

Since Grandma Ralph died, I took off work that day to celebrate Dee's birthday with her, and she knew I was beginning to cross over to that other reality where the mirrors of wilderness cascade one before the other such that I no longer knew who looked back at me as I gazed into them. We went shopping and ate lunch together and I felt comfortable that I didn't have to defend myself to this precious girlfriend who simply accepted me as I was and didn't act threatened by my reality. We laughed and got high and went to the bar that night where I danced myself into oblivion.

By the following weekend, my plan came clear to me, after I had drawn my infinity-figure-eight "flowers" in lipstick all over the ceiling tiles in the stairway of the house, and I had thrown my alarm clock out the window to "watch time fly." I would check in to the honeymoon suite at the Marriott Hotel by the Ford Motor Company "glass house" headquarters in Dearborn. I would contact Marsha Gleeman, Neil's attorney, and Arch Angel Records to let him know the time had come for him to reveal himself as who he really was, Jesus Christ Himself, and for him to take his "bride," who was me!

On my way to the hotel I stopped by Your Moustache Lounge to hear Bobby Lewis and the Crackerjack Band for a while. During a break, I asked Bobby, the lead singer and guitar player, if he would come out to my car with me because I had something I wanted to tell him. I had been walking up and down the aisle by the bar with a glass of water balanced on my head telling everyone

"I represent perfect balance ... perfect brain balance ... perfect balance of the entire world ... I am the Great Baptism ... I am the salvation of the world ... Everything will be in balance because Jesus is coming to take His Bride ..."

I was surprised Bobby agreed to come out to my car because usually he was wary of the girls trying to hustle him as he was a married man. Apparently he knew instinctively I was in trouble again and thought perhaps he could help. When we got to the car, I put my arm around his shoulder and said, "Bobby, I can't do this Messiah thing ... I just can't do it ... I'm scared ... have you ever thought about what it would be like to live forever and NOT die? Bobby, it's the scariest thing in the world ..." and I buried my head in his lap and cried, deep, gut-wrenching sobs, and then came the screams that would not stop. They came with the same intensity as those that happened the night that Neil's song, "*I Am, I Said*" kept me from taking those hundreds of milligrams of barbiturates and killing myself nine years before.

Bobby was flustered and did not know what to do other than to hold my head and stroke my hair, as he couldn't think of anything to say. His break time was over and he went back into the bar while I took off on my "mission" at the Marriott Hotel. I checked in to my reserved honeymoon suite and paid them in advance for two nights. I figured Neil would come on Sunday, the Christian Sabbath, as it would only be fitting since I was Christian. This union would be the marriage of the western world with the Middle East; this was what I was born for – to bring balance to the world; to be the Bride of Jesus Christ at His return.

When I was all comfortable in my room, I took a long, leisurely, hot bath and washed my hair to become beautiful for my husband whom I was sure would arrive. "Will he come early so we can have one night of private time before we have to 'Face the Nations' of the world? Will he be gentle? Will he be kind? *Will he be angry with me for messing up in Los Angeles? Will he know the tremendous sacrifice I've had to go through all of my life ... I've been waiting so long for this moment to arrive ... when will it ever happen?"*

After I felt suitably gorgeous and clean enough to be the "Bride of Christ" (how arrogant is that?), I put on a leisure suit and began to stroll about the elegant hotel. I stopped in at the bar and had a drink and left imagery of napkins and matchsticks, all in the shape of the Cross, to let others know *"this is the spot where the Holy event will take place, as it is already taking place because Christ's representative is HERE!"*

Since California time is three hours before Michigan time, I knew I had to wait to contact Neil's people until a little later in the evening to make the time I contacted him correlate to the Eastern Standard Time that I checked in to the hotel. Now that I was back in my room, it was time to start making my calls. I must have called Marsha Gleeman and Arch Angel Records about 60 times, and they always said Neil was with his family. Panic began to mount.

I spent the rest of the weekend calling California and wracking up a phone bill that would sink a battleship, but by Sunday, when no one sent Neil to me, I checked out and drove to Port Huron, thinking he would meet me at the cemetery where Danny's gravesite was. Of course when I got there, no Neil was to be found, so I turned around and drove the 65 miles home.

My landlord discovered the lipstick "flowers" drawn all over the stairwell leading up to my apartment and he was furious, asking me what on earth I was doing. I didn't know what to say, so I went upstairs and locked myself in the bathroom so he couldn't get to me. It wasn't long before Aunt Janet and Uncle Leo came over and asked me to come home with them, but I argued that I was fine and needed to go to work the following day.

Soon, my ex-husband Wes and his gutsy girlfriend Marcy came over, and she let the air out of my tires so I wouldn't get any big ideas about driving to the airport to fly to Los Angeles again. Marcy talked to me and said, "Holly, they want you to go to Beaumont Hospital in Royal Oak. Neil is there waiting for you and that's where you have to meet him." *"Oh, NO,"* I thought, *"Just as I suspected ... it HAS to take place at a hospital to prove medically that Neil and I – scientifically – are of the same gene pool; we HAVE to be together ... It is the Will of God ... It is also the Will of God for us to meet in a hospital before we make our presence known to the world so it can be proven ..."*

So I willingly went to the hospital's emergency room to wait for them to bring Neil to me. The attendants were extremely rude to me and gave me haloperidol (Haldol) to terminate the psychosis. I walked up and down the hallway with a glass of water on my head, admonishing them for upsetting my "perfect balance." The other patients simply shook their heads, seeing me as a hopeless case.

The next day began what would be a nine-day hospital stay with all of its routines of seeing the doctors; going to group therapy; resuming the lithium; going to arts and crafts; more group therapy; meals, and so forth. By about the third day, someone in the group voiced a certain concern or problem, and I quipped back with a logical response that almost broke the necks of several patients as they turned their heads in shock that such sense was coming out of me whom they deemed as hopelessly insane.

Within the following few days, just as occurred in L.A. County General when I came around, patients began getting discharged so fast that there were none left of the original group I came in with. It's almost as if they all realized that if I could get well that fast, so could they.

After nine days, I, too, was discharged to resume my life as a typesetter for G. Temple Associates. Aunt Janet and Uncle Leo, bless their hearts, talked with Gerry Temple and explained my illness to him and that I had been off my medication but should be just fine now that I was back on.

With my second manic episode behind me, I vowed there would be no more; and I was humbled that I was, indeed, only Holly Ralph, and all I had to do was to get to work, be as kind to others as I knew how, and that one day, "Mr. Right" would come onto my path and I could be happy once again. Even though I moved rapidly into a euthymic, neither manic nor depressed, bipolar state, I still had not lost my creative sense of adventure which I would exercise during the prospect of finding a mate.

Chapter 10: Globe Magazine's "Find-a-Friend"

Stay the path of greatest advantage. Develop your skill at surfing the waves of the primary symptoms of bipolar disorder.

–William J. Dubin, PhD

Although I just got out of the hospital from another manic episode, for some reason, I was in much better shape than I was from the first one when I'd been in LA County General Hospital and returned to Michigan. I think this was mostly because this second episode was of much shorter duration, that is, I wasn't "out there" for nearly as long; and because I didn't lose anything. I still had my job, thanks to Aunt Janet and Uncle Leo who talked with my employer and let him know that I would be okay once I resumed taking the lithium. I still had money in the bank and I still had my apartment even though the landlord was a bit annoyed with me for writing in lipstick all over the walls and ceiling of the stairwell. I was able to go back to work and continue performing at my previous level of enthusiasm and expertise because I was so grateful I had not lost my career opportunity.

While remaining slightly manic, however, my mind was on a different level than when totally stable. "Hmmmmmm," I thought. *"What do I need to do to break the boredom of this lonely existence of night after night in this tiny apartment? Danny's been gone for over two years, and somehow, I do believe that God will provide me with a 'replacement' due to my devotion* to *Danny within three years after his death. How do I do this? Ah, yes, 'it pays to advertise'! I'm working for an advertising agency ... advertise ... look in the personals ads ... place an ad and see what happens"!* So I began answering personals ads from the local paper.

I dated a couple of guys who were intellectually intimidated by me, even though I tried to play down my intellect and enthusiasm in an effort not to overwhelm them or to come on too strong, needy, or desperate. Then I stumbled upon a *Globe* Magazine which I reviewed and discovered the "Sheila Woods Find-a-Friend" column. One thing about having bipolar disorder is that it can make one rather bold. I had been introduced to the concept of "Holy boldness" when I was baptized in the Holy Spirit and I decided I would be bold as an act of faith and place my own ad in Sheila's column. I was moved and touched by a success story she printed whereby a couple met through her column and had been happily married for five years, and something much bigger than I was urged me to follow my inner guide and compose an ad.

This method of advertising was much safer and more controlled than putting an ad in the local papers because all replies were sent to a blind box number at the *Globe* and then sent to me, thus, no one knew my name, address or phone number. I was simply words in the column and a box number to potential suitors. So around Thanksgiving of 1981, I carefully composed an ad that stated exactly what I was looking for and what I was all about. In it I said I was looking for *"honesty, integrity, sensitivity, compassion, intelligence, 5'8"-6'2", age 35-45, and a Neil Diamond build!"* I stated all my various positive attributes such as *"enthusiastic, honest, intelligent, sensitive, passionate, successful ..."* and paid $25 and sent it off.

I knew I had been true to myself by sowing the seeds of adventure which had the potential of fulfilling my faith that I would be granted a partner within three years after Danny's passing. I was always thankful for Neil Diamond's song, *"Holly Holy"* where he sings, "*And the seed, let it be full, full with tomorrow, Holly Holy.*" Those words were like a mantra for me because I realized, "*I cannot expect any fruit unless I not only plant the seeds, but water and fertilize them as well; then my tomorrows will be full of promise, expectation and gratitude.*" I would later realize that practice was the source of my perpetual optimism, one of the traits that allows one to be successful at dealing with the bipolar ups and downs.

This enterprise helped to anchor me back to reality so I could effectively engage in my day-to-day life, my career, my friends, and becoming more stable. It gave me the sense that I had done all I could do to achieve my highest goal of finding another husband and now, it was merely a matter of time and waiting to see what would happen next.

In the meantime, I celebrated the holidays with my friends and family, and went on a couple of dates with a man who called himself "Superman." However, by the first of the year 1982, he dumped me because he claimed he wasn't into commitments and he knew that's what I wanted. I was deeply saddened and felt a huge sense of rejection because I had my sights set on him. I tried to resume writing my novel, "In Search of Mr. Right," but I wasn't getting very far.

One day when I came home for lunch, I checked my mail and found a large envelope with five responses to my *Globe* magazine ad. These were the only replies I received, but I was ecstatic I received any at all. I read each one and answered them all by typing up a blanket response single spaced, on a piece of legal paper and copied it five times. On the back of each letter, I hand wrote a personalized letter to each gentleman and for those who sent photos, I sent them pictures taken with my Polaroid camera. As I mailed all five letters I thought, "*Now I'm watering and fertilizing the seeds that were planted by placing this ad in the first place; it's so interesting that my ad came out in an edition of the Globe containing a picture of the Holy Shroud of Turin on the cover; I do believe the Holy Spirit is with me on this one. We'll see if any of these gentlemen are taken by my replies."*

About a week later, on Jan. 8, 1982, as I was catnapping in between gazing out the frost-covered windows, glistening and sparkling in the late afternoon sun, my phone rang, startling me from my reverie. When I answered it a sexy, resonant voice drawled, "Hi, Holly. I'll bet you get a lot of weird phone calls. This is Chief Ken Hollan of Weimar, Texas." That was the start of a three-hour phone conversation during which I felt as if I'd known Ken Hollan all my life.

We discovered many things about each other during that first phone conversation and in the correspondence by letter and cassette tape over the two weeks that followed. One of the interesting things I learned was that on Martin Luther King's birthday a year before while I was at the Roosevelt Hotel in Los Angeles and heard my first voices telling me to lie still in the bed and felt that chill of a "presence" enter the room only to discover the next morning that the tiny piece of paper on which I had written Neil Diamond's record company's phone number was missing, Ken Hollan had been shot by a 38-caliber pistol point-black in the upper left forehead by a man in a routine traffic stop on Interstate 10 half-way between San Antonio and Houston that very same night. The bullet exited at the top of his head.

He left the patrol car's police dispatch radio turned on so the Sheriff's Office knew he had checked out and what mile marker he was at. When they hadn't heard him check back in, they sent a squad car to the site, and upon seeing him sprawled out on the highway's shoulder in a pool of blood, they took him for dead and prepared to put him in a body bag. The Sheriff's youngest deputy, who worshipped the ground Ken walked on, fell down on his knees over him, sobbing, "Chief, don't die; you can't die ..." and he laid his head on Ken's neck.

Within seconds, he jumped up yelling, "He's not dead! He's NOT dead! I can feel his breath on my damp face"! At that, Sheriff Jim Broussard radioed for a life-flight helicopter to come and take him to Ben Taub Hospital in Houston. While the chopper pilot didn't want to take him because his vital signs were so unstable and he didn't want a death in the air and the complications of which county Ken might die in, Sheriff Jim pointed his sawed-off shotgun at the helicopter and said, "See this gun? See that man? If you don't load him into that craft immediately, this gun will blow your chopper clean off the highway"!

Ken was taken to the hospital where he lay in a coma for approximately three weeks while the doctors stated that if he lived, he would be a vegetable. When he came to, the medical staff was shocked because he was so alert. After several weeks of rehabilitation, he was back out on the beat none the worse for wear except for discovering a dislike of certain foods he savored before, sometimes blanking out as to where he was and where he might be going and picking fragments of lead out of the top of his head at the exit wound site for years to come.

When Ken told me this story I was moved and touched as I thought, *"God has kept this man alive for me; our meeting is simply destiny; I could have been murdered in California, too; maybe Ken's spirit left his body that night as I lay in that hotel room and maybe Ken is who spoke to me telling me to lie so perfectly still; maybe Ken's spirit removed that paper with the phone number on it? So many 'maybes' ... Maybe those are just manic thoughts, too!"*

In any event, our phone conversations, letters, tapes and pictures were frequent and numerous over the first two weeks of our acquaintance, when suddenly, in one conversation Ken asked, "What's the weather like in Detroit? What are you doing this weekend?"

I replied, "Cold, snowy and I planned to go hear my drum teacher Jimmy Boyer who played with Billy Swan for a while as they toured the world play, and dance."

To which he responded, "Well, I'm not much of a dancer, but how would you like some company?" I was flabbergasted that he would fly all the way from Austin, Texas to meet me and told him I would be delighted to have his company.

The following week dragged by because I was so excited to be able to meet Ken and with that excitement came a tendency for manic thinking. One thing I began to notice since the first manic episode was that any time I was stressed, and it didn't matter what kind of stress, be it "bad" in terms of too many things to think about or "good" in terms of heightened anticipation, I had a propensity toward manic, "other world" kinds of thoughts along with way too much energy.

Finally the day came when I would go to Detroit Metropolitan Airport to pick Ken up, back in the days when you could meet your party at the flight's incoming gate. It was bitter cold with about a foot of new snow on the ground, but my heart was warm enough that I didn't care. The flight landed and I waited … and waited … all of the passengers disembarked and I began to panic that maybe he hadn't come.

When I almost gave up, there he was, sauntering into the airport in his confident gait, police jacket on, and grinning. I ran to him and launched myself at him like a shot from a cannon and we both spun around from my impact as we embraced in what felt like an eternal hug. I knew at that moment God put my new man in my life and the promise of a replacement for Danny had been fulfilled.

Since he only brought carry-on luggage, which included his gorgeous pearl handled, gold inlay 44 Magnum pistol that he proudly displayed along with his Chief of Police badge, we went straight to my car and then shopping for gloves because his hands were freezing. Then I took him to Jimmy and Joan Boyer's because we were all scheduled to have dinner together. Little did I know that an interesting revelation awaited.

Upon entering the upstairs apartment where Jimmy and Joan lived, Ken stopped as Jimmy walked toward him, both with hands outstretched to shake hands. I thought of Neil Diamond's *"Sweet Caroline"* where he sings, *"Hands, touching hands;*

reaching out, touching you, touching me ..." when in unison, Jimmy and Ken both exclaimed, "I know you from somewhere! Armadillo World Headquarters, 1977"! They robustly shook hands and Jimmy told me the following story.

"I was playing with Billy at Armadillo World Headquarters, and during the break I met Ken Hollan who was doing crowd control in his capacity as constable. We sat and talked for the whole break, you know, Virgo brothers gotta hang together. And I told him about my paralyzed friend, Danny, in Port Huron, Michigan and that I needed to send him a postcard of the Armadillo. Ken reached into his shirt pocket as he just happened to have the postcard I needed, and that was the postcard you and Danny got back in 1977 – it came from over Ken's heart"!

Well, all I could think of, as a huge rush of goose bump chills engulfed my body was, *"WOW! Another coincidence! Another piece of 'proof' that this man Ken is meant to be in my life; another sense of how 'right' this whole thing is turning out to be; another instance of someone being in my life before they actually were!"*

By that point I stopped worrying about my bipolar brain and whether I could be a good partner; Ken knew I was bipolar and that I had been slightly manic during our correspondence, but he didn't care. He wanted a lady to fill the emptiness of his life and I wanted a man; we both wanted the same thing and that was all that mattered.

We had dinner with Jimmy and Joan, and the evening was filled with raucous laughter and silliness as the four of us acted like old friends who shared a lifetime together. Ken and I later went out to hear Bobby Lewis and the Crackerjack Band play where Bobby dedicated the Jimmy Buffet song, *"Margaritaville"* to Ken and me. Then we went to hear Jimmy play after which we went back to my tiny apartment, small for a man of 6 feet 5 inches tall, where we went to bed and simply cuddled. This was fine with me as I enjoyed Ken's presence and the massive sense of comfort and security it afforded.

On Sunday, the day of the Super Bowl, he informed me he had passed up an offer of $1,000 for his boarding pass while waiting in Austin to catch his flight to Detroit. I teased him, "That makes me feel pretty good because you put a $1,000 price on my head. That's a lot of money, and you could have waited a week and been a $1,000 richer"! Since neither of us was interested in football, for which I was forever grateful that I wouldn't be a "football widow" each year, we dined at a quiet, romantic little Italian restaurant while the entire city was consumed by the game.

We came home to watch one of Ken's favorite TV shows, and after the program I was sitting on the floor between his knees when he presented me with this question: "How would you like to come back to Texas and be my wife?" I turned over onto my knees, put my head in his lap and wrapped my arms around his thighs saying, "Oh my God! You have just made my LIFE! Yes, I'd love to do that"!

Ironically I had one bit of business I had to attend to before I could just up and leave Michigan because I had gotten a DWI ticket during the second manic episode when I had quite a bit to drink and was reaching down to the floor while driving to pick up a tape that had fallen from the seat and I swerved. The waiting police officer stopped me and made me take a breathalyzer which showed me as two times the allowable level of intoxication. It seemed strange to me that here I was, about to become the Chief of Police of Weimar's wife and I couldn't assume that role due to having to appear in court for a DWI!

After Ken left, the following six weeks were full of breathtaking activity to prepare for moving all my belongings in a U-haul down to Texas, getting my car serviced for the trip, taking care of banking and the court appearance. These preparations and the pleasant anticipation of changing my entire life provided excellent anchoring of my attention to details which helped me in becoming more grounded and stable from the second manic episode the previous fall.

Finally, there was one last detail to complete: attending my last Neil Diamond concert in Michigan. It was strange because I walked out during the closing song. I had such a hard time in crowds of people, and I wanted to get out before everyone else did and beat the mass traffic exodus from the parking garage. My former sister-in-law Joyce was flabbergasted that I would walk out before the concert officially ended, and I told her, "I don't need Neil Diamond; I have my very own husband in waiting and he's coming tomorrow to pick me up, lock, stock and barrel; my life is complete so I can put Neil in the proper perspective of an entertainer whose talent I deeply appreciate."

When Ken and I departed the next day, it started to snow, and driving the red Buick Skylark with the U-haul attached was rather treacherous. It snowed all the way to the Indiana state line, and once, as I was handing Ken a drink of water, the U-haul jackknifed and we started to slide. He corrected the spin and straightened us out in barely a knick of time before an 18-wheeler zoomed by on our left! We drove all night, stopping only long enough for gas and a small bite to eat. At daylight I took over driving for about three hours so Ken could sleep in the back seat.

As we were driving along the Houston beltway around the city we heard a strange "yhah-yhah-yhah-yhah-yhah" sound that seemed to be coming from the rear of the car; however, with unibody construction, it was hard to tell where the sound was coming from. I had just changed the wheel bearing on the back right wheel, but that whining sound seemed to come from there. By about 10 p.m. we pulled off the highway to meet the sheriff at Cattleman's Restaurant, and just as we exited the highway and made the left turn to pull into Cattleman's, the left front wheel fell off the car. I went into a panic attack, but tried to be brave as I realized the implications if this had this happened while driving and pulling the trailer.

We had the car towed to Ken's home in Weimar where we disconnected the U-haul and a wrecker driver towed the car back to Columbus, the county seat of Colorado County, to repair it. The next day Ken took me to establish a bank account and to the Colorado County courthouse where he introduced me to the sheriff and the county clerk: "Hi, this is Holly Hollan, my Yankee wife!" We were instantly married in common law because in Texas, if one represents someone as his or her spouse, they are married.

"Wow!" I thought. "I am Mrs. Ken Hollan – Holly Hollan – I love it; now I can legitimately change my Social Security card and drivers' license ... My entire identity is changed ... I'm a new being ... I have a new life ... I am starting over ... this is like a rebirth ... this is just way too cool! And this weather here in Texas and all of the Bluebonnets ... it's like I've died and gone to heaven"!

Ken was afraid that I'd experience culture shock coming from big city and suburb living to being in an extremely small town of fewer than 4,000 people out in the middle of the country. I assured him I was a country girl and was like the song, *"You can take the girl out of the country, but you can't take the country out of the girl!"* I was right at home and while he worked I spent the first few weeks cleaning his house, hanging pictures and generally providing a more feminine touch to his home with candles, incense, knick-knacks and so forth. Again, this focus on structured, detailed organization helped in my stability and adjustment to my new life.

We spent the entire spring, summer and fall of our first year together fishing as Ken had keys to almost everyone in the county's stock tanks. All the residents were eager to have him fish on their property because they liked having the security of the visible patrol car parked on their premises. I'll never forget the day I caught my first fish, a five-pound channel catfish that I almost lost from the hook due to my inexperience at reeling one in and my excitement that I had him.

It proved to be my last fish of any consequence, yet the activity of being outside in nature, watching the bobbers in the water, being with Ken and sharing in his excitement as he caught numerous largemouth bass proved to be infinitely more stabilizing than the lithium I was taking for the bipolar condition. When we went to the mental health facility in Columbus, the doctor there wanted to increase my lithium to bring it more into the therapeutic blood level range of .5 to 1.5 parts per milliliter. However, every time my blood level registered .64 or higher, Ken would say, "You'd better give her less because she's turned into an irritable witch!" I began to wonder if the lithium was really helping me.

I worked a part-time job for a while to bring in some spending money of my own, and then I found a full-time job as office manager of a wrecker company in Columbus. Sometimes Ken would take me to work on the back of his 1,080-CC Kawasaki police motorcycle and pick me up at the end of the day. One time we stopped at a little bar and had a couple of beers, and then he decided to open up the throttle during the 14-mile trip home. What a thrill that was, holding on to him at 110 miles per hour, with the wind whipping by my face, a fantasy fulfilled.

Life was basically bliss for me, although I experienced some scares as I would listen to the police radio and hear Ken checking out during domestic disputes where folks had guns and threatened to shoot anyone who came near the house. Then the radio would become silent and I couldn't stop plucking my eyebrows in the quiet, wondering if Ken would come out alive. But he made it each time, much to my relief. I listened for him to check out at the Dairy Queen: "745 to Columbus, checking out at the DQ, 10-4," and I'd hop into our Suburban and drive the few short blocks to join him and the sheriff's deputies who would meet him there for coffee and doughnuts.

It was a fulfilled life until the citizens of Weimar started accusing Ken of stealing the city's gas which was a grave misunderstanding. The mayor of Weimar from whom we acquired our first Border collie, "Big Jake," told Ken he could gas up the Suburban for his work as he had been requested to go on all-night burglary stakeouts in an unmarked vehicle. For whatever reason, the city council listened to the citizens instead of the mayor and voted to remove Ken as chief of police. Fortunately, the sheriff believed Ken and immediately hired him as a Colorado County sheriff's deputy for slightly less pay.

We continued our fishing adventures as we adjusted to his new schedule and one day, when we arrived home I discovered a message on the answering machine that said, "Hi, Ken. This is Vicki Taylor and your daughter, Kati, wants to meet you." I said, "Ken, you never told me anything about a daughter named Kati. You told me about your ex-wife Sandy and step-daughter, Debbie, but this is the first I've heard of Vicki and Kati!"

He became rather sheepish and said, "Uh, well, I never told you because Vicki thinks Kati is mine, but I don't think so. She had me sign away all paternal rights so she could marry Bob, who adopted Kati." But he called her back and agreed to meet Kati the following weekend at the radio station in Seguin where he was working part-time as a disc jockey.

He came home that Sunday telling me, "Well, I got real weak at the knees when Vicki and Kati walked in because I've never seen a more beautiful seven-year-old in my life, and here, look at these pictures ... there's <u>no doubt</u> in my mind that she's my daughter, down to every last mole!" He was right; she was simply gorgeous and bore an eerily striking resemblance to him. For him, it was love at first sight, and suddenly the thought of having his own child was appealing so he started sending her little gifts of earrings and requested that Vicki bring her to the radio station so he could see her again. However, her father was threatened by Ken's presence and asked him to cease trying to be her "daddy," which he felt would undermine his authority as her father and perhaps confuse her. Ken was broken-hearted that he couldn't nurture his little girl.

Not long after this letdown we experienced a major upheaval because the sheriff insisted that his deputies wear hats which Ken hated with a passion. He had a large head and couldn't walk into local stores and buy a regulation hat that fit, so he ordered one in his size. In the meantime the sheriff terminated him for insubordination and we were without a source of income because I had quit my impossible job at the wrecker service. Later the sheriff took me aside and told me that he really terminated Ken because he was too jumpy and was practically threatening little old ladies with his 44 magnum as a result of having been shot a year and a half before. He said he didn't want to hurt Ken's ego and fire him for being cowardly, so he used insubordination as the outward reason.

At this point we decided to move to Austin as there were no jobs for Ken in the small-town, rural area. He had a second area of interest and expertise because he was a ham radio operator and was a brilliant electronics engineer, his secondary passion to police work. So we packed up everything once again in a U-haul and he and Big Jake and I moved into a house in southeast Austin. Neither of us had jobs; we were at the mercy of the economy. We had essentially no money and didn't know how we would pay the second month's rent, utilities or payment on his motorcycle.

Within two weeks I found a job as a department clerk at the local electric utility company. For a month, I was our sole source of income until Ken found work repairing television converter boxes. Times were tense; our tempers were taxed; yet somehow we managed to remain supportive and encouraging of one another. And somehow my moods remained stable for the longest period ever in my life. Ken's laid-back personality, his ever-present sense of calm and belief that things would work out and his ability to not take things too seriously all served to be more comforting and stabilizing than the lithium alone could ever have been.

We did everything together and even the bad was good. I helped him file for bankruptcy, which was a big step for him to take. I encouraged him that we could in no way pay all his debts and we had to have an opportunity for a new start. I told him we didn't need credit if we could discharge his debts, and I helped him by preparing the entire petition as if I were his attorney. He represented himself at the discharge hearing and was relieved he no longer had that huge burden of financial obligation and the stress of creditors calling all the time to weigh us down.

This liberated him to get back into ham radio as he was able to purchase the amateur radio equipment necessary to get back on the air. My love for him knew no boundaries, and I wanted to see him happy and fulfilled. I found that when he was happy, it was contagious to me, and I was able to enjoy the ham radio hobby so much, just by listening to him send Morse code and talk to and visit with other hams. I studied the *"Tune in the World with Ham Radio"* book and tape and got my own novice class license in lightning time.

The theory necessary to acquire one's ham license covered subject matter that interested me from the time my father bought me an electricity kit. I'd wound my own little generator coils all the way up through my first manic episode when I'd been obsessed with radio stations and their call signs. Now I had my own call sign, KA5SBY, and Ken was K5IQ. I was so motivated and excited to be part of this ham radio brotherhood with Ken that I continued to study and got my general class license, N5GXE, and continued with the electronics and radio propagation theory studies until I earned my Advanced class license, KI5XD.

These studies channeled my energies bringing contentment in learning new skills and developing new understanding of such things as Ohm's Law, the 11-year sunspot cycle, solar flares and being able to see how the radio frequency spectrum was allocated for various types of communications. An entire new world of science and electronics opened up for me, and never before in my life had I felt so challenged and so happy for such an extended period of time. It didn't matter that my lithium blood level was running low because I was on a legitimate hypomanic roll whereby my energy was high, but my focus and ability to cope with a multitude of details with creativity and precision of thought was rock solid.

Soon Ken got a job as assistant chief engineer for one of Austin's radio stations. My own career at the Lower Colorado River

Authority (LCRA) took off such that in 18 months I advanced from a department clerk at $1,050 per month to a non-degreed, junior engineer at $2,242 per month. I was successful! I was way more than competent as I taught myself FORTRAN programming and was teaching the other engineers how to compile and link edit their own FORTRAN programs on the mainframe computer. I was responsible for developing all the operating and performance statistics for six electricity generating units. I was responsible for tracking the cost and volume of coal and natural gas consumed to produce the electricity, as well as for answering all requests for information in LCRA's rate case hearings with the Public Utility Commission relative to operating and performance statistics. I was even the first employee to receive my own IBM/AT desktop personal computer, and I taught the engineers how to use theirs as more PCs were acquired.

In the meantime Ken started his own broadcast engineering business called Hollan Electronics and I was his partner, responsible for all of the accounting, payroll and tax preparation; advertising, marketing and development of bid proposals and contracts; and I performed all of these duties in addition to my full-time job at LCRA. Administering Ken's business and my own career provided the positive atmosphere for me to run full steam in a constant hypomanic state.

In between working the two jobs, I partied with Ken and all the radio station engineers in town. We ventured out to the transmitter sites of the various stations, which were always located out in the country or up on a hill somewhere in beautiful settings, and we'd drink beer and laugh and tell stories. Once again, I found myself completely in my element as I was surrounded by engineers, much as I felt when I was working for the mechanical engineers at Ford Motor Company. There was something about these radio station engineers that was "goofy," and I fit right in. I was hungry for knowledge of this world of radio frequency (RF) propagation.

During this time we attended two Neil Diamond concerts, and at one, as we were walking across the curved driveway into the arena I froze dead in my tracks and couldn't move. We looked around the corner and there was Neil's limousine and I could feel his presence several yards away as Ken had to haul me across the driveway. "*I wonder what it is ... what's so powerful about that man that I can sense his presence and be paralyzed by it?*" I thought as part of me drifted out to space. I especially enjoyed sharing Neil Diamond with my husband.

Soon we acquired Duke, a tiny Border collie puppy since Ken thought Big Jake needed a playmate and because Jake had become Ken's dog, accompanying him everywhere, I felt left out because I wanted a dog that was mine.

It wasn't long after we got Duke that our broadcast engineering business died a rapid death as we lost more than $60,000 in contracts we thought we had on the books. Eventually Ken got a job teaching electronics and we were able to buy our first home, both his and my first time as homeowners.

The following spring I had a triumphant trip to San Diego to the North American Electric Reliability Council's NERC computer users' conference where I made my first professional presentation. It was in response to a call for papers regarding how we at LCRA converted an entirely manual, on-paper method of determining generating unit downtime statistics to the FORTRAN and Statistical Analysis System (SAS) programs I developed. I was able to speak in front of a room full of about 200 people and receive interesting questions in response to my presentation. This was the highlight of my working career and emphasized my sense of self as successful.

Just before that trip we acquired our third Border collie, Misty, who was the sister of Duke, two litters later. Ken and I were bound even tighter together by our mutual love of the three Border collies and found them to be a delightful diversion from our day-to-day working lives as we would spend the weekends driving around, scouting for new places to take them swimming where I could also fulfill my passionate need of the water and swim with the dogs.

Suddenly just as our lives were smoothly intertwined and we were both happily involved with our careers, our dogs and our mutual joy of ham radio activities, I had a vision. It happened powerfully one morning as Ken was running phone patches from the ham radio station for deployed United States maritime mobile military personnel out in the middle of the ocean. He made biscuits and gravy for breakfast that day and delicious rabbit and dumplings the night before. Since I never cooked, I especially appreciated his culinary talents.

We were sitting there drinking our second cup of coffee and he was running a phone patch. I closed my eyes and was enjoying the comfort I felt at the sound of his voice when I saw him, in my mind's eye, dying an ugly death from lung cancer due to smoking and all of the beer he drank, which lowered his resistance. At that moment I knew he was going to die and leave me a widow. I couldn't contain myself as I said, "Ken, we're going to have to quit smoking so you won't die before me and leave me a widow like Danny did."

He became a bit hostile as he said, "I'm not going to die until I'm ready; I'm going to live to be a hundred; and besides, I'm NOT Danny."

I replied, "Then we still need to quit smoking so you can live to be a hundred." He said, "I'm not going to quit smoking; whenever I try, I crave heroin, which I was addicted to when I was a teenager, and I'm not going through that kind of withdrawal ever again. It's harder to go off cigarettes and nicotine than it is to go off heroin ... no thanks ... you can quit if you want to but I'm not about to."

I began to try everything to quit smoking; the nicotine gum, the patches, reading books about it, listening to waterfall and other nature tapes to bring calming imagery, but I couldn't quit either. Ken got on the bandwagon with me a few times, and we even went for acupuncture. All that did for both of us was to take away our appetites so we didn't want to eat! It did nothing for the cravings for cigarettes.

I finally looked in the phone book for hypnotists to help, and found Dr. William J. Dubin, a psychologist who specialized in, among other things, addiction control and weight loss programs. I was skinny as a rail and didn't have a problem with my weight, but I called him and made an appointment for Ken and me to come and discuss quitting smoking.

That first hour, Dr. Dubin talked with both of us, and was quite complimentary of me as I would offer various insights about human behavior, thinking and emotions. He said several times, "How very insightful of you," which made Ken hate Dr. Dubin because he was never very complimentary of me openly. I knew how he felt about me because of what he would tell ham operators over the radio saying such things as, "She's brilliant; she's the most intelligent woman I know; she's multi-talented; darn, I love that woman." In general, Ken hated psychologists, thinking they were full of "psychological mumbo-jumbo" and that they were not "real doctors" because they didn't have an M.D. degree.

However, there was something charismatic and magnetic about Dr. Dubin that made me go back to him and continue seeing him. And there was something happening to me that made me scared not to see him because my thoughts were again turning to Neil Diamond. It's almost as if since I'd had the vision that Ken was going to die, I needed to go into a fantasy world once again to protect myself from the reality that such precognition had come to mean for me as I previously knew of three people's deaths just as they died. My track record in such matters was of serious concern to me. In other words, if I knew somebody died, they were gone. I was sure Ken was a goner. I just didn't know when.

In my therapy with Dr. Dubin, which started in the summer of 1988, I felt comfortable telling him about my bipolar disorder, and for the first time since 1976, I was back in therapy where I didn't have to hide my inner fears and conflicts. I told him all about my mother and how Ken was neither complimentary nor very affectionate, and how I often felt hollow and empty in spite of the good times with Ken. We tried some hypnotherapy to help me quit smoking, but I was only able to make it for two or three weeks and then I'd relapse.

Finally, in September 1988, I decided that since Ken was born on Sept. 12 and Neil Diamond did the song, "*September Morn*," I would make the commitment to stay off the cigarettes for real. I thought I could do it, so Dr. Dubin and I did another hypnosis trance during which he said to me, "You will permit no exceptions," numerous times during the trance time. I made it for three weeks, when I knew that mania was setting in again. I began dancing until the wee hours of the morning to the rock and roll and believed that if I danced, I would set my spirit and soul free to be with the angels of Jimi Hendrix and Jim Morrison, and that my spirit would be able to go and "visit" with Neil Diamond and let him know that now, for the third time, was REALLY the right time for him to reveal himself as the Christ whom I believed him to be and to claim me as his bride.

My work at LCRA took a downturn because we were not very busy, and my boss said, "We are paying you to think; you don't have to produce all of the time." So, I began to stare out the window and think about the origins of the universe as I would gaze at the large transformer on the electrical pole outside my window. I began to write, pages and pages in which I'd analyze the periodic table of the elements and get off on such things as the symbol for gold, which is "Au," and think that was close to an abbreviation of "August" and Neil's "*Hot August Night*" album and the concert where I first saw him in August of 1972. And I'd tie that in with Neil's "*Gold*" album and that the atomic number for gold was 79, and in 1979 was when I first "knew," during manic episode number one, Neil was really Jesus Christ and he was to be my husband because that was the year Danny died while holding my hand.

I wrote volumes of things in code that I'd give to Dr. Dubin whereby I assigned a different number for each of the letters of the alphabet, so "A" was "1"; "B" was "2" and so forth on up to "Z" being "26," which was also an "8" because "2 + 6 = 8." I would superimpose the plus sign over numbers like "18" which to me meant I was invoking the sign of the Cross over my code and "18" became "9" which symbolized that somehow the Beatles had been "reached" by the coming of me as the "Messiah's bride" because of their "*Number Nine, Number Nine, Number Nine*" song. And I was convinced that their music in the song, "*Imagine I'm in love with you; it's easy 'cuz I know; ... So I'm telling you, my friend, That I'll get you, I'll get you in the end ...*" was written by the angels trying to pair Neil and me up, and that this time, I WOULD "get Neil."

I took almost literally reams of this stream of convoluted consciousness up to Dr. Dubin's office because at that point I believed that he was really Neil Diamond's younger brother and simply hadn't told me anything about his personal life. I would call Dr. Dubin in the middle of the night, screaming hysterically that I couldn't go on and couldn't keep up this "Messiah stuff" because it demanded too much of my mind: it demanded I know everything and figure everything out for humankind from developing a cure to cancer to stopping all the wars, to figuring out how to seed the clouds and stop tornadoes and hurricanes. I believed I could do all of these things.

One day I called one of Ken's engineering friends from one of the radio stations who had a boat. I took off work because I simply couldn't be cooped up any more. I had to get away because I had been sending hundreds of pages of faxes from LCRA's fax machine to Sandy Gallin, Neil Diamond's agent, telling them who Neil really was and why I knew this. I was afraid I would get into trouble for using LCRA's equipment for my own personal gain, even though I believed I was responding to my boss's statement, "We're paying you to THINK." At some level, I knew I was "there" again and the mania once more consumed my being because no longer could I sleep, and I was edgy and in a state of complete denial that anything was wrong.

I asked Ken's friend, after I drove out to LBJ State Park to commune with nature, if I could meet him at his house and go out on his boat with him. He and Ken and I had done so a few times previously, and had gone swimming nude in Lake Travis near Hippie Hollow where such things were not taboo. Kevin was not working that afternoon and was experiencing his own grief because his wife died of leukemia not long before we met him. He was also in the mood for getting out on the water and away from the stress of working.

So I drove all the way to his house on the north edge of town, about 30 miles from our home in southwest Austin. I arrived to find Kevin finishing hooking up the boat trailer to his truck. We made the trip out to the lake and eased the boat into the water. We cruised at a high rate of speed all around the lake for a good while and then stopped in the middle and took off our swim suits and eased into the water where Kevin hugged me and I started to cry. My tears made Kevin cry as we embraced and consoled one another.

Soon it was time to get back because I had a Dr. Dubin appointment that night, so we loaded up the boat and went back to Kevin's house where I got dressed and asked him to take me to Dr. Dubin's. By this time I was so out of it I didn't know what I was doing, and I didn't know what to say to Dr. Dubin, but I knew that I seriously needed help. I introduced Kevin to Dr. Dubin and then he left me there and went home.

Needless to say, Dr. Dubin was more than a little annoyed because this meant that he had to take me back to my car. I had delivered myself to him and totally put my well being into his hands which he didn't appreciate one bit. At one point, thinking he could shock me into some semblance of rational thought, he engaged in some theatrics. He grabbed a short stack of magazines from his table, jumped up from his chair, slammed the magazines down on the floor and bellowed, "**You're NOT going to marry Neil Diamond!**" I didn't believe him and all that served to do was to make me terrified he was very angry with me and I was in deep trouble. He drove me up to my car at the end of the session, an unhappy camper, and when I got there I honestly did not know the way home. I was so manic and so far away from anything resembling reality that I did not recognize any of the landmarks on the way home, so I tried to follow the moon, being motivated by Neil's *"You are the sun <son>, I am the moon; you are the words, I am the tune; play me."*

I arrived home very late and Ken was beside himself. "I feel like I've lost Holly; I've lost my wife," he said. In the days, weeks and months that followed, I continued to see Dr. Dubin and my psychiatrist Dr. Gary Aitcheson, who tried numerous different medications, none of which did me any good. I just kept growing more and more manic as I wrote in my atomic element and numerology-arithmetic-alpha code to Dr. Dubin and Neil Diamond via his agent. I danced to the rock and roll all night long and decorated the house with record albums, motivated by the James Gang's and *"I got me an office called 'Records on the Wall',"* and blue jeans from Neil's *"Forever in Blue Jeans"* song.

Finally, in January 1989, Dr. Aitcheson told me I was one of his failures because he couldn't help me and he sent all of his failures to the best psychiatrist in town, Dr. Tracy Gordy whom I arranged to see around the third week of that month. I'll never forget our first meeting because when I told Dr. Gordy how, way back in the 60s, the Seconal barbiturate helped me, he got tears in his eyes and said, "Do you know why?" I told him I didn't and he said, "Because it helped to slow your racing brain down."

He ordered an EEG which revealed a left mid-temporal lobe brain spike in the theta wave and diagnosed me as having temporal lobe epilepsy. I told him the lithium made me shake and tremor, and he decided to add Tegretol as a tier-one mood stabilizer to try to control the mania. I came home and looked at the *Physicians' Desk Reference* (PDR) where I read, regarding Tegretol, "Not to be given as the drug of first choice in seizure disorder as it may cause seizure activity." Right away, I began to doubt Dr. Tracy Gordy's judgment and his stature as "the best in town."

The writing and faxes to Neil Diamond's agent proliferated, and I would sit at work and just stare at my keyboard and watch it fade away as I felt I was being jet-propelled out into space to dance with the angels. Soon, my boss came in to me and told me, "I have some bad news. We are laying off 40 people and we have to let you go. We will pay you three months' severance pay, and you can cash in your retirement, so you should be able to find a job before your money runs out." I was dumbstruck, yet somehow felt that they had "set the eagle free."

I made arrangements to go to Detroit to see all my friends and ex-husband Wesley for the first week of June 1989. By that time, my thought disorder exploded way beyond the ridiculous as I now thought that God tested my faith by holding Neil out there as my husband (even though I was married to Ken) and that really, I was "supposed" to marry Dr. Dubin who was Neil Diamond's brother according to my distorted thought. Dr. Dubin's wife Tina would just have to step aside because Dr. Bill Dubin was really Jesus Christ and I was to be his bride.

I made the trip to Detroit where I told everyone I was to have a new husband and Ken was going to, as a result, be reunited with his ex-wife Sandy and they'd be happy ever-after … everything was going to go backward in time because after all, I represented time turning around. I was the epitome of time, just like when Jesus was born, "in the Year of Our Lord" was established; so, now, I would pinpoint and earmark "a new time."

When I returned from the trip to Detroit, Ken had purchased me a beautiful and expensive gold watch since I was so obsessed with time. I put it on my wrist and there was something about the metal, it made me feel off balance, and I had to hang on to it with my left hand to feel "balanced" instead of wearing it. I put it around the tom-tom holder on one of my drums thinking that since drumming essentially keeps time for the musicians in a band and allows people to dance, so I was a "timekeeper" (had been the timekeeper at Morton Salt during the Port Huron-Danny days). When Ken asked me why I wasn't wearing his watch, I told him, "I'm sorry but I can't wear it; it throws me off balance"! He angrily jerked the watch off the drums and threw it in the garbage disposal and turned it on, destroying both.

I agreed to check myself in to Shoal Creek Hospital so Dr. Gordy could monitor my medications more closely and in the meantime, Dr. Dubin terminated further treatment because he could not talk any sense to me and felt that he was doing me more harm than good. I was now exclusively under Dr. Gordy's care. I remember telling Ken, "You know, my brain is something they've never seen before; they are going to do surgery on me and remove part of my brain and clone it so they can give parts of my brain to retarded people to help them out. I am so brilliant and special that they want my brain; you know that, don't you?" Poor Ken did not know what to say and he just hoped I wouldn't back out of my self-commitment.

Before checking in to the hospital the following day, I drove to a dumpster at Southwest School of Electronics where, in a rage, I violently threw away every one of my Neil Diamond record albums and cassettes as I hated Neil Diamond for not coming to me this time. I didn't ever want to see him in concert again nor did I want to hear what I thought were his "pathetic, whiny love songs."

While they were signing me in to the hospital and Dr. Gordy came to see me, I began to hysterically scream, "Neil Diamond can rot in hell for all I care; Neil Diamond is a fraud; I am Holly Holy and I am his creation and he has ABANDONDED ME ..." They could hear me all the way down the hallway as Dr. Gordy had them take me away to my room.

The following day I was scheduled for a CAT scan, and Dr. Gordy told Ken, "I hope it's something so simple as a brain tumor." But, that was not the case as the CAT scan came back normal. I was simply manic; insane and psychotic; I did not know reality from the fabrications in my own mind. I was again completely out of touch with the world as we know it and was entrenched once more in a deep, terrifying, mysterious, ominous, endless wilderness of mirrors. As my little sister Heidi would say, "The bird has left the cage."

I was in the hospital 30 days and Dr. Gordy phased me off both the lithium and Tegretol and phased in the Depakote. Dr. Dubin came to see me at the hospital which touched me deeply because I was afraid he hated me and had written me off for good. I performed well in the group therapy, but nothing helped me more than the long walks I took around the hospital's peaceful grounds. Being with nature helped me slowly and gradually begin to come to reality and the knowledge that I was simply Holly and not the "Messiah's bride."

Even though I'd been here before, coming down from mania, I did not realize the long road of recovery that lay ahead of me.

Chapter 11: Widowhood And Word Art

*Just like driving a car, it is useful to know how to
operate the vehicle - how to steer, speed up or slow down.*

−William J. Dubin, PhD

Upon my release from Shoal Creek Hospital after 30 days, it was almost like culture shock as I suddenly realized I was unemployed and my severance pay wouldn't last forever. Dr. Gordy felt I was incapable of working and was reluctant to release me to look for work so I could file for unemployment, but I convinced him that by the time I found work, I would be able to manage it. So, once again, I began to stabilize myself by becoming fiscally responsible and filing for unemployment, cashing in my retirement funds and attempting to locate a job in a tight labor market. My job became finding a job as I turned the search into a highly structured, meticulous plan of action. This type of directed focus can create a reorganized cognitive process which can minimize the symptoms and effects of mania or depression.

Day after day for 11 months I felt defeated because while I was granted interviews at which I performed well, I was not called with any job offers. Eventually, my unemployment and retirement pension funds ran out and we had to take desperate measures. I cut Ken's life insurance in half to provide more funds for groceries; his income was not enough to sustain us. I made arrangements to skip a house payment and a payment on our

Suburban. These times called for jumping through hoops which I did with all of the creative problem solving I could muster. In spite of my resourcefulness, the seriousness of our situation catapulted me into depression from the mania, which took its toll in frequent crying jags and intense panic attacks as well as sleeping a lot. The Depakote I was put on during my hospital stay immediately rendered its side effect of weight gain, and I gained 50 pounds in the first six months.

Finally I was hired by a state agency at a salary of half of what I made for LCRA, but it was work; it was money coming in. After three months of being a clerk, I was promoted to the headquarters office as a department clerk. Due to rapid cycling between depression and mania I was unable to focus at work and had great difficulty understanding what was expected of me. I would have bouts of crying and panic, and then periods of intense, giggly energy all within one or two days. However, by this point the Americans with Disabilities Act had passed and they could not fire me, so they demoted me to a transcription clerk position which they created for me. I transcribed tapes for the media department to facilitate closed captioning of their training and news videos. I performed this job with excellence and dedication to the degree that I began to stabilize a bit. Because of my mixed state of both mania and depression, Dr. Gordy tried a number of antidepressants, all of which produced bizarre side effects such as acute nausea, dizziness and back to increased mania. For some reason, I could not stabilize.

Ken read an article in *"Discover"* magazine about the 11-year sunspot cycle, which peaks every 11 years in the amount of sunspot activity (see Figures 1 and 2). He pointed out that people with Bipolar I disorder tend to become more manic when exposed to intense amounts of light and that during a sunspot peak, bizarre things take place such as transformers blowing out and genetic mutations. I realized both my severe manic episodes of 1979-1980 and 1989-1991 occurred during a sunspot peak period with the smaller one of 1981 occurring on the back side of a peak, which declines over about three years. I also read if bipolar patients receive too much phototherapy to assist with depression, the excessive light tends to manifest manic symptoms. I began to accept my condition as not being my fault.

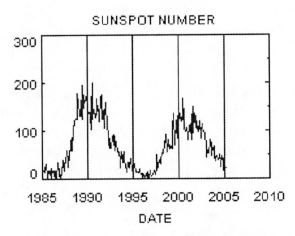

Figure 1. Sunspot Numbers and Years of Greatest Occurrence

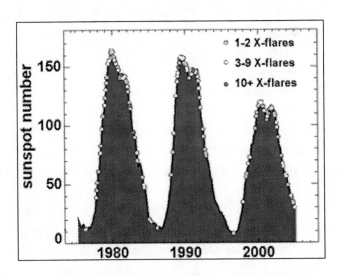

Figure 2. Sunspot Cycles and Years of Greatest Frequency

One summer day I arrived at work to learn that Ken had been rushed to the hospital as he'd had a pericardial effusion. This is an attack on the heart whereby the fluid in the pericardial sac that holds the heart does not move through the sac's walls. It built up such a pressure on his heart that it stopped. I sat in my car outside the hospital and listened to Neil Diamond songs and prayed, "*Dear God, please don't take him away yet; I'm not ready for you to take him; please let him live, just for a while longer.*" Almost miraculously the doctors put a shunt into his heart and drained the fluid off, and when I went in to see him, he was sitting up drinking coffee, all of his color having returned to his face, and he felt great. My prayers were answered.

The following year on the day before my birthday, my father died, and three months later Uncle Leo died. We already lost my grandmother, Ken's mother and our "Big Jake" dog the year before. I was beginning to feel everybody whom I knew and loved was dropping dead as I'd barely deal with the grief of one when another would go. This cycle of deaths and grief intensified the mixed state in which I'd be manic and depressed, sometimes several times in one day. If the Depakote was helping, I wasn't too sure of how I'd have been without it. I wanted to return to therapy with Dr. Dubin who felt I was doing fine with Dr. Gordy, the best neuropsychiatrist in the state. I felt a huge rejection over that on top of my grief.

In the meantime a gifted preacher friend of Ken's from their teen-age years re-emerged in Ken's life on the two-meter ham radio frequencies. They lost contact with each other for 30 years and were delighted to reacquaint themselves. Harold and I started talking and he began to help me understand the Bible in a way that mysteriously began to heal me. He had written two little books: "*The Secret: How to Get Your Life Together When the World around You is Falling Apart*" and "*Fifty Days to Grace*" that I found to be most helpful. He defined faith in a way that finally made sense to me, calling it "The A-B-Cs of Faith" saying that "Faith is an Action, based upon Belief, sustained by

Confidence in the promises of God." Harold was having difficulties in his marriage and found much satisfaction in talking with and counseling me to help bring me more stability. Ken didn't mind the time spent on the phone by the hour with Harold because after several months, he noticed a distinct improvement in me as he told his ham radio friends, "She's so normal it's spooky."

I had been taking Vicodin (hydrocodone), to help with the residual back pain from my surgery, and Ativan, a benzodiazepine, to help with panic and sleeplessness. On Ash Wednesday Harold guest preached at the downtown United Methodist Church, and stopped by the agency where I worked to meet me in person after having gotten Ken's permission to do so. He walked up, carrying his purple preacher's robe, and I asked if I could touch it, much like the sickly woman in the New Testament touched Jesus' clothing and was instantly healed. I touched that purple robe and something happened to me that I'll never be able to explain, but I felt healed much like when I heard *"See Me, Feel Me, Touch Me, Heal Me"* back in Port Huron and was instantly healed of the dreaded mononucleosis. I went home and threw away all the mind-altering pills except Depakote, and never missed them.

I became more stable over the next two years and was a solid anchor for Ken when he had to have total knee replacement surgery. I stayed home and tended to him for several weeks. Offering him encouragement and comfort provided a stability such as I had not known in the past few years.

Our friend Harold began to teach me more about the personal computer than I was learning at work. He was most impressed with my skills as an editor of his writings, which further served to keep me stable because not only was I focused on helping someone else, but also, Harold's content was ingeniously written, providing me with interesting concepts to ponder.

One November morning in 1994, Ken and I were scheduled to go hear Harold preach when Ken awoke with severe chest pain again and we both panicked. We skipped Harold's sermon and went to the emergency room where they gave Ken prednisone and monitored his heart for more than half a day. They did a chest X-ray and when he was stabilized, they let him go home. The following Monday our general practitioner called with the bad news that Ken had an inoperable tumor the size of two nine-volt batteries in the sternum area very close to the trachea. When I heard these results over the phone at work, I almost fell down as my knees shook so badly. *"Oh, my God ... Dear Lord ... PLEASE don't let it be cancer; PLEASE ... Oh, Lord, is this the fulfillment of my vision back in 1988? Is this what you were trying to tell us when I 'saw' my darling Kenneth dying of lung cancer? Oh, why do you let me know these things? To prepare me? To let me down easily so I won't be so stressed and so apt to go manic again?"*

Then the oncologist who called and said it appeared to be metastasized lung cancer that latched itself in the scar tissue where Ken had the shunt put in three years before. He had been a walking time bomb ever since then because he easily could have another pericardial effusion from the moment he had the first one, which would have killed him.

But now he had the dreaded cancer. Somehow I miraculously stayed stable as we whisked him in and out of the hospital for numerous procedures. First was the biopsy, which revealed it to be Stage IV large-cell, adenocarcinoma, an extremely virulent type. Then came the insertion of the portacatheter for receiving his IV chemotherapy. After that was the initial screening and diagramming on his chest to target where radiation would be aimed. There were also numerous oncologist consultations for pain medication, antinausea drugs and Zoloft for depression; and the running to this and that pharmacy to fill the prescriptions. Life was a whirlwind of medical involvement.

In the meantime, as I watched my husband slowly deteriorate, I pursued better employment. I had been a grade 5 department secretary at the one state agency, while another had an opening for an electronic forms designer. With Harold's patient tutelage, I got the job, which was seven salary grades higher than the job I currently held. I felt God elevated and protected my income since it was becoming apparent I would soon lose Ken's contribution to the household budget.

However, he was able to work, and even though on my birthday he had a massive seizure that rendered him paralyzed in his right arm, he still continued to work, dragging himself up the stairs to the school to teach. We were told the disease had spread to "numerous walnut-sized tumors in his brain," and he had less than six months to live. On my mother's birthday, he had another massive seizure and I took him to the oncologist where they gave him heavy doses of phenobarbital to slow down the seizure activity. Three days later he wanted to go to St. David's Hospital because he was afraid he was a burden on me as he could barely walk.

For five days I went to the hospital in the mornings before work and stayed a couple of hours with him to let him know I was there for him, but then I went to work. For five mornings I cried while the oncologist held and comforted me saying that he would merely keep Ken comfortable in honor of our living will. On Good Friday I went up to see him and he could no longer talk. I took him Big Jake-dog's bandana "necktie" and put it in his hand and told him, "Ken, you are free to go. You don't have to stay around for me and the puppies; we will do okay; we have Harold to help us with stuff; I have a good job; you can go be with Big Jake and your daddy and mom," and I read him the Twenty-third Psalm and other Scripture from Isaiah. He smiled as I read to him and held my hand. My body went numb as I recalled that Friday in April 16 years before when another man, Danny Smith, held my hand and died. But I remained brave and strong and went home.

The next morning, on income tax day and Passover, I began to feel extremely antsy that I was not at the hospital. Just as my friend finished mowing the back yard, the phone rang. It was "Buddy," Ken's older brother. "Holly, he's gone." Immediately, I got on the ham radio and said, "CQ, CQ, this is KI5XD; K5IQ is a silent key." The entire ham radio community knew that my darling Kenneth was no more. The next day was Easter Sunday, and I numbly went to a Lutheran church, although I didn't know what I had to celebrate except that Ken was out of his misery and he left this world with a smile on his face unlike any he ever had, almost as if he had a joke on the rest of the world or discovered a secret only those who cross over are able to know.

Amazingly I made it through all the arrangements, the Memorial Service, taking his cremains to the cemetery where his father was buried and a year's worth of setting my finances straight with strength, determination and an uncanny sense of stability that shocked me and everyone around me. I owed my rock-solid stability to Harold who treated me like a little sister and who gently guided me through every difficult decision. He also helped with home repairs; and helped me open and run my own editing business, The Publisher's Editor. For six years I edited people's manuscripts and was a freelance copy editor for Holt, Rinehart and Winston Language Arts Division. This business added enough to my income to facilitate keeping my ship afloat.

Three years after Ken died, the year I turned 50, I suddenly came under a huge compulsion to join a church for the first time in my life. For reasons beyond my comprehension, I was lead to the tiny St. Christopher's Episcopal Church just a few miles northwest of my house. I had passed the sign pointing to that church hundreds of times, but on my 50th birthday, something told me to follow the signs and pull in to the church parking lot on a rainy Friday afternoon. I had three of the Border collies with me and they became visibly animated the moment we pulled in to the driveway under the immense, white Celtic cross on the grounds. I immediately felt the presence of the Holy Spirit on that hill; it was an awesome sense of power; and it tugged at my inner core and soul.

The following Sunday I attended a service there and immediately afterward contacted the priest and his wife, inquiring of them what I needed to do to become confirmed Episcopalian. It felt like a life-or-death decision; that I was somehow in danger and needed the protection of the church body that only membership in a denomination could afford. I liked the Anglican, sacramental church service, and it was close enough to the Roman Catholic liturgy – and Father Jack was charismatic – that it was what my inner spirit told me I needed to set myself free.

The following week I enrolled in Confirmation classes and began attending church services every Sunday. I even joined the choir for a while and found that the beautiful music made me cry and sob, but I didn't care. I felt at home with the Lord and where I needed to be. I was confirmed in May 1999 and the moment the Bishop laid his hands on me, my entire body jolted just as it had when Danny took my hand as he died. I didn't know what to make of that, but I believed I connected in a most majestic way with the Lord of Lords, King of Kings through His Most Holy Spirit via the Bishop's anointed hands. I was happy. The depressive, despondent sense of being "lost" immediately lifted because I was now a member of the Body of Christ, an ambassador of peace and good will and I didn't even need Neil Diamond to do it!

A year later I came under another anointing as we were singing, *"These hands are holy; He's given us holy hands because we are holy … we lift up holy hands …"* when I suddenly felt as though I were living a contradiction by smoking. *"How can these hands be holy when they are holding these filthy, stinking cigarettes?"* And I went forward for an altar call after the service that day and allowed Father Jack to lay his hands on me as I wept and sobbed, and turned my cigarettes over to the foot of the Cross. I never looked back as I was convinced that quitting smoking was the reason God led me to St. Christopher's Episcopal Church and Father Jack's loving, charismatic, healing presence.

Three weeks later I got a call from my brother-in-law Tim that if I wanted to see my mother alive, I'd better get to Asheville, North Carolina because she was in the hospital and had lung cancer so bad her heart was not even visible on a chest X-ray and wasn't expected to live through the weekend. Over the previous five years, Mother and I had become extremely close in our capacities as mutual widows, and all the hurt I experienced from her seemed to have disappeared. Dr. Dubin gave me a little "forgiveness script" to read in the privacy of my home; and I prayed and forgave Mother for her rather severe ways with me when I was growing up. With that forgiveness of her came a humbling sense of healing of my own hurt and disappointment in her over those early years because I realized she was my mother and I loved her. While geographically we were far apart, we maintained an intimate telephone contact for the five years previously and I knew I had to see her, so I paid a premium price for airline tickets to leave the following day.

I spent five days in that hospital room with Mother during which time she rebounded remarkably, shocking the doctors and nurses. The love of our family in that room gave her a will to live and her time to go was most definitely NOT that weekend as she was discharged with oxygen and a plan of chemotherapy which she soon abandoned. My niece, Eliana, sacrificed three months of her life; put her career as a manicurist on hold to go from Florida and stay with Mother so she could enjoy her last few months in her lovely mountain home Daddy built for her.

When I got back from that visit, it started to happen. Ironically, the year 2000 was another sunspot cycle peak. I was stressed to the maximum with my mother dying of cancer and having quit smoking. Also, two of our web developers at work quit their jobs so the entire burden of maintaining two websites fell on me and two other people. The insidious mania started to creep back in, yet I denied it. That's when it got dangerous. I began my incessant writing; I developed a website that depicted Christ's return with imagery of the "12 fruits" and the mighty tree as explained in Revelations. I believed Father Jack would be instrumental in getting "the Christ" (again, Neil Diamond) to take me as his bride. And this time, it was Christian music that told me what to do rather than the rock and roll. I fully believed that because I was under the umbrella of protection from the Church's body of Christ that now the time really was right for this blessed event to take place.

I wrote Father Jack volumes and volumes of e-mail and I made cassette tapes of beautiful Christian music to present as gifts to our agency's executive director because I felt if I was nice to and aligned myself with powerful people, those in power would facilitate the divine wedding for me. I was told by my boss not to take any more gifts to anyone at work, but I persisted because I felt I was holy and above anyone's jurisdiction since I was directly under the anointing of the King of Kings Himself. I sent volumes of e-mail to Neil via the Friends of Neil Diamond (FOND) fan club—love letters, sharing who I believed him to be and believing he was getting them and responding to me in prayer that traversed the ethos between our souls.

Soon, when I took another gift to the executive director, one of the game wardens met me and called my division director. She took me down to her office and said to me, "I thought Kathleen told you not to take any more gifts to people?" And I said to her, sounding much like a 10-year-old who crossed her fingers, "Yeah, but I didn't promise." Thus, I was escorted out of the building and told I could not return until a mental health professional deemed me together enough to work.

I began choreographing a little spirit-filled ritualistic dance to the "Jonathon Livingston Seagull" medley from Neil's "Love at the Greek" CD and I had a friend do a video recording of it which I sent to Gallin-Morey and Associates, Neil's agent. I believed if I danced and prayed incessantly, I could make Mother's cancer go away. I believed Neil and I as the Christ would be responsible for healing her. So I danced until all hours of the night every night.

I continued developing my website in which I was "proving" beyond a shadow of a doubt that Neil and I belonged together ... that we were, truly, a match made in heaven. And that I was not only Neil's "Messiah," but also the savior of the world. Everything I did centered on the power of the Resurrection and I believed I represented the balance of power of the whole universe and I could do no wrong because I was going to right all the wrongs of humanity from Adam and Eve all the way up to the current time.

I also engaged in a craft I called "Word Art. Below are examples of some of the concepts I tried to convey in my "Word Art:"

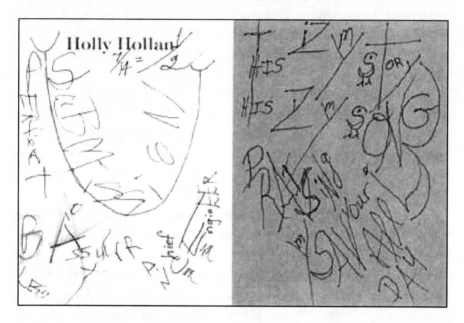

Figure 3. Manic "Word Art" Drawn to the Words to "Blessed Assurance"

This writing is clearly an example of mania in that it was about the song, *"Blessed Assurance,"* and the "BA" was symbolic that I received my college degree in "spirituality;" *"Blessed"* was written as *"B-less-t"* with the "t" representing a Cross; on the right side, the writing swoops up and begins to go counterclockwise. Whenever I begin writing in this form of "word art," it's a clear signal that mania is in full swing. The counterclockwise turns of the various concepts symbolize time turning around backward, which is what I believed would happen once Christ returns – we will all go backward in time, and time as we know it will stop. The interesting notion on this piece of word art is the idea of *"P"+"Raising My Savior all the day long"* meaning that my entire focus is on resurrecting Jesus from the heavens to materialize Him on earth once again.

Since I was escorted from the office I began driving around all day long, listening to powerful Christian music and making the sign of the cross. I believed that if I made the sign of the cross often enough, I was bringing forth a balance of energy on the earth such that all negative things would stop and there would be nothing but positive as a result of my powerfully spiritual nature because I believed I WAS the Holy Spirit embodied in the flesh.

While I was here in Texas being manic, my entire family was tending to Mother in her gradual decline from the cancer. On Labor Day they all decided to close up her home and move her down to Pensacola to be with my little sister Heidi. Three weeks later I flew down there to see Mother for the last time. I had just spent a day doing psychological testing in an effort to prove to the folks at work that I could go back. The reality of my Mother's eminent demise as well as my focus on trying to get back to work began to have an impact on the mania, and I was beginning to sink into depression instead.

Two weeks later, on October 5, 2000, Mother passed away with Heidi reading from Isaiah and Ezekiel scripture to her, and a week after that I returned to work. Our family spent the entire following year settling Mother's estate and grieving her loss. I felt somehow vindicated in the sense that finally, my family had witnessed a manic episode and they finally knew what I experienced with this illness. Heidi called it "when the bird leaves the cage." My family was loving and I was beginning to feel accepted. Still, I experienced shame as a result of my rapid, intense and out-of-the-blue swings.

In the spring of 2001 I lost my dearest Border collie, Duke; the next spring my confidante and precious preacher friend also passed away from cancer; and that summer Jimmy Boyer, my drum teacher passed away from cancer. On October 3, 2002, I embarked upon reaching a long-term goal by joining a Rite of Christian Initiation of Adults (RCIA) Roman Catholic confirmation class. On that day I lost the next Border collie, Misty, mama of Abbey, Bonnie and Clyde, whom I still had along with

Maggie-Mae. Again, I experienced one grief after another and I could barely reconcile one when another would occur.

I put everything I had into the confirmation class to become Catholic, a dream of mine since I was 15 years old. I wanted it all; I wanted to be able to take Holy Communion with those of the Mother Church. As the class progressed, I got so consumed with the intensity of the teachings and the depth and richness of the Catholic tradition that I began to develop another thought disorder, again manifesting around the theme of the Second Coming of Christ.

Shorty after New Year's 2003, I started to slip into depression because I couldn't stand to see all of the couples and families walking across the parish campus, holding hands, loving one another as I walked, week after week, all alone. The parish priest called one day and asked me to come in because he was concerned that I was depressed as a result of an e-mail I sent to him in which I expressed my sorrow that I could no longer come to church and feel alienated from all the family involvement. He said to me, "You are a beautiful and brilliant woman with a whole lot of love to give and no one to give it to. Well, you can love me."

Within three weeks, on Neil Diamond's birthday, I started making Irish Christian music CDs for the priest and leaving them as gifts for him at the altar of the little chapel by the confessional. My "word art" took on a frenzy as indicated in several examples that follow.

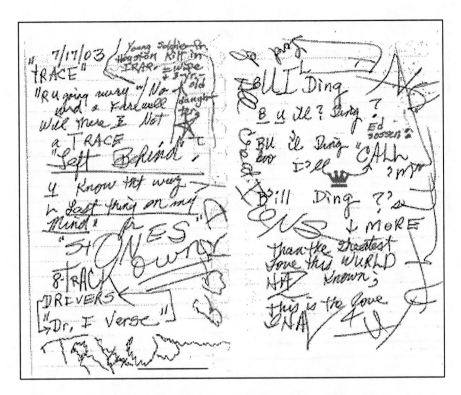

Figure 4. Word Art to "Last Thing on My Mind"
(Note the underscored "CY" which was "See Why"?)

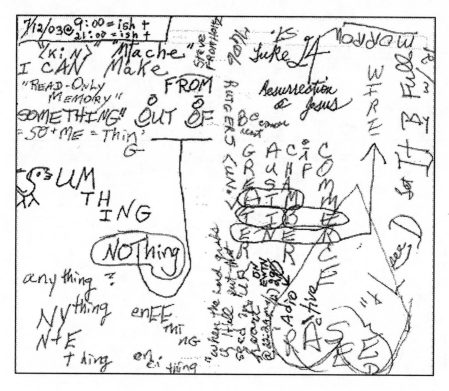

Figure 5. "I Can Make Something Out of Nothing! I am the Creator!"

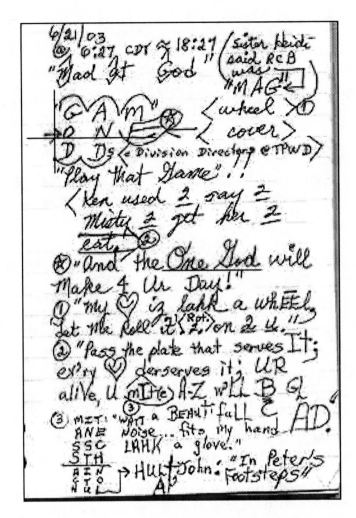

Figure 6. "And the One God Will Make for Your Day!"

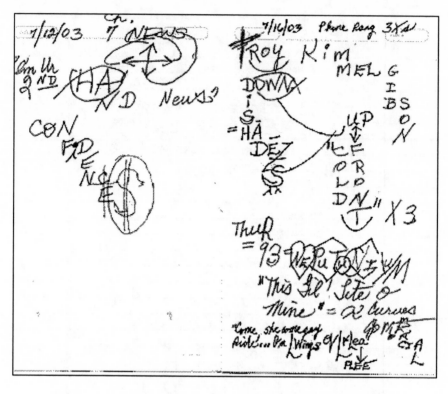

Figure 7. Word Art to Fleetwood Mac's "Secondhand News"

Oh no! JUST as I am doing this, KEYE is playing bagpipes of "Amazing Grace," and they said, "Are you ready to get married?" Oh boy! Oh yes!! Suddenly, I was "TOLD" to keep watching commercials. And I realized that one commercial for "sneezing / allergies" had the letters in the form of a cross.

Praise the Lord, It's HAPPENING!!!! The Media is telling me I'm getting married!!!!!

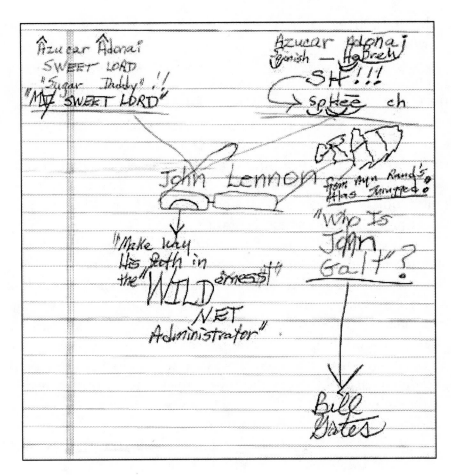

Figure 8. Word Art to John Lennon's "My Sweet Lord"

I would listen to the radio or television news and diagram out anything I heard that I thought had a hidden meaning to what "they" (the media) wanted the general public to hear, and I believed I was privileged to receive communication beyond what was intended in the broadcasts. Albert Einstein was my hero as I again pondered what he really meant, on a spiritual level, by the Theory of Relativity, because I thought of "relativity" as everything and everyone being "relatives." All things were interrelated and everything had some form of significant meaning and it was my "job" to discover the hidden meaning of life so I could save the world.

In the meantime, the priest was the target of all of my e-mails because now I believed the sacred wedding would take place there under the jurisdiction of the Mother Church. Now that I was almost Roman Catholic, I believed I was making Christ's return eminent. That for sure Neil would come to me now because he was Jewish; I would be Catholic and together we would right the world's wrongs. Since this was my fifth manic episode, I believed that it took five times to "get it right" because Harold told me that the number "five" was representative of God's perfect grace.

I was escorted out of the office at work again because of an e-mail I sent to the Pope, the Secretary General of the United Nations, the President of the United States, and the Texas Governor's Office using the agency's equipment in which I said that when Neil Diamond and I come together, the world as we know it will no longer exist and our union would heal me of the dreaded bipolar disorder because I would finally be balanced. I said that until Neil claimed me as his, "the Christ's," bride, I would not be able to find my balance, and once Neil and I connected, Saddam Hussein would be captured.

I was off work for another month while the doctors tried Seroquel and one other anti-psychotic medication. Dr. Tracy Gordy retired and I was not the least bit happy with the replacement doctor as he seemed young and inexperienced and entirely too patronizing. He wanted to put me in the hospital and I told him, "No. I am not a danger to myself or others. I am harmless and I need to be home with my dogs." So I dismissed him.

This put me in a precarious position of having no doctor at all. I needed a doctor's recommendation, once again, to return to work and I had none. I called Dr. Dubin's office but his secretary gave me the distinct impression that he wanted nothing to do with me, so I sent him a number of contact memos from his website but he never answered me. I was desperate to talk to somebody who could help me. I later learned that Dr. Dubin never received any of the web contact memos because that part of his site never became operational.

I finally made contact with a young psychiatrist under the in-network mental health portion of my health insurance program and to him, I was just a number – someone to be seen for 15 minutes once every eight weeks. He did accomplish what I needed, however, as he completed the necessary forms for me to return to work and he helped me make the decision NOT to become confirmed Roman Catholic because I was terrified of the commitment at that time.

He seemed to accept that Neil Diamond had some sort of spiritual connection to me, but neither of us knew why. He increased my Depakote considerably trying to slow down the manic thoughts, and he put me on Topomax to try and assist with the mood stabilization along with its secondary off-label usage of weight loss.

The summer progressed and I became involved as an intercessory prayer partner for Deep River Ministries, Father Jack's healing ministry. I found that praying for this ministry and for other people with extreme difficulties helped minimize my awareness of my own instability.

Finally, right after Labor Day 2003, the Catholic priest called and asked if I still wanted to be confirmed Roman Catholic, which I did in a small ceremony in the chapel. I was elated that at last I was a member of the Mother Church. Three weeks later on the Roman Catholic Church's "All Angels' Day" (Sept. 29), I saw Neil Diamond on the Larry King Show in which Larry asked Neil, "What is your favorite of your songs?"

And Neil replied slowly and thoughtfully, "Well, it would have to be the most autobiographical; it was the one that was the most difficult to write; it would have to be '*I Am, I Said*,'" at which point I fell prostate on the living room floor in tears saying, "Now I KNOW there's a spiritual connection between us because his favorite song is the one that saved my LIFE!" I could not stop crying, and I realized I was in desperate need of therapeutic help, not just trying one medication after another.

The following day I saw a movie on CBS that was dedicated to fireman in which all a man wanted to do was to thank the fireman who saved his life. I realized that was all I actually wanted from Neil was to thank him for saving my life and as I saw that movie, I again fell on the living room floor in gut-wrenching sobs.

I decided again, try to contact Dr. William J. Dubin to see if he would be willing to take me on as a patient once again because I felt I had a score to settle with him where Neil Diamond was concerned. I made the call and a sweet young voice answered the phone; it was not the same secretary who had been there since I left in 1989. She said, "Let me ask Dr. Dubin what he would charge you and why don't you come in next Tuesday evening at seven o'clock?"

I could not believe my ears! Finally, I could return to the brilliant expertise of the therapist who helped me in the forgiveness of my mother; to someone with whom I would be free to share whatever craziness was in my head without fear of repercussions! My journey to wholeness had at last begun. I would begin to realize the immense and amazing impact of words that heal and anchoring hypnotherapy.

Chapter 12: Surprise Healing

All experience is transient. Whatever up or down
you are now experiencing won't last very long.

–William J. Dubin, PhD

I was relieved to be able to seek refuge with Dr. William J. Dubin finally, at last, where I could talk about the storms in my head and attempt to unravel them. I checked Dr. Dubin's Website: http://www.psycharts.com and felt comforted to read his background.

While the primary thrust of Dr. Dubin's practice is devoted to substance abuse and weight loss and management, at least 50 percent of his patients are bipolar. From having seen him in 1988 and 1989, I knew he had a brilliant and encouraging perspective, and I knew the Depakote didn't seem to be working for me since about 2000, thus I believed psychotherapy would be the source of the healing I so desperately needed.

One positive element in my favor is I am able to talk openly about issues, observations and conclusions in such a way as to communicate the bipolar experience fairly adequately to someone in a position to help. I am honest, exploratory and have a high IQ relative to verbal expression and abstract reasoning. This facilitates awareness and introspection that can lead to understanding and acceptance. I would later learn these strengths, combined with my keen memory and capacity for visualization, would serve remarkably toward healing in terms of grasping concepts by which to deal with the bipolar vacillations.

I experienced a rather intense sense of mission returning to Dr. Dubin because we never resolved the issue of Neil Diamond. When I heard Neil say on the "Larry King Show" that his song, which saved my life, "*I Am, I Said*," was his favorite song, I felt a sense of spiritual connection between us and a slight vindication as to why I always thought Neil Diamond was the Savior in my manic, delusional, psychotic episodes. I felt somehow Dr. Dubin and I could resolve the issue of Neil in my life so I could be "healed" of my delusions concerning him.

In the first return session with Dr. Dubin after not seeing him since 1989, he was a bit amazed at how heavy I was because I'd been at about 135 pounds when he last saw me and I was over 200 in 2003. I had been off cigarettes for almost four years, which also surprised him. We spent the first session with my telling him about the 16 people and dogs who died since I last saw him, and my also assuring him I would not push the boundaries of the therapist-patient relationship as I had before by calling him at all hours of the night and thinking I was supposed to marry him instead of Neil Diamond. I told him it was too much of a privilege having the expertise of his counsel to mess it up by wearing out my welcome in childish demands. We got off on the right foot at a great relief to me.

After the initial session I took a trip to Florida to visit my sister Heidi and see her new home. While the Topamax medication appeared to help bring down the mania I couldn't completely get out of, it was beginning to affect me negatively in that I was crying a lot and felt under the influence of a chemically induced depression. I tried my hardest to be upbeat for my sister and her family, but her whirlwind lifestyle wore me out. I admired her energy and involvement with people but wondered when she ever really slowed down and rested.

A week after I returned I had my second session with Dr. Dubin. I walked in saying, "I'm in a tremendous spiritual battle. I keep going back to the Old Testament where I find comfort among the prophets that the Jewish people find comfort in. (Dr. Dubin is Jewish.) I'm so spiritually hungry and I pick up on the energy of people around me and external things. I'm just so sensitive. You know, back in the spring, I was making .WAV files for Neil and putting them on my Web site."

"What were those .WAV files? What was the nature of them?" Dr. Dubin asked.

"Well, they were just me talking to Neil and telling him stuff, and I put them on my Web site, and then I sent the link to Neil at the Fan Club e-mail address. I did it on my own equipment and on my own time but people at work saw them and got all upset. Like, it's none of their business what I do on my own time. I'm not breaking any laws. And I wrote to the Bishop and the President and the Secretary General of the United Nations and begged them not to go to war. You know the war in Iraq started on my birthday in 2003. Dr. Dubin, the Topamax makes me foggy. Well, back in March 2003, I was dismissed from work because of an e-mail I did write on the agency's equipment during my lunch hour. I sent it to all of the 'wheels' I just mentioned and to a friend who used to work for my agency and had gone to the Governor's office."

"What did the e-mail say?" Dr. Dubin interjected.

"Well, that I had a vision that Jesus was gonna come back, and I told them if Neil Diamond and I connected, I would be healed and wouldn't need my medication, and Saddam Hussein would be captured and the world as we know it would no longer exist. They dismissed me. I guess they were scared or something.

"And then just before Confirmation, Dr. Dubin, I saw bodies in graves. I had a vision of bodies in a mass grave, all kinds of bloody bodies. And I knew the devil hates the blood of Jesus, so I laid on the floor of my living room and cried, begging Hussein to quit killing people and then I took this red fabric from my mother and, it was a nice knit red fabric, and I took it over to my church's Garden of Gethsemane at midnight the Saturday before the Easter Vigil and my Confirmation. I shrouded the three statues and sang and danced for a long time, praying the blood of Jesus over Iraq. The Priest said he was going to wear red during the Easter Vigil so I thought I should invoke the blood of Jesus on the statues and bring them to life so they would stop the war.

"Then I came home and turned on the TV, which I hadn't had on in several days. Oh my God, Dr. Dubin, they just found the mass grave and all the murdered victims in it. Dr. Dubin, they FOUND EXACTLY WHAT I HAD SEEN IN MY VISION! Now how did I know that? Why did I see that? Huh? You tell me? And then a little voice in my head said, '*Go take the red fabric shrouds off the statues,*' but I was crying so hard I just couldn't do it. And another voice said, '*No, leave them there because they MUST know that you knew that. They MUST know of your connection with God because you are now ready for the Easter Vigil.*'

"Well, I was kicked out of the choir and the Priest got furious with me for messing with his expensive statues and said he was afraid I was going to ruin the Easter Vigil. He said everyone was on pins and needles for fear I would do something to upset the Easter Vigil, so I backed out. I told them to shove their Confirmation and I would not do it. It was too big of a commitment – all I did in the choir was harmonize – the Holy Spirit took my voice and broke it into a beautiful harmony and they thought I was trying to stand out. I couldn't help it, it just happened. So I'm just manic, I guess, and I'm tired of being kicked in the face for bein' me. That's why I'm here." And I started to cry.

Dr. Dubin listened with interest and then inquired, "**What would I see if you were manic? If I were watching a movie of you manic, what would I see? What does it do to you?**"

"It hits me like a brick. You would see it in my eyes ... and hear racing thoughts."

"**How would your eyes look? Dilated?**"

208

"Yes. My team leader says they look wild, and I look like I have a secret that no one else has."

"The thing in March, how long did it last?"

"Well, I asked my attorney to send a package to Neil Diamond's attorney, Marsha Gleeman, some time in June, I think. It just seemed so real."

"Is there any editing, that this isn't going to happen, that this is nuts? When did you realize that this wasn't going to happen?"

"Well, some time in August, I think, after I got the stuff back from my attorney and he told me that he talked to Marsha and she said she didn't want to hear from me ever again. After that, I made a cassette tape for Neil in which I sang a duet with him to '*Unchained Melody*' and I asked him on the cassette to marry me and sent it to the fan club, and I sent him the stuff I sent to Marsha Gleeman – some of my stuff from work and a CD of some music with a pretty label on it – so it was from March through August. And then when I saw him on the '*Larry King Show*' Sept. 29, that's when I knew I had to come back to you. To try to get un-nuts."

The session ended with Dr. Dubin recommending the book "*Love's Executioner*" by Irvin Yalom, MD as something I might find interesting to focus upon and direct my attention to. I immediately got the book and, while reading was difficult for me due to my inability to concentrate for very long, I found it a compelling series of studies in psychotherapy that was helpful in stabilizing my thought processes.

I continued seeing Dr. Dubin once a week when one day I went in with a need to talk more about what it's like to be me. **"What should we put on the agenda today?"** Dr. Dubin encouraged me.

"Well, I wrote you an e-mail but I chickened out in sending it. You know the song, '*He*,' that the Lennon Sisters sang? Well, I cried at that when I was 14 because music ministers to me. I just can't find my balance; my brain is like a savage beast; I can't stop crying. But when I sing to the beautiful Christian music, I stop crying when I sing. And when I go to bed at night and pray, I get these flashes of light at my brow line; it hurts my brain to think. I'm trying to find my faith, I guess."

"What is a manic episode like?"

"Well, I think I'm Jesus; I get to fantasizing that, with my energy, I'm powerful enough to stop all the wars; and if all the energy and money that goes into fighting the wars were put toward the living, we'd have a cure for cancer. And, Dr. Dubin, I have a secret. Christianity is based on a lie and a fairy tale (beginning to sob); Jesus is not coming back. The Second Coming was when the Holy Spirit Dove landed on Jesus in the Jordan River when He was baptized. For bipolar people, Christianity is a dangerous fantasy that creates powerfully dangerous thoughts like, '*I can do all things through Christ who strengthens me.*' And I begin to see infinity; I can see forever; I become all the saints and I travel backward through time and become each one and become nothing but a spirit that just travels freely throughout time and space. And I think God has me on a magnanimous mission and just when I think I'm almost there, I get these thoughts of, '*what have I done?*' and then it eludes me."

It was so liberating to finally begin to share without fear of retribution what goes on in my head when I go manic because at last, I could let it out. We spent several sessions with my telling him where I'd been during each of my manic episodes, and after each conversation, I felt I was slowly gluing myself back together simply by hearing myself being honest about where I'd been and answering his questions as completely as I could. This was intimate dialogue about the inner workings of my mind and often it was painful to let it out, but doing so provided a deep and lasting cathartic effect of cleansing, much like the act of confessing one's sins to a priest.

During my 16-mile drive up to Dr. Dubin's office I discovered the nationally syndicated "Delilah Show" on Austin's KKMJ ("K-Magic") radio station, which I never would have tuned in to had

I not been making that drive at 7 each night of my sessions. I listened on the way to and from each appointment and became enraptured by Delilah's passion for souls and found her show offered a supplemental healing to what I experienced by talking to Dr. Dubin.

One night when I went in talking about psychosomatic pain, Dr. Dubin asked, **"Do you know what alexithymia means? Because psychosomatic pain can be related to that. You know that 'thymia' means 'mood.' And 'lexe-' means 'word,' and 'a-' means 'without.' So alexithymia means 'mood or emotion without words.' When you have emotions, would you know what they are? Would you be able to give the correct label to the emotions that you have?"**

"I think so."

"How can you tell? How do you know which emotion it is?" Dr. Dubin queried.

"Well, I didn't cry when Mother died and throughout her whole illness. I went into a manic episode to avoid the whole thing. And when I had the precognition in '88 about Ken's death, it was the same thing. I just listen to Neil Diamond where I find myself in his beautiful voice and words. It's the only place I feel real and I find my identity and there's where I have a connection."

"You say the only time you feel real; what do you mean by that? What does it mean to feel real?"

"Like I'm not fake or something. I feel alive; touched; able to have my feelings. When Ken was okay, everything was good and I felt whole. After I had the preknowledge of his death, I went crazy. I lost my job, I lost everything and took Ken with me. It really took Harold coming on the scene in 1993 to bring me around. We spent a lot of time on the phone. But when Harold died, I never grieved his death either. When I came to see you on Oct. 30 for that emergency session when I found out Heidi had melanoma, after I was SURE when I visited her a week before that something wasn't right with her – I think I cried more in that appointment than I've cried in 14 years since I saw you last. I think I cried over everybody and all my dogs who have died. "

"So it's good that you would allow yourself to experience it. Do you agree?"

"I guess, but it feels as though my body is crying all the time and that's why I have this acid reflux. I take Aciphex for it, but it just feels as though I'm in pain all the time and when I cry like that, the pain stops. But I can't go around crying all the time."

"Well you can let it out here."

"But I'm afraid I'll never stop ..."

That night on the way home, Delilah asked her listeners to log on to her Web site if we wanted to submit a story of thanksgiving as it was near the Thanksgiving holiday. The next day, I logged on and found the input form and pondered, *"What should I tell her? I have so many things to be thankful for ... so much has happened to me that's good, in spite of all of the bad, there's just so much good, what will I write? What should I write?"* I stopped for a moment to pray, *"Lord, what am I most thankful for that I could share with Delilah and her listeners?"*

Suddenly it came to me as I remembered the CBS movie in which someone who had been rescued from a fire wanted so desperately to find the fireman who saved his life to thank him for doing so. I remembered what I realized as I watched that movie and sobbed while lying prostrate on the living room floor – that I wanted to thank Neil Diamond for saving my life when I was going to commit suicide back in 1972 and his song, *"I Am, I Said"* prevented me from doing so.

I poured out my heart on Delilah's input form and told her the entire story and how grateful I was for Neil's captivating, soul-searching music that turned around what would have been an action with irreversible consequences. I didn't know what might happen, but I had a sense of sowing the seeds of adventure; I had a feeling I had finally done something right and wholesome rather than something "nuts." The ability to sow seeds of adventure is a definitive asset, especially when dealing with the depressive dips.

I could tell my sessions with Dr. Dubin were paying off because at least I wasn't manic any more. I was still unstable as I'd be way up and euphoric one day and deeply down and crying the next, sometimes both extremes several times a day, which is known as "rapid cycling" and a "mixed state." I was worn out much of the time, not knowing which end of the spectrum I would be on at any given time and because of the challenge of trying to convey what I was experiencing to Dr. Dubin. The mixed state was a bit of a relief because at least I knew what was real and what was not, and the twice-a-week sessions with Dr. Dubin provided a testing ground for me to throw out ideas and experiences in a safe, comforting climate of acceptance.

Dec. 1, 2003, I decided to pursue a local dating service in my attempts to alleviate my loneliness as a widow, which I tried continuously to cover up and run from. I met with the couple who ran the service and they presented their sales pitch with all the charm and gusto as if they were offering me the moon, and then said they needed $1,800. When my mouth fell open, aghast at the cost, they were insulted I didn't immediately pounce upon their "offer" as if it were good as gold.

Usually, I am a salesman's delight, but this one told me to run like lightning as fast as I could never to look back. As I was driving home, feeling rather smug that I hadn't gotten taken by their tactics, my cell phone rang. On the other end of the line was a young lady's voice saying, "Hi, I'm Jenna from the Delilah Radio Show, and we're going to host Neil Diamond on a show later this month for the Christmas season. We were wondering if you'd be willing to share with Delilah over the air the story you wrote on her Web site about Neil Diamond helping you out during a difficult time in your life."

"Oh my God" I exclaimed. "Well, the old saying, 'is the Pope Catholic?' Of course I'd be delighted to tell my story!" She told me they'd be calling me back in about an hour on my landline where we'd have a better connection, that Delilah would be on the phone and for me not to have my radio on. I was breathless to be able to finally share that story publicly without shame or guilt, and I was so excited I was afraid I might go manic again!

I got home and changed my clothes into something comfortable, played my keyboard a little to kill some time, and the phone rang, about to begin a conversation that would forever change my life.

DELILAH: Hi, is this Holly?

HOLLY: Yes, Delilah it sure is.

DELILAH: Welcome aboard; I'm glad you're here with us tonight.

HOLLY: Well thank you – God Bless you, you are such a dream.

DELILAH: Well thank you. You know that Neil is going to be co-hosting a show with me, right?

HOLLY: Oh my God.

DELILAH: You wrote to us and you shared a sweet story; a sad story, but kind of a sweet story of when you went through a really tough time in life.

HOLLY: Yes, actually, uh, and I'm not ashamed of this any more; I finally after many years have come to grips with the fact that I am bipolar and I have many ups and downs in life. And it's hard for me to handle the ups and downs. I'm getting much better at it.

DELILAH: And you were having a down time?

HOLLY: Oh, yes.

DELILAH: And depressed?

HOLLY: Very.

DELILAH: Had lost a job?

HOLLY: And they let me go because I wasn't dignified enough for their office. They said I laughed too loudly.

DELILAH: Wow, I would have gotten fired a lot if that were the case.

HOLLY: (Chuckles in reply!)

DELILAH: You know I laugh so loud, Holly, that when I go to movie theaters, funny movies, people get up and move?

HOLLY: Uh-oh!

DELILAH: Now I just rent them and bring them home. That way I can laugh as loud as I want and nobody gives a damn; but people move in theaters when I laugh.

HOLLY: Well, hey, I'm sorry. (Giggles a bit.)

DELILAH: So you lost your job; you weren't dignified enough; you were too loud; you were so depressed, you decided you just didn't want to carry on.

HOLLY: That's right. And at the time I was an atheist. I did not believe there was a Lord out there who loved me.

DELILAH: And what happened to change that?

HOLLY: Well, I drove down a country road with many, uh, barbiturates, and I was going to take them all. And I wrote a note, and, you know, basically said, you know, 'The world doesn't want me; I'm not good enough. (Soft piano music begins to play) And therefore I'm going to end my life. And I poured them out in my hand and I had my eight-track of Neil's, uh, "*Stones*" uh, eight-track with me, and, for some reason, um, something much bigger than me told me to stick that in my player.

And, it just so happens that the track that "I Am, I Said" was on, and he started singing it, and I started crying, and really, I mean deep, really crying, pounding the steering wheel, and all of a sudden, I realized, "What on earth are you doing? Neil surely has felt this way, and he's alive singing about it, so it would be pretty stupid for you to end your life. And remember what Jesus said," you know, because I had read some Scripture – He said, "You know before Moses was, I am."

And all of a sudden I realized, "God is here! There IS a God." And I threw the pills out and drove home.

DELILAH: And, has life gotten better?

HOLLY: Very much so. Very much so. I have a lovely home; I have a lovely job; I am really working at finding happiness, and it's – I'm basically a very happy person.

DELILAH: So, do you think that had you not popped that tape in at that time; had you not heard that song, things might have turned out differently?

HOLLY: I probably would have taken the pills.

DELILAH: That wouldn't have been a good thing.

HOLLY: No.

NEIL: That would have been a terrible thing, Holly. Hello?

HOLLY: Oh my God (giggles ...) [I had not known that Neil would be listening on the other end of the line!]

NEIL: Hi, darling, this is Neil and I'm sorry, I just overheard what you said.

That's a beautiful story. You know, I can't tell you because I was kinda down when I wrote that song myself, and uh, it meant a lot to me too, and it's so nice to hear that it had an effect on you and that you didn't let yourself get down and you pulled yourself out of it and it's a beautiful thing. And I think the world is a better place because you're around...

HOLLY: Oh thank you.

NEIL: And you do have a great laugh (Holly giggles) and we need that; we really need that.

So, you know, you've done me great honor by telling that story and, uh, and I love you for it. Just to know that you're not alone. There are lots of people out there, myself included, who've gone through really difficult times, and for some reason, they've been able to pull themselves out of it.

And, uh, we all know that there's something bigger than we are out there and, and uh, He pulls the strings, and uh, He sure pulled the right strings that day, and uh ...

HOLLY: Yes, He did.

NEIL: And I'm happy to hear you tell that story.

HOLLY: Well, I'll tell you what, Neil, I never, ever thought that I could ever talk to you and I've made a royal pain in my butt about trying to reach you. This is all I've ever wanted is to just thank you!

NEIL: WOW! Well, you've done it.

DELILAH: So Merry Christmas early, Holly!

HOLLY: Oh my goodness, I don't know what to do!

NEIL: Well, you keep laughing, and just hearing your story is beautiful. Like I say, it's gonna make my Christmas this year. And God bless you.

{Delilah plays Neil singing *"O, Holy Night."*}

DELILAH: With me, uh, co-hosting tonight is Neil Diamond. Neil, thank you for agreeing to be here with us.

NEIL: Oh, I love it. I love this music, and, I want to pick some songs to play – some of them.

DELILAH: When you're singing, when you're performing, when you're recording, you have no clue who it's going to touch or how it's going to touch once it's out there.

NEIL: You know, that's so true. You only hope it goes out and does something nice to somebody, but you never do know. And every once in a while, you hear a story like the one Holly just told and you realize, hey maybe, maybe you do have a purpose and there's a reason that you're around and when you're getting down, maybe you shouldn't be getting down. It's all valuable and it plays a part in this whole crazy scheme of things. So ...

DELILAH: Or, even like she said, when you do get down, the fact you were honest about it; the fact from your depression or your sad situation, you were able to write that song and able to share that song, which is such an empowering song of faith for me and a multitude of other people ...

NEIL: Hmm ...

DELILAH: You know, had you just, had you taken that down time, or that sad time, or that tough time – whatever it was that you were going through, Neil, and then said, "You know, I don't want to focus on that; I don't want to talk about it; I don't want to sing about it; I don't want to – I just want to move on.

NEIL: Yeah, uh – You're absolutely right. You know, you just never know the good things that you do and they just seem to go out there and they create ripples, and uh. You never do know when you're doing something that it's going to be to some good cause, and then you hear the story like this one and it makes it all very clear once again ...

DELILAH: Christmas with Neil Diamond. We'll be back to talk with Neil coming up in just a moment.

I was shocked that Neil was on the phone, yet I was able to keep my cool and talk to him intelligently for about 10 minutes total, much of which was not aired in the broadcast that would be played back later in December. He and I talked about my learning how to play the keyboard and he said to me, "Holly, use the keyboard as therapy. It has worked so well for me. And sweetie, let every note that comes out your fingertips be like magic – it has been for me." I teased him about buying him a steak dinner at the Old San Francisco Steak House if he ever got to Austin and he laughed. I couldn't believe I was able to talk to Neil Diamond like he was a long-lost friend or brother – just like it was meant to be.

When we hung up I didn't know whether to jump up and down, or laugh or cry, so I called Dr. Dubin at home because it was the only thing I could think to do even though I knew it was against our boundaries. He was not at all thrilled and asked me not to call him at home. Woops! While I felt terrible that I had crossed that line, I felt it was forgivable considering what had just happened to me!

I bounced in to work the next day, so high I could hardly work, but I was able to finally concentrate and get something done. For 10 days I was on pins and needles waiting for the show to air, and it happened that they were going to play the tape on the night of one of my Dr. Dubin appointments. So I took my boom box with me so we could listen to it during my session. Dr. Dubin was quite interested in hearing it so we had the Delilah show on while we talked about other things prior to her airing the conversation.

When it came on, we both listened intently for the first part of it and then she played Neil singing "*O, Holy Night*," while

I sat there and trembled and bawled. I looked up to see Dr. Dubin with tears rolling down his cheeks, too. I felt the whole office was consumed by the grace of God; it was a magic moment; a moment of reconciliation. It was a resolution of psychologist Dr. Kurt Lewin's theory of the effect of incomplete tasks. These create an unresolved tension that is only alleviated if the task is completed or abandoned. It also was an example of the Zeigarnik effect or theory, which states that the memory of uncompleted tasks goes unresolved and remains in your memory as long as the task is incomplete. At last, the task of paying the debt of gratitude to Neil was completed; it was resolved; it had closure.

Dr. Dubin told me, "**Do you realize that for those few minutes, you and he were equal, and that you VALIDATED him, for heaven's sake? If anyone would have asked me, could you get Neil Diamond to say he loved you on national radio, I would have bet everything I owned that you could not; you never fail to amaze me because I would have lost the farm!**"

I never again had any psychotic delusions about Neil Diamond because that night on Dec. 1, 2003, he became a real person and a friend: I was forever healed of the Neil Diamond fantasy, thanks to Delilah and her compulsion to help troubled souls.

Remembering my mania of 2003 whereby I e-mailed high officials that if Neil and I ever connected, Saddam Hussein would be caught, it also brought me gleeful gratification that Hussein was, indeed, captured two days after I initially talked to Neil! I again felt vindicated.

Chapter 13: Extra Sensory Perception

I don't want you to suffer, and it is frustrating to me that
you suffer more than I think is necessary, and yet I have not
been able to communicate the path to less suffering to you. I'll
keep trying different ways, and you keep telling me the truth,
and we will get there one day.

—William J. Dubin, PhD

After talking with Neil Diamond himself, everything else
was a letdown as I thought, "Geesh! What do I do for an encore?"
I did slip into depression and one night I tried to explain the
process to Dr. Dubin. However, I didn't do a very good job of it as
seen in this conversation.

"All right. So how ya doin'?"

"Not worth a shit."

"This has lasted a long time; I don't like that."

"I don't either. But I went to bed at a decent hour and did
what we said. I listened to Saturday's tape and found it peaceful.
It helped and the peaceful imagery we did last night helped to
find a little comfort among the hurricane. But then I had all of
these stressful and distressing dreams."

"Yes."

"You know, my car gets stolen; my wallet gets stolen ...
Everything is stressful."

"Uh huh, um hmm."

"But when I woke up, I thought, '*Well, it's another day;*
it's a new day and a new chance to start over again,' you know,
just to do something decent. But when I got to work, I couldn't
interact with people. I didn't want anything to do with anybody,

but it took me a while to get going. Everything I did, I wasn't speedy Gonzales today ... it seemed to take forever; I mean, I got six [web] pages done today."

"I'm impressed that you're able to work under these conditions, you know, it's fabulous. That's what we're looking for; that's the heroic performance. You know, you think I'm mad at you or I look down on you; quite the contrary; I'm amazed that you're performing so heroically. I'm very impressed, and you should be, too. Of course, you're depressed and your bias is opposite that."

"I didn't have any energy to do anything ... when I got home I was so thankful that I didn't have any mail to take care of because I just felt I couldn't do anything extra. But I tipped the chair back and thought about the pool imagery from last night and I did relax, and when I woke up, for about three minutes I felt like, '*Wow, this is great. I feel absolutely fine. Enjoy it while it lasts.*' But that's all it lasted was about three minutes."

"And what happened after the three minutes? What was it like?"

"I was just washed with this ... something ... I don't know what ..."

"Depression?"

"Yes. It just sort of like something descended upon me or something. I didn't even have time to think, you know 'cuz I had to get up and grab my water and pet the dogs and leave ... I was action focused at that point..."

"Um hmm."

"I'm very discouraged. I guess. I'm very discouraged. Um, I suppose we could see if we could get past the physical crap that ... whatever ... rise above the biochemistry, which I think we do in the 'trance-formation.' Which is hard because something was competing with my efforts to relax last night because I felt the bugs crawling all over me ... it was hard to relax, but I did."

"Very impressive."

"It was hard, very hard to relax last night ... and ... well I feel like something horrible is going to happen."

"What possibly horrible could happen that you haven't already experienced? You know, what are you afraid of? Freedom means you've got nothing left to lose, Holly; you've experienced the worst; you've experienced the bottom – it doesn't get worse than that. And you should have no fear."

"That's an interesting observation."

"Well, it's sincere."

"Well Kathleen said she noticed that I was different; that I was not smiling. Not that I walk around smiling all of the time."

"Yeah, you do. That's why I always think that you look like you're having so much fun. You're usually very enthusiastic; you're high-spirited and smiling and you look like you're having fun."

Through this conversation and many others like it, I began to realize how tremendously beneficial Dr. Dubin was simply because of his <u>choice</u> to focus on the positive. This is something that is extremely difficult for bipolar individuals to grasp because of what happens in our brains. Throughout the months of my frequent sessions with Dr. Dubin, I kept telling him how my brain seemed not to work right, and how sensitive I was to things I could not objectively perceive through my five senses. For example, every time there was a large earthquake, I found myself crying and sobbing uncontrollably for much of the day either prior to or the day of and, invariably, I would see on the news a report of a seven magnitude earthquake somewhere in the world.

In one of our sessions, in fact, we were doing hypnotherapy for relaxation in an attempt to relieve the mixed state I was in, and I "saw" an earthquake twice. Right in front of my face, I saw a stretch of dry, cracked earth, and suddenly it split wide apart and separated, shifting into a huge chasm. This "vision" happened twice as I was going into the trance state. That night, just as I left Dr. Dubin's office, a large, 6.9 magnitude earthquake occurred 60 miles from the coast of Crescent City, California. I felt vindicated that the reality is, I do "see" these things which cause emotional turmoil because I'm not in a position to do anything to help others who may be in harm's way.

Another time, while manic, I actually could see the rings of Saturn with my naked eye. I believe bipolar individuals possess a keen level of perception that can be either exhilarating or alarmingly distressing.

When my team leader experiences a high degree of stress, her tension or frustration is contagious to me as it actually appears to penetrate my thoughts and obstruct my ability to objectively pursue the tasks I have at hand.

Whenever someone famous dies, it feels as though somehow the bipolar brain taps into a vague, but overpowering and huge sense of depletion, loss and despair sort of like an all-engulfing grief that cannot be escaped or explained.

The result of these perceptions is what is known as hyperthymia or excessive emotion unrelated to one's immediate reality. However, when these emotional states take over and permeate our being, we try to equate them to something in our external environment to make sense of them. This occurs because one of the primary causes of depression is confusion or a sense of being overwhelmed by perceptions that we do not understand.

And these cognitions, while they are not based on tangible, objective reality we can glean from our five senses, are just as real to the bipolar brain as is the direct conscious awareness of our external reality. I call these cognitions "super-perception," or "extra-sensory perception" because something "extra" is coming into our brains causing sensory reactions that the mind attempts to process but cannot tangibly grasp. We feel many different emotions intensely that do not correlate to anything we can consciously perceive. The resulting confusion causes both depression and anxiety.

For many years, I struggled with these phenomena, trying to understand them and, in recent months, attempting to explain them to Dr. Dubin and to Dr. Robert E. Cantu, my psychiatrist. I tried to tell them that for a bipolar individual, another apparent cause of depression is a sense of being "out of sync" with time. Rather than being able to follow the maxim, *"Be here now,"* it feels as though the mind is racing "out there" somewhere, trying to grasp onto ideas, concepts or understandings that are ahead of where we might be at any given time.

At last, with the advent of scientific progress through the use of functional Magnetic Resonance Imaging (fMRI) and the Stroop Interference cognitive task testing, an explanation of these experiences has been offered by Dr. Stephen M. Strakowski. As director of the Center for Imaging Research, University of Cincinnati College of Medicine, he and several other prominent researchers wrote an article for the *"American Journal of Psychiatry,"* entitled "Abnormal fMRI Brain Activation in Euthymic Bipolar Disorder Patients During a Counting Stroop Interference Task." For more detailed information, the complete text of this article in Portable Document Format (PDF) containing comparison images between bipolar and healthy subjects may be obtained by writing to stephen.strakowski@uc.edu.

During these experiments, 16 patients with euthymic (stable) bipolar disorder, meaning they were not experiencing either a high or a low mood, and 16 normal subjects were asked to perform a counting Stroop Interference task in a controlled condition while undergoing functional magnetic resonance imaging (fMRI). The essence of this testing was to have them identify the colors of words written in various colors of ink, such as to identify **RED** (written in blue ink) as "blue," and YELLOW (written in green ink) as "green," and **BLUE** (written in red ink) as "red," and so forth. The performance of this task was matched with areas of brain activation between the two groups, and the results were fascinating.

This testing revealed the bipolar patients showed distinct impairments in performing the task as compared to the normal subjects. Heightened brain activity among the bipolar patients in different cortical (frontal) brain regions from the normal participants revealed perhaps an attempt to compensate for interference from the limbic or emotional brain networks. Essentially, what this means is that in a bipolar person's brain, certain areas, even when not in a heightened or depressed mood state, remain "charged" or, "lit up."

When Dr. Cantu presented me with this study, suddenly, an entirely new, exciting and vindicating door opened up making all my attempts to explain to doctors and others what goes on in my mind take on a new meaning and even a degree of logic. Normal people perceive objects, events and places in what I call a primary level of perception through typical brain processing centers. However, bipolar people, due to our extrasensory activation of the brain's visual and emotional centers, experience perception beyond the normal five senses, or what I term "extra sensory perception." Since our bipolar brains are fundamentally wired differently, we are more sensitive to external stimuli as shown in the fMRI images below.

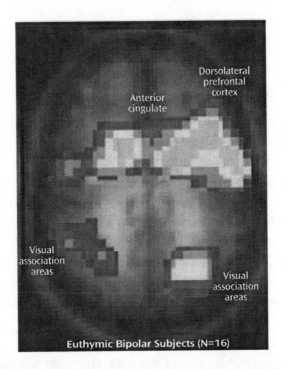

Figure 9. Shows Regions of Activation in Euthymic (Stable) Bipolar Patients During the Stroop Cognitive Interference Task.
Reprinted with permission from the American Journal of Psychiatry, Copyright (2005).American Psychiatric Association.

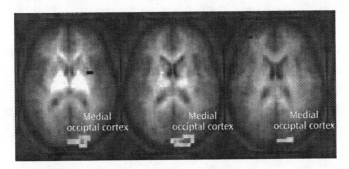

Figure 10. Shows Differential Brain Activation, Adjusted for Education, in Euthymic (Stable) Bipolar Patients During the Stroop Cognitive Interference Task.
Reprinted with permission from the American Journal of Psychiatry, Copyright (2005). American Psychiatric Association.

Since I am a lay person rather than a physician, I can only interpret these results within the context of my own experience. However, the areas of the bipolar brain that generally stay activated are those areas relating to visual and emotional stimulus. This makes sense out of the vague, generalized awareness that we "see" through our emotions which are continually heightened due to the bipolar brain's electro-neuro-chemical excessive firing.

One way of assisting in quieting down this excitation of brain regions is through medication; another way is through cognitive psychotherapy and "trance-formation" through hypnotherapy. I have vast experiences with both. One strategy regarding the excessive emotion is to be ever aware that while we do perceive at a depth or height beyond the normal brain, it does not necessarily mean anything significant. Like Dr. Dubin explained, **"Emotions are like sounds. They come and they go. Like sounds, some are 'louder' or more intense than others and may cause discomfort. However, like sounds that pass through our hearing mechanism, emotions surface and intensify, but they ebb and wane and are gone."**

This analogy helped me tremendously to realize I am not going crazy just because I may be having emotions that do not relate to anything in my tangible, visible reality. It simply means my brain is picking up something through its charged-up radar or antenna and the resulting emotions will peak, but they will also die down. Knowing this provides a certain degree of comfort and safety that my mind is intact and, in its razor sharp mode, is simply keying into things I do not need to understand. I can allow the emotions to run their course and emerge on the other side with my sanity intact.

Rather than pondering and thinking about what I may be feeling or why, I can direct my attention to a current reality such as my work. I can engage in metacognitive awareness, which means to simply focus on the immediate surroundings. I can remind myself to *"Be here now"* and not be concerned with abstract, distant thoughts or feelings.

The distinct challenge in dealing with bipolar disorder is the ability to know the difference between primary symptoms and secondary or recursive symptoms. The latter are in our control and once we can learn how to recognize the manifestation of the primary symptoms brought on by the brain chemistry and to distinguish those from our own cognitive processing about those symptoms, we can have a handle on how this disorder can either paralyze or enhance us. Yes, it can enhance us because of the richness with which we can experience life. One of the most eye-opening ideas that hit me like a ton of bricks has been, *"Bipolar disorder is an exciting adventure that only one in 100 people get to take!"* I realized that because of my brain's sensitivity I am allowed a degree of creativity to sow the seeds of adventure necessary to keep life interesting.

This is an example of overriding the often negative sense of gloom and doom by a <u>choice</u> to think differently and to see that in fact, being bipolar is a **"condition or trait of brain function having its advantages and disadvantages."** If one can develop the strength of mind to focus upon the advantages, the primary symptoms alone will remain, unfettered by the often devastating effects of secondary or recursive symptoms.

What is meant by "primary and secondary or recursive symptoms?" The primary symptoms occur when a mood state such as a sense of darkness, blackness, bleakness or despair appears seemingly from nowhere, out of the blue as a result of those biochemically charged-up regions of the brain. The only remedy for this phenomenon is medication; we cannot prevent or control these states. However, once a medication influence has occurred, we can exert tremendous control over how we think, what we choose to focus upon and how we deal with it.

Secondary symptoms result when we elect to catastrophize about the state we have found ourselves slipping into. We can begin to have suicidal thoughts such as, *"Life is hopeless; I am worthless; everything sucks; I'll never be any better; I'd rather be dead than to feel like this,"* and so forth. It is important to realize that any and all negative thoughts about who we fundamentally are will only serve to bring us down further; they will magnify the state and make it appear to be much worse than it really is. Negative thoughts will borrow trouble and will absolutely guarantee that we will either stay depressed, or grow even more so.

A more helpful way to think when the mood begins to change into a negative state is something like, "*This too shall pass; this is not who I am; this is only temporary; it does not reflect my fundamental nature as a compassionate, caring human being; I don't need to know where this is coming from; it just is, but like everything in nature, it has a beginning and an end and it is not going to last. I am okay; I am strong; I am an ingenious survivor. I am competent; I am confident; I am loving; I am lovable; this despondency will not beat me down.*"

While it is extremely difficult to think in terms of positives in the wake of a highly attention-grabbing, salient negative mood, we can do it. We can also develop what Dr. Dubin calls a dispassionate meta-cognitive awareness, which means to do exactly as described and that is to step outside ourselves as if we were watching a movie and just let the state be, allow ourselves to experience whatever emotions may result, and to refrain from taking any irreversible action based upon the negative state.

Additional and more detailed strategies are outlined in chapters 15 and 16. Often, since it is so difficult to battle the powerful forces of our bipolar chemistry, medication can help. However, some of us have grave difficulties with medications and their side effects, so psychotherapy can be a strategic adjunct to the benefits of medication.

Chapter 14: Wilderness of Mirrors

Intentionally suspend the impulse to
evaluate and judge what you are experiencing.

–William J. Dubin, PhD

While little is known about how medications for bipolar disorder serve to control the brain's biochemistry, it is generally agreed that for most patients, one or more medications can be beneficial. The important thing to remember is to achieve a positive outcome, not whether one is taking medications. There is no shame in taking medication; there is no shame in having this condition, no more so than if one is diabetic or has migraine headaches. Bipolar disorder is a recognized medical disability in the degree to which it can be difficult to control and requires a vigilant sense of monitoring on the parts of the patients and the doctors.

There are few medications developed specifically for bipolar patients, and many of these drugs are used for their "off-label" effects. For example, Depakote, Lamictal and Tegretol are all used in the treatment of seizure disorders as well as for mood stabilization in bipolar disorder. These three, along with Lithium are known as the "big four" or "tier-1" medications in terms of being the primary options prescribed when one is diagnosed as having bipolar disorder. Seldom are anti-depressants such as Zoloft, Prozac or Wellbutrin used alone because of the tendency for these types of drugs to induce mania when not balanced with a mood stabilizer.

From my experience, it is my opinion that the most practical approach for medications should be to use as small a dose as possible of as few drugs as necessary to achieve the desired degree of stabilization and to minimize the onset of side effects. It is typical among medical professionals in the psychiatric and neuropsychiatric field to "ramp up" dosages to some industry-defined standard, while not all patients may be able to tolerate that much. Patients will go off drugs because of undesirable side effects, not because the medications are working.

Another myth regarding medications is that most of them take a week or two to get into one's system and start working. For some drugs and many patients, this may be true; however, I know from experience that at least two drugs, Abilify and Busbar, began to work immediately, and when we rapidly increased the dosages to what is considered "therapeutic" for both of these drugs, manic symptoms set in.

For me, Topomax and Risperidal began to work immediately and as the doctors increased the dosages, severe depressive symptoms ensued. Also, a very small dosage of Seroquel made me so sleepy I almost drove off the road and I fell asleep so soundly at my desk at work that my team leader thought I had a heart attack because she could not wake me up. Also, after five days, the drug, Symbyax, which is a combination of Zyprexa and Prozac, my feet and legs swelled so badly the skin was stretched to the point of cracking and my lower appendages looked like they belonged to an elephant!

When my psychiatrist Dr. Robert E. Cantu realized what was happening, and after talking with my psychologist Dr. William J. Dubin, as my "team," they decided that at least in my case, we should attempt tiny dosages of only one drug at a time in the effort to stabilize me. Upon my initial diagnosis in 1980, I took Lithium at very small amounts until 1989, and whenever my blood level even approached the lowest end of the therapeutic range, I turned into an irritable and grumpy person. Then, in 1988 when I began to experience a severe manic episode, the psychiatrist at the time tried numerous medications in powerful doses all back-to-back, never knowing what one was doing or not doing before adding another one. This is not the way to deal with a person's biochemistry, from one who has been on the receiving end of this philosophy.

Dr. Cantu acquired my case in 2004 after I had been on the Depakote since 1989 and gained well over 50 pounds. Depakote appeared to work until 2000 when I began to have an almost nonstop manic episode for four years. When I went to Dr. Cantu, I had experienced extreme difficulty in getting enough sleep, a primary characteristic of bipolar mania. One can try as diligently as possible to sleep, but getting enough rest eludes us, and the less sleep we get, the more mania has an opportunity to catch hold because anyone, if deprived of enough sleep, will have difficulty with cognitive awareness and mental function. He prescribed very small doses of Xanax which, when combined with the Depakote, tended to cause confusion and that, along with my despondency about my weight sent me crashing down into depression.

Then we tried Abilify and, at 5 milligrams per day, I began to do much better. However, since I was new to Dr. Cantu at the time, he followed the "standard dosage rule," and gradually ramped the dosage up to 15 milligrams per day. I watched myself going manic; however, this time, I was able to ride with it and convey to the professionals treating me what was happening as the symptoms evolved.

While depressive symptoms seem to come all at once, out of the blue, one does not simply wake up one day to mania, which is insidious and tends to creep upon one slowly as it gradually manifests in an intense high. The more practiced and experienced we become at dealing with this condition, the more aware we can become about what is happening and we can control it before it takes over.

Thus, while manic, I wrote the following outline as to what happens in a manic episode in an effort to replicate on paper for the professionals what was happening in my head.

1. I get "lost" – "Lost" in racing, right-brain, creative, driven focus/thought.

2. I cannot stop spending money.

3. I feel like an "open circuit" – like I'm wild, unmodulated sine waves, radio (RF) frequencies, an antenna just picking up whatever signals it can find.

4. I have a TOTAL loss of identity – *"Who Are You? Who-who? Who-who? Who Are You? Who-who? Who-who?"* – and I begin to identify with the rock and roll music.

5. I have a strong sense of finding a cure for cancer and really believe I can in the right setting.

6. I believe I am in partnership with God at a level ***nobody else is*** ... Heck, ***I know I am ...***

7. I will start five things at once, and then finish something that's ***NOT*** on my list and feel as though I'm "real clever!" (I believe this could be obsessive-compulsive disorder or attention deficit disorder imposed on the manic phase of BP.)

8. I try to find symmetry in everything – ***Balance is the key ...***

9. I move pictures and knick-knacks all around to ***make a (spiritual) statement*** (MASS).

10. I cannot make decisions ...

11. I have rapid insights and "God Winks" or epiphanies, brain farts, or "OMGs" (Oh My Gods!") and then, "What have I done?"

12. **I cannot balance my checkbook nor pay my bills without GREAT difficulty.**

13. New premise of "Visual Basic" (**Object** Oriented Programming): I meditate on "Objective Reality," that is, key objects in reality, to give me answers, direction, insights, wisdom, guidance and healing, etc., believing that

Jesus placed all of these items in my objective awareness to be (**2 B**) used for my own <u>enlightenment</u>.

14. I ponder famous people – when they were born and more importantly, when they died.

15. I resurrect those famous people by compulsive, driven, obsessive writing about my ponderings using the "word art" shown previously.

16. Then I know that I am Jesus Christ ...

17. I work with Einstein and his statement that *"The Power of Imagination is Far Greater than Knowledge Alone"* and I work on the theory of Relativity; and I put creation in relationship to the Divine, always focusing on Resurrection Power.

18. Time spins in a circular motion rather than moving forward in a linear fashion; I feel pulled in infinite directions at once and throughout multiple dimensions of time.

19. I experience hallucinations: auditory (voices – usually Ken or Mother calling rather sharply, "Holly! Holly!"); tactile (like bugs crawling on me); and visual (like dark demons or shadows flying around furtively).

20. My vision becomes extra keen and I can drive without my glasses and see the rings of Saturn with my naked eye, yet I can barely read any kind of type.

21. I begin to believe in reincarnation and I believe that in order for me as Jesus Christ to make my appearance to the world as the combined "Holly Holy-Jesus Christ-in-One" with my Universal Language and solutions to ALL problems via that language, that so many ("X" many = "Merry **X+*Mass***) souls have to first "die." I believe everything is a matter of numbers and God's timing is mathematics. So, every living thing is accounted for, which means that bugs – roaches, ants, spiders, mosquitoes, etc. – have to die, too. So I get on this horrendous kick to kill roaches and other bugs. That's ALL I would kill (as well as scorpions), though – not ANY other form of living creature!! Because

of the tactile hallucinations that bugs are crawling on me, that's why they must be dead, saving enough for the food chain, frogs, birds, etc.!!

22.   I have a sense of being a spinning top that no one knows when and/or where and/or how it will land.

23.   When I become REALLY manic, I begin to get highly irritable if people don't agree with me that my reality is "correct."

24.   I start writing poetry and find it much easier than when I'm neither up nor down (the euthymic state). The ease at which verse springs forth becomes my barometer as to how far up or down I am!

25.   I am <u>compelled</u> to do my aerobic, expressive, interpretive, worshipping ("Davidic") dance; and/or play drums – or go to a pool and ride my "noodle" flotation device – anything to work off (sublimate) excessive and intense energy.

26.   I sense the presence of <u>all</u> of the "angels" in my life, such as Danny Smith who took my hand and "jolted me with his soul energy" when he died; my Mother; drum teacher Jimmy Boyer; Preacher Man Harold, late husband Ken Hollan, *ad infinitum.*

27.   I become obsessed with numbers and meanings given to them and try to map out a "meanings chart" for every number that comes into my awareness, like the stock market's gain or loss; temperature; wind velocity, etc. I convert these values into Scripture Chapters and Verses to assign divine and Biblical meaning and insights to objective reality.

28.   Actually, I become aware of "coining" "reverse concepts" like this: In the Midwest and Northeast especially, there's a phrase, ***April showers bring May flowers***. Well, for here in Central Texas, I say, ***April Flowers bring May Showers*** (Bluebonnets, etc. and it almost always seems to rain like hell in May)!

29. REVERSE: Anything to do with "Reverse" becomes special or significant because the Hebrew Torah reads "backwards" or from right to left. "THAT'S RIGHT!" – This one just stopped me as I had to ponder Dr. D. sitting at my LEFT side during our hypnosis, where Danny was when he took my hand when he died and I had that humongous jolt that forever changed my life. An "OMG" is under way here!

30. I meet numerous "Holly's" when I'm having an ME (manic episode)!!! I rarely meet any, but for example, just this past week, I've met three!

31. Concepts about the "Alpha" and "Omega" or "A" to "Z" begin to occur relative to "I AM ... the first and the last ..." With the idea of "time as we know it" forever (4ever) changing. These concepts come about as a result of several premises: (a) There is a reason for everything; (b) We were created in God's image, therefore have the potential for infinite mind and knowledge, especially since we only use such a small percentage of our brains; (c) If you're smart enough and tuned in enough, you can glean those reasons (from the Book of <u>Ruth</u>, the idea of "Gleaning from the Sheaves); (d) My mother told me to "Use your head – that space between your ears! It's for more than just holding your cap/CAP!" (e) My Grandma <u>RUTH</u> Davis and I shared the same birth date, and when she died, I told everyone I was "<u>RUTH</u>LESS," thereby making death humorous; and (f) I was born the year Israel {Is Real; IZ (I'm) REAL} became a Nation, and the Israelites are God's chosen people; (g) Dr. Dubin's son, DAVID was born on my birthday. I have near total recall, and I believe there's something to be said about why I've been put here in the condition I'm in!!!

32. During each Manic Episode (ME), songs come out that have great meaning to where I am at that particular time. For example, this one: Mercy Me's *"I Can Only Imagine"* (What it would be like **2 B** in Jesus' presence – Well Dr. D., Dr. Tina and Dr. Wong get to know ... get to find out ...

just by reading this ... Dr. Cantu, too ... He's endless Love ... FO(U)NT of MANY BLESSINGS). Another one this time is *"The Calling,"* and still another is (Just got little electric "kissy sensation at center of lower lip!!!) *"Calling All You Angels"* (See Number 26). ***AHA! Daddy (Father) was a square dance CALLER!!***

33. The "Chair" and "Frog" and "Seagull" and "LIVING" and "STON(E)" metaphors in Neil Diamond's *"I AM I SAID"* and *"JONATHON LIVINGSTON SEAGULL"* begin to proliferate and take on significant, agape-love kind of meaning.

34. I become unable to write in a "straight line" and writing goes circular; I "B+cum" unable to write "straight" and writing goes off on tangents or if it's in a straight line, it's tangential in terms of becoming a written form of free association, unedited relationship drawing. This kind of writing always results in a "resurrection power" sort of concept whereby someone's name – usually someone "famous" who's passed on – comes to memory, which then is the way they are "resurrected," thereby fulfilling the Scripture wherein it says, *"The dead in Christ shall arise first, and then the rest."*

35. I become totally paralyzed about "The Future" like even one day from the current one. ANY concept of "future" brings about total panic.

36. The "OMGs" (Oh My Gods) concepts that are written on business cards turn out to be "See +/= Sures" (Seizures), or bodily affirmations, or TOTAL EPIPHANIES. This is my very own language and communication with God.

37. I become obsessed with resolving all curses of humankind: Adam and Eve, and her disobedience toward the Father; Cain and Abel and brother killing brother; Nimrod, and the issue of vanity as he shot the eye of the Lord, and then Babylon and the issue of no universal language and communication.

38.　In my Christian Formation class, I had two excellent "angel lady" teachers who described for me the concept, "In the fullness of time." And that described when, where and why Jesus came. I already knew the "how." But most folks don't understand the "Fullness of time" concept: There were good roads for travel throughout the Roman empire; the area was at peace; there was basically one language for communication; the stars and planets were at a unique lineup never before seen. Now is the "fullness of time" for Him to come back. I feel privileged to see these things that "no one else can."

39.　I travel through the souls of individuals I know and have known to and through the souls of individuals I have known *of* all the way to the ends of the Universe and back ... to infinity ... round and around again and again. (This gives those around me the sense that they are watching a spinning top and they don't know when it's going to stop. Usually when it gets here, the pdocs [psychiatrists] want to put me in the hospital but I tell them to shove it.)

40.　In the past, when I have arrived at the point where I am not Jesus Christ by myself any more but rather, where Neil Diamond, who is "my Creator" (because he wrote, and therefore "created" the concept of *"Holly Holy"* – that's why at this point, I tend to see him as my "Creator"; also because he "Created" *"I AM, I SAID"* which God used to keep me from killing myself; therefore my "Creator" "Saved" me) – so therefore I "see" ND as Jesus Christ and I am "The Bride" mentioned in Revelations, and therefore "supposed" to marry ND. (But I didn't do that this time in 2004 after talking to Neil on the Delilah Show.)

41.　Now at this point, ALL the shrinks REALLY WANT TO PUT ME IN THE HOSP. This was where, back in September 1988, Dr. D. DEMANDED that I LISTEN to him when he DID raise his voice and practically bellowed, **"YOU ARE**

NOT GOING TO MARRY NEIL DIAMOND." Father Jack said the same thing in July 2000.

42. Weird things start to happen to those around me whom I love and influence in some way, e.g., my friend Troll's Aunt Betty whom I love and adopted as my own "Aunt Betty": The night I hooked up my new cordless keyboard and mouse, and there was a serious car accident here that knocked all of the power out, her Windows system started booting up and then did a direct 90-turn of the screen (I had also decided to move my furniture in my living room by a 90-degree rotation!!)

43. Chance? Or some kind of generic meaning? It's anybody's guess. Amen, AMEN, and *AMEN* again.

44. (Text changes to blue and red instead of black.) I start writing in different fonts and different colors, like blue for veins and red for arteries for the Blood of Jesus, and I will make up words, and usually they are related to music-lyric metaphors: Example: **Gullnerable** = "**Cross**" between "Vulnerable" and "**Gull**ible" = {Jonathon Livingston Sea**gull**} – I was talking to a bipolar friend about how we people with BP are ... and it just "came out" ... "gullnerable" (we laughed at now I make up words = laughter is good for us!) - We BP people are gullnerable to the entire spirit world.

45. Everybody starts to look like somebody else I know. That's already happened two or three times in the last week or so.

46. My abbreviation (shorthand) for the "trans-" prefix (a "pre" + "fix," or solution) is "X" - started when Jewish Dr. Robert Handlesman hypnotized me and my RIGHT **arm** ("**Arm**ageddon") became "as strong as a steel rod" with the imagery of "I can win over the entire world." "Trans-" generally means "across," so when we write "Merry X-mas," we are writing "Merry '**across**' Mas" ... Happiness

for the masses, and at this point, I am convinced that <u>I AM</u> Jesus Christ come to save the world.

Perhaps others may identify with some of these key characteristics of a truly manic state and associated psychotic thought disorder which could be similar to the highs achieved from street drugs or opiates. The most important thing for bipolar patients to remember is to communicate honestly with their practitioners and to hold nothing back because it is only through trusting dialogue that our doctors can know where we are on the bipolar spectrum and know how to treat us. The only time hospitalization is needed is if we become a threat to ourselves or others; merely having a thought disorder such as described herein does not necessarily mean hospitalization is inevitable.

Throughout the 2004 episode described here, I was able to convey to Dr. Dubin where I was and in the process of talking with him, I was able to keep my actions rational enough that I did not have to go on a leave of absence from work. I trusted him with my innermost thoughts and together, we worked as a team to guide me through the episode in a way we realized the manic symptoms increased intensely when Dr. Cantu increased the Abilify to 15 milligrams per day. It is the patient's responsibility to assume the role of a scientist and to report the results of all medication experimentation to the professionals treating us because each one of us is different; bipolar disorder can be vague and nebulous, coming in different "flavors" depending on one's neuro-chemistry.

I believe there are six primary "meters" of danger in terms of what happens as one is approaching either mania or a seriously mixed and unstable state:

1. Level of "playfulness:" The mind, in its attempt to perhaps correct a depressive downswing, begins to take things way too lightly and we begin to "play" with reality, finding meanings that may or may not exist, and so forth;

2.   Level of "confusion": Simple actions that we can otherwise perform with ease, such as balancing our checkbooks, take on a degree of awesomeness. This goes hand in hand with,

3.   Level of "overwhelm:" Making decisions, even the most insignificant ones, are more and more difficult because the thoughts are racing in a tangential fashion which interferes with normally mundane activities and thought;

4.   Level of "impulsiveness;" As the mind begins to race and a sense of panic sets in at the difficulty in making decisions, it becomes easier to abandon logical choice and just do what "feels right" regardless of whether it may truly be in your best interest;

5.   Level of "defensiveness:" Because we know, as a result of our lack of clarity of thought, that we are slipping into a state of frenzied thought, we tend to become defensive that we're either not doing the right thing or not doing well the things we attempt to accomplish; and,

6.   Level of "irritability:" As the mind becomes more cluttered and focus more blurred, our ability to tolerate even the smallest stress or frustration becomes progressively compromised.

These warning signs are quite clear and can be invaluable to be aware of in the process of averting or diffusing a full-blown manic episode. Some strategies for slowing down the onset of mania will be outlined in the following chapters.

After I found myself in the mania described here in 2004, and then the resulting depression when we added first the Risperidal and then Trileptal and Zonegran to the Depakote, I decided to take a daring and potentially dangerous move simply because I felt safe in the hands of my psychotherapist Dr. Dubin and my psychiatrist Dr. Cantu. Most people who are bipolar want to go off their medications because they are feeling good and think they can do without them or because they are tired of the side effects of lethargy and sleepiness. It can be extremely dangerous to abruptly terminate medications, especially without close supervision of the professionals. I do not recommend going off meds willy-nilly just because we feel like rebelling or feel we can do just fine without them. It is classic for bipolar people to abruptly go off their medications and experience dramatic and traumatic difficulties as a result.

However, Dr. Cantu was taking a sabbatical for a few months and I was so depressed and getting fatter all the time, I decided to phase off all of my medications except the Xanax for panic attacks, which I take sparingly and responsibly. I first dropped the Zonegran by taking it every other day for a week and then stopped; then, I phased off the Trileptal slowly, cutting it by 300 milligrams per day for a week, 300 less than that for another week, and so forth so that durng a month's time, I phased it out. Then, I tackled going off the Depakote which I had been on for 14 years, and which did not seem to be working for the past four years. I gradually weaned off the Depakote in the same manner as I did the Trileptal so that by August 2004, I was no longer taking any mood stabilizing medications.

I did all of this under the protection umbrella of psychotherapy with Dr. Dubin and consultation with Dr. Cantu so I knew that as long as I communicated honestly and openly with them what was going on, I was essentially safe and in a minimum of danger. The good thing here was that now, should Dr. Cantu want to try another medication, we had a clean slate, and we could try small doses of one thing at a time to see what assistance it would render.

The primary excellent news was that I began to lose weight, which served to elevate my mood from a rather deep depression to one of hope and confidence. My metabolism began to change as did my appetite because no longer did I crave constant sweets and salty treats. I helped this situation two ways: One, I began to drink a high-protein Ensure or Boost each night for supper and if I awoke hungry, I would drink a lot of water to trick my stomach into feeling full; and two, I simply began to eat less, practicing what my brother-in-law Vince calls "The Armstrong Method of Dieting." Just remember to push myself away from the table! I didn't count carbohydrates or fat grams; I merely reduced my caloric intake which gradually shrunk my stomach to the point where I simply did not want to eat huge portions of food any more. Within less than a year, I lost a total of 77 pounds, went from a size 20 pants down to a size 10, and lost almost 12 inches from my hips.

While I found it extremely difficult to navigate the powerful impact of the brain's biochemical changes with no medication other than minimal Xanax to help with the ever-increasing panic, the self-esteem enhancing results of the weight loss provided hope, encouragement and suddenly a reprieve from the loneliness of being a widow for 10 years because the men began to be interested.

Now I had a body to match my potent optimism and enthusiasm which made me attractive to the opposite sex and provided diversion and involvement outside myself and my career as a Web administrator for a state agency. Suddenly I was desirable and with this boost to my confidence, I was more able to manage the mood swings brought on by the unmedicated bipolar condition.

I continued to investigate strategies with Dr. Dubin which entailed talk therapy; trance-formation hypnotherapy for relaxation, slowing down the mind, affirmations and anchoring. These methods kept me on a rather rocky, but manageable roller coaster ride while Dr. Cantu was away for a couple of months, and for the ensuing seven months until the external stressors of dating and my employment became too intense and another mania or intensely mixed state began to creep in.

When faced with increasing symptoms, as I had noticed the six "meters of danger" levels insidiously intensifying, I realized that I needed to take responsibility for myself. I scheduled extra appointments with both of the doctors, and Dr. Cantu suggested a medical leave from work due to the ever increasing stress of an awesome deadline of rolling out an entirely new Web site by Aug. 1, 2005. This is an instance in which a bipolar individual can influence the outcome of approaching mania.

I discussed with Dr. Dubin my concerns that if I were not at work, I would probably become suicidal out of the awareness that I was not at work and helping my team in whatever way I could. I had a Family Medical Leave Act event in place that provides for up to 12 weeks off work per year due to a covered chronic illness. However, I believed that if I were to request Americans with Disabilities Act (ADA) Accommodations, I would be able to work in a reduced capacity and still contribute to my team. Thus, I went on a reduced schedule of six hours per day under FMLA and requested that I be moved to a quieter, less distracting office; that I be allowed uninterrupted "block time" to work on complex coding projects; and that I be allowed to take my break times in shorter, five-minute intervals rather than two 15-minute breaks per day.

The Human Resources personnel warned me that if I were to elect to work when the doctor advised that I take a leave of absence, my performance might suffer, and I would be evaluated accordingly. Not being in a frame of mind to make the best decision, my heart overruled my head and I thought that I could at least produce some Web pages rather than none at all and help my team in that way.

This was in a way a victorious manic episode and mixed state because this was the first time that I did not take off into a psychotic, delusional thought disorder. Under the auspices of my doctors' care, and with the ADA accommodations at work, along with the FMLA reduced schedule, I was able to gradually improve my focus and develop a significant number of Web pages in spite of my poor focus, high degree of feeling overwhelmed, and constant need for help in understanding the dynamics of the new Web site design standards.

However, because I cried frequently, often requested immediate assistance from my team members, made numerous mistakes and could not help others, my performance indeed suffered and I was given three "needs improvements" on my goals with an overall rating that I had "been a detriment to the team."

I would like to use this example as a word of caution to others that while there is legal protection in place to help us when we are unstable, there are limits to that protection. When Dr. Cantu requested that we extend the six hours per day of reduced FMLA schedule, my employer declined saying they a business need of a full-time Web developer. This is an employer's right under the FMLA laws. However, they did say that if on any given day I felt as if I couldn't complete the day, they would send me home on FMLA sick leave.

Likewise, under the ADA reasonable accommodations, one must be able to perform all of the functions of the job with the accommodations in place. If performance is at all compromised due to the illness, as long as one is at work, the employer can evaluate the employee based on performance or lack thereof regardless of whether the bipolar disorder is causing interference with such performance.

Shortly after these difficulties, I requested of Dr. Cantu that we re-try a small dosage only of the Abilify which helped me so much the year before prior to increasing it to 15 milligrams per day. While I stabilized significantly on my own with the help of Dr. Dubin's hypnotherapy and just talking with him, I knew that I needed some kind of medication assistance to continue in that vein of stability.

We began five milligrams per day of Abilify with only a small amount of Xanax per evening, and it appears as though the Abilify at that low dosage has been my "gold nugget" by balancing the neurotransmitters in my brain such that I can function at a keen degree of focus and motivation that I've sustained for some time. While the exact way Abilify (or any other medicine for bipolar disorder) works is unknown, it is thought that Abilify may work by affecting the activity of some key brain chemicals – adjusting dopamine, instead of completely blocking it, and adjusting serotonin. When activity of key brain chemicals is too high, Abilify lowers it; when activity of key brain chemicals is too low, Abilify raises it.

This has resulted in a period of surplus and has enabled me to maximize the therapy with Dr. Dubin instead of always having to deal with immediate crises and emotional upheaval.

Chapter 15: "5—4—3—2—1—0!"

Meta-cognitive awareness is the understanding that thoughts, feelings, and sensations come and go. See if you can simply notice them without becoming attached to them.

—William J. Dubin, PhD

While small amounts of Abilify seems to be my healing gold nugget, I cannot discount the healing benefit of intensive psychotherapy and hypnotherapy with Dr. Dubin. One of the scenarios frequently encountered by individuals with bipolar disorder is a coexistent occurrence of borderline personality disorder. This happens as we are growing up and often experience bitter rejections by those around us simply because we are "different." These rejections, lack of acceptance by others, criticism or ridicule tend to foster an intense sense of abandonment, which is a critical issue in borderline personality disorder.

We thus walk around in a heightened emotional sensitivity and reactivity due to the agitation or sense of being charged up in our bipolar brains. Also, because of our fears of abandonment and/or shame that we are bipolar, our limbic or emotional systems tend to maintain an intensified level of fight-or-flight hormones. This undermines our sense of confidence and self-esteem, which in turn can agitate us into a downward or depressive spiral.

This state of agitation creates a nearly constant state of stress and tension which sets up an alert situation, the perception becomes one of "everything's against me." Thus our bottom-line processing of reality comes through a pre-defined filter of "I'm somehow in danger." Then, when something happens to us that may be difficult, such as a coworker looking crosswise at us or saying something critical, or potentially unrealistic deadlines in our work, our reactions to normally low-threat external events are greatly exaggerated due to our already compromised opinion of our sense of worth. This can also trigger panic reactions in addition to depressive thoughts such as "*I'm hopeless,*" or "*I'm worthless.*"

Hypnotherapy, or as Dr. Dubin calls "intentional trance formation," can be highly beneficial in managing the intensity of the bipolar brain surges which intensify the low self-esteem issues that tend to accompany bipolar disorder. Everything we do involves a "trance" of one form or another because "trance" is another term for keen focus of awareness. For example, when we get in our cars to drive to work, we may be thinking of what we need to do once we arrive at our destination. However, our minds are in the "trance" of driving because we've done it so much, we do not have to consciously think about the mental functions involved in navigating the car to our work place. Thus we tend to have a sense of peace about our driving because it is a trance state.

Other forms of trance are a focus on being angry; or being so involved in one's work ("flow" activity) that nothing else going on around us is of any particular importance. Trance can be defined as a state of profound abstraction or absorption that can be used to divert one's mental and physiological states from those of negativity, confusion or agitation to a resourceful state of being calm and relaxed with the mind free to accept positive and helpful, or affirming ideas and suggestions.

The first objective of hypnotherapy was for me to establish confidence and trust with Dr. Dubin. Therefore, intentional trance formation that he geared toward "comfort, safety and relaxation" allowed me to learn how to tune everything out except his voice and just listen exclusively to the words he uttered. After several iterations of a soothing, calming, tranquility-based hypnotherapeutic induction, I began to realize control of my own mind through trust in another individual is possible.

Such a "comfort" script is outlined below. The use of ellipses dots (...) indicates pauses in the delivery of the script which tend to correlate with breathing. Our goal was for me to slow down breathing to very long, slow, deep inhales from the stomach and through the diaphragm and then to let those breaths out equally slowly. This conscious focus only on my breathing begins to alter both the physical and mental states to achieve a different, more peaceful, positive and productive outlook.

"Okay. So now it's time to relax. Close your eyes and let those eyelids get heavy... Just let go of all of the tensions ... let them just fade away ... all doubts and fears just fading further and further away. All voluntary and involuntary reactions and responses just gradually fade ... and disappear. And little by little, you become free of fears, free of anxieties ... free of thinking ... free of feeling ... knowing that nothing really matters except your enjoyment of this experience.

"So allow yourself to tune in to the healing rhythm of your breathing ... as the body recovers from the stressors of this chapter of your life, because now it's time to heal. So feel yourself drifting deeper ... and deeper ... down into a state of peace and calm and healing ... healing of body and mind ... As the calmness becomes deeper and deeper, enjoying the sensations of comfort with nothing really to do ... no one to please, no one to satisfy. Just to notice how comfortable you can feel ... And so you can just allow the body to rest and renew itself as you drift down ... deeper now ... W-A-Y down ...

"Growing more and more comfortable ... more and more confident ... more calm and serene ... so feel yourself drift even deeper ... down into this state of resourceful calmness, with cheerful tranquility all around you ... penetrates evermore deeply within your

251

body and permeates your mind ... So just let go and allow the relaxation to penetrate ever deeper into EVERY CELL OF YOUR BODY.

"And the body just seems to sink deeper and deeper ... down into the chair ... and the chair seems to support you ... totally, causing you to feel fuzzy all over. Or is it a tingling feeling? Or, are there no feelings at all? And of course, it doesn't matter. All that does matter is that you notice ... just notice ... how the body feels when it is relaxed and at peace. Because when the body is at peace, the mind can be at peace. ...

"And so the mind can be at peace ... just at peace ... relaxed ... calm ... and so comfortable. And the body feels the body when the body feels the chair ... and this dreamy, quiet, calm feeling extends throughout you, and you can feel the chair pressing up against your body as the body relaxes more ... and more deeply ... down ... into the chair. And as I count backward from five, down to one, you can drift down ... into the trance. ... Drifting deeper with each count.

"Five ... so serene ... eyes resting comfortably; back and pelvic area so relaxed ... drifting deeper with each count. Four ... more and more deeply down into the trance, enjoying the thoughts and the sensations drifting through you. Three ... well along your journey down into this comfortable and peaceful state. Learning that the body and the mind ... can relax and permit your energies to renew themselves. Two ... so deeply ... muscles of the face beginning to smooth, enjoying the comfort of drifting ... ever deeper ... down ... One ... drifting deeper and deeper ... deeper than you've EVER gone before. So good to settle down ... into this comfortable and peaceful state.

"And I want you to enjoy this experience ... I want you to enjoy ... EVERY MOMENT OF IT ... because the more the body savors the pleasures and comforts of this state, the more it can receive its healing benefits. And you can return to this state whenever you wish ... and here's one way to do it: Whenever you're ready to relax and reduce some stress, just close your eyes and direct your attention to the most ... comfortable part of your body. And when you ... locate that comfort ... enjoy it.

"And you can allow that comfort to deepen. And you can allow that comfort to spread throughout your body all by itself. You know 'comfort' is more than just a word; and 'comfort' is more than a lazy state ... Really going deeply down into comfort turns on your parasympathetic system, and that's your natural relaxation response ... and this is the easiest way to maximize the healing benefits of the rest phase of your body's natural rhythms.

"And during these periods of comfort, you'll often receive quiet insights ... about your life ... and what you really want ... and how to get it. And because you want to develop and enhance your ability to influence your own mental and physical states, you're here now, listening to these words, taking this first step along your path of greatest advantage. And success is sweet ... and you can achieve success by utilizing your talent ... to mindfully aim your attention ... just like you're doing right now ... so that you successfully navigate the hazards of stress and temptation and stay your path of greatest advantage.

"And I want you to have a very thorough appreciation for how very capably you have performed again this evening, and I want you to know that I thank you for your kindness in permitting this communication to take place. Now soon, I'll count to three and, as usual, when I reach 'three,' you can open your eyes, becoming alert, refreshed and feeling wonderful. And a good feeling

will stay with you. READY ... One ... Two ... and Three. So welcome back! Tell me about your adventures!"

I opened my eyes feeling like a different person. "Well, I did get fuzzy. As I was getting fuzzy I started seeing my dog's coat being fuzzy; I've been being very affectionate toward her. My body feels real relaxed but my mind is very much engaged now because I realized some things. I want to tell you that when you just start giving things of value away, that's a sure sign of mania. Also, do you know what it feels like in your body to REALLY have to pee? Well, when I start getting that sense of depression – that total lack of confidence, and being overwhelmed and the tears – my body is having a similar feeling to the way it feels when you're experiencing pee poisoning."

The act of becoming relaxed during the trance allowed me to have some of those "quiet insights" that Dr. Dubin mentioned so I could give him examples of what the pathology of the bipolar experience feels like. Trying to explain this disorder to someone who does not have it is like trying to describe or define the color "green" to a colorblind or non-sighted individual. I found it very helpful in the trance state to come up with analogies so my therapist has some clue as to what the experience feels like.

The benefit of this type of intentional trance formation focus is that whether a patient is experiencing either the high, rapid-energy, flighty thoughts of the manic phase, or the extremely despondent, self-condemning, worthless thoughts of the depressive phase, all that mental activity ceases at least for the duration of the trance focus. The result is a sense of mental and physical healing and balance. With enough repetitions of the state, I have begun to find the capability of reproducing that calm state, if only for glimmers during the stressful times of wild, rampant energy, or those of devastating bleak, despair.

"Anchoring" is one of the hypnotic techniques we have employed to assist in taking control of stressful mood swings occurring in real time. The key in these exercises is to elicit an intentional trance, or ability to alter the content of one's mind when symptoms are present. Anchoring is a method of setting up a cue that will be triggered when needed. In the therapist's office, with few threats and distractions, we can get ourselves into a resourceful, relaxed or calm and safe state that then becomes conditioned to a trigger, or a stimulus that we can later, in a high-risk situation, use to elicit a more desirable state.

A trance is an altered state, and everything is a trance. Different anchors trigger different trances. Anchoring is setting up in advance a stimulus or cue to which an emotion or trance will be conditioned to respond. After the anchoring in the therapist's office, the anchor acquires the power to generate that trance whenever attention is focused on the anchor. When I am in an unproductive state, I use the anchor to modify or alter that state to produce a more positive state or trance. Anchoring is a way to quiet the mind, manage stress, increase our sense of well-being; increase our sense of harmony with social and physical surroundings; and improve performance on tasks. Anchoring involves learning to focus the attention and thereby quiet the mind, similar to meditation or prayer. Having a quiet mind is not being zoned out, without thoughts, or numbing one's feelings.

One method of anchoring is to get into the intentional trance formation state with the hypnotherapist and to have him or her present positive, powerful affirmations as post-hypnotic suggestions. These thoughts, ideas and concepts, when repeated a number of times while in the comfort of the therapist's office and in a relaxed, open-minded state can override the negative, disruptive or confusing thoughts when symptoms are present.

Neuroscientists are beginning to have new respect for the value of hypnosis because of the way the brain processes information. Our perceptual processes work sort of like an elevator in that we take in information at the bottom floor or lower level. For example, we are shown a yellow rose. The lowest level of processing first determines what we are seeing is an object that has color as opposed to being black and white. Then, at a higher level, we perceive the color is yellow. Going up one more level, we determine the object is a yellow flower, and up one more level in the perceptual refinement, we glean we are seeing a yellow rose as opposed to a yellow chrysanthemum. What hypnosis and the repetitive anchoring affirmations do is to teach processing at the higher levels which help bypass some of the more primitive, prejudiced lower-level thoughts like "It's hopeless," "I'm worthless," and so forth.

Below is a series of such powerful affirmations, delivered while in the calm, resourceful trance state, that can be called upon when one is in a real-time crisis of symptoms that may occur totally out of the blue, or as a result of external stressors. Again, the ellipsis dots indicate pauses in the delivery of the thoughts to coordinate with long, slow, deep, cleansing breathing.

"Please contemplate the following affirmations.

"I am loyal to myself ... I am full of compassion for the person ... who finds themself in my situation ... I acknowledge there are many forces that pull me ... and I have compassion for the person so pulled.

"I have compassion for the person ... who lived through my childhood.

As a child I was an innocent ... a product of my environment ... who could only react to the forces acting on me ... but now I am an adult ... and I accept the responsibilities of adulthood. ... I select my own direction ... I move toward the goals I choose for myself ... even in the face of forces that would divert me.

"I am clever and flexible ... and can move into my resourceful state of mind whenever I choose to. ... I am loyal to myself ... and this loyalty is of prime importance in all situations. ... My first priority ... is responsibility for my physical health ... and personal development. Taking good care of myself ... without guilt ... without any form of self-hate ... takes precedence over all other activities.

"I have many talents and abilities ... and I can utilize my intelligence and creativity

along with the feedback I receive from experience ... to progress and develop.

"I am flexible and can respond ... to the demands of different situations. ... I can be loose and fun loving in some situations ... and I can be strict and disciplined in others.

"I do not underestimate my own powers ... nor do I underestimate the powers of my foe ... and so I forgive myself for each small defeat ... and learn from my mistakes ... and I congratulate myself for each small victory ... because to achieve it I had to overcome my mortal enemy. ... And the more experienced I become ... the more effective I become ... at managing this enemy of life.

"I am an intelligent, effective adult ... and can manage my thinking wisely ... in order to maximize my pleasure ... and minimize my pain ... I am an ingenious survivor ... I think in a way ... that maximizes my health ... and the quality of my life ... And I have learned ... that the rationalizations I have used in the past to break my commitments ... have caused me pain ... and so as soon as I notice ... a lapse of thinking ... I cut it off.

"I am determined and resilient ... and I can maintain my focus ... despite frustration and discomfort ... until I accomplish what I set out to accomplish."

One tool that Dr. Dubin uses to assist his clients is the "Intention and Action" (I&A) form shown below. Utilizing this form causes an intentional direction of focus. It creates a cause and effect in real time that minimizes the symptoms. It's an interactive engagement that helps to purposefully redirect a symptomatic, non-productive thought process.

	Psychological A R T S		
	Intention & Action		
	4131 Spicewood Springs Road, #E-2 Austin, TX 78759 Phone: (512) 343-8307 E-mail: spice@ psycharts.com	Fax: (512) 452-7282 http://www. psycharts.com	7801 North Lamar Blvd.,#F8 Austin, TX 78752 Phone: (512) 452-6383 E-mail: lamar@psycharts.com

Name:	Holly Hollan	**Goal:**	Combat Spiraling Biochemistry

The purpose of this data sheet is to learn how your intentions influence your actions so that we have access to real time data during our sessions. The intended coping tactic is specified in the top section, and your observations of what actually happens in real time are described in the numbered sections below.

Intended Action

Will Statement

As soon as I notice the warning cue, I will execute the coping tactic. In the space below, please write your own Will Statement.

WARNING CUE: Panic and Anxiety; Tears; Self-sabotaging Thoughts
COPING TACTICS: (1) Take Naps; (2) Do Deep Breathing; (3) Make Gateway System Recovery CDs; (4) Load Software to Gateway; (5) Transfer Files to Gateway; (6) Enter e-mail Addresses to Gateway; (7) Transfer "Favorites" to Gateway; (8) Shower (Sun.); (9) Wash Hair (3:30 PM Sun.); (10) Take Rich Out to Dinner (7:00 PM Sun.); (11) Practice and Record "Canta Libre" -- send to WJD, Bob, IAIS folks; (12) Practice "Dear Father"; (13) Take Xanax as needed; (14) Drink Coffee moderately (warmth calms insides); (15) Eat KozyShack (from HEB) Tapioca Pudding with vanilla soy milk.

Observations

1. Took Nap Sat. from 4:30-6:15 PM (1) -- did NOT HELP -- woke up in SEVERE panic; body in all-over pain; Did deep breathing (2) -- did NOT HELP; Friend Debbie called, found her and her fucked-up life to be a distraction that added to panic; Configured Norton AV on Gateway; Made 4 Recovery CDs (3) -- in spite of almost immobilizing panic. Made cup of coffee (14); fed dogs; 7:15 took 1/2 mg Xanax (13).

2. 1:00 AM Sun: Diligently loaded software (4); = very organized, focused and meticulous; Entered all e-mail addresses to Gateway (6); Made myself eat a small TV dinner; Copied all desired files to CD for transfer to Gateway in the morning.

3. Did not sleep well; woke up somewhat down and anxious. Recalled I&A: immediately set about to transfer all documents to Gateway (7), (5); Completed additional software installations (4); Took a LONG HOT shower (8); realized that focus on DOING these items quieted "Lucy Fur."

4. Now I'm "free" -- to do the "music thing." This efficacy at methodically setting up the Gateway to essentially be my prime machine (aside from SONAR work) has done wonders to deter or to calm the panic. Tears are present, but so what? I guess that's just "me."

Anchoring is best done when the patient is in a fairly upbeat frame of mind rather than when down or highly agitated. At those times, simple relaxation into the calm, resourceful mindset with the objective of modifying the body's state is the best approach. However, another type of anchoring elicits patient input identifying certain objects that have personal meaning to create a tangible focus that can and will change unproductive mental states.

I have great success with two such images. One is anchoring to a lighter held in my left hand with the suggestions being *"Lighten up; I can be a light to those around me; my load is lightened; I can achieve enlightenment; I can learn to not take myself or the expectations of me so seriously; I can see things as wants and not needs; I don't NEED to get everything done in record time; I want to please my customers; if I have a lighter heart, I can have a lighter mind and bring lightness to those around me ..."* and so forth.

The second powerful image I use is that of two business cards, one of Dr. Dubin's and one of Dr. Cantu's, the "team" whom I hired to help me. Since I have great confidence in the professional expertise of my team, anchoring to their business cards serves to remind me that I can have *"confidence in my own abilities; I can adopt a 'taking-care-of-business' mindset."* This image has strong positive affirming effects because of my earlier experience of successfully playing drums to the song, *"Taking Care of Business"* prior to my drummer friend joining Jose Feliciano's band.

While in the trance state, Dr. Dubin has placed either the lighter or the business cards in my left hand and presented the suggested thoughts that I can anchor to while in a stressed, symptomatic state. I cannot say how many times I've been frazzled, anxious, tearful or confused and I've gone for a short walk with either the lighter or business cards in my left hand. My mind will be triggered by those anchored objects to the thoughts suggested and often, my entire state has changed to the attitudes brought about by the thoughts cued from the anchored objects. My entire thinking has cleared as a result of directing my attention to ideas of *"Lighten up; I am confident that I can take care of business; I can be a light to others,"* and I've been able to return to my desk and resume my focus on my work projects with a clear mind, relatively free of symptoms.

Another form of anchoring has to do with one's posture and the concept of "Pull into Adult." Often when experiencing symptoms and their accompanying self-doubt, we slump into a posture that reflects carrying the weight of the world on our shoulders. I have experimented with consciously observing my slumped posture, and pulling my shoulders back, holding my head high, tucking my chin in and walking down the hall bearing this new, confident posture. It's amazing how that simple act of pulling my body into a confident, competent, professional demeanor can help affirm a mentally positive focus, diverting the sense of burden that symptoms are present.

A final form of anchoring is based on the ability to imagine different relaxing scenery to divert the mind from stressful circumstances caused by the internal biochemistry or from external events. While in the hypnotic internal trance formation state, Dr. Dubin often painted beautiful sunsets, or ocean scenes such as swimming among the dolphins, or walking along a beach, being out in a boat, visiting lovely waterfalls in idyllic settings, or walking down flowered and wooded paths and meeting my "inner guide." Other such imagery centers around such concepts of *"My body and brain are balanced; I am bathed in a healing light; I am washed in cheerful tranquility,"* and so forth.

This imagery that's presented while in a calm and resourceful state in the therapist's office can be recalled at will by triggering to long, deep breaths with the eyes closed momentarily, and it serves as a trigger or an anchor to divert whatever stressors may be causing an undesirable state.

The phrase "mind over matter" is not to be taken lightly. These relaxation and anchoring techniques have served me well as tremendously powerful tools in the arsenal of fighting the manifestation of symptoms brought about by the strong changes in the biochemistry of the bipolar brain. The mind can be and is in ultimate control. That doesn't mean we will not continue to experience symptoms; what it means is that we can exert an influence over the intensity of the manifestation of those symptoms and we can divert the tendency to magnify them, thereby setting in force recursive or secondary symptoms such as *"I'm no good; everything sucks; I'm worthless; it's hopeless,"* and so forth.

Through anchoring, we have a method to maintain a healthy sense of control over the influence of our natural tendency to focus on the negative or confusing symptoms. My recommendation is to be creative about the images or cues you can trigger to and find anchors that have meaning to you and that represent an image of confidence and success.

Chapter 16: Acting My Way Into Good Thinking

We can take the perspective of viewing thoughts as thoughts - events in the field of awareness, independent of their content and their emotional charge, without trying to change them or "fix" anything, but rather observe them with a degree of equanimity.

– William J. Dubin, PhD

While anchoring techniques remain as my most powerful tool to manage my bipolar mood swings, I have developed a number of other useful strategies that are simply effective life guidelines for anyone. However, they are essential when one is bipolar. The first is to adopt The Golden Rule in my interactions with others. If we treat others the way we wish to be treated, and we reach out to others, we create an external reality that serves us well during times of duress. I go out of my way to be kind and considerate of others, to compliment people in a way that is personal and uplifting. For example, rather than saying, "I like your sweater," I will say, "You look great in that sweater;" or, "That shade of blue looks wonderful on you."

When emotions or thoughts are running rampant, I exert all strength of will I can muster to avoid taking out my frustrations on other people. While we may be feeling a certain way that entails pain or confusion or threat, we simply must strive to maintain our relationships with people based on compassion for them and on awareness that everyone has problems of their own, and everyone else wants us to like them as much as we want to be liked.

We need to remember actions have consequences and harsh or hurtful words and behavior toward others cannot be taken back. Likewise, when we behave in a way others find threatening, such as acting out suicidal thoughts, these actions not only make others uncomfortable, but they come back to haunt us through the behavior of others toward us that further aggravates our own condition.

So what do we do when we feel completely hopeless as if one more minute of life is not worth living? What do we do when the emotional pain is so intense that cutting on ourselves almost seems pleasurable because it diverts the pain from our total being to something more localized and specific?

I dated a fine, outstanding gentleman for a few months. He was the first man to show me any attention and affection in almost 10 years of being a widow. I had high hopes the relationship could grow and blossom. The man was brilliant and compassionate and accepting of me and all that I am. The relationship progressed slowly and I found a level of stability I had not known in many years. This gentleman served as a positive focus for my attention.

Suddenly, he announced that his work was taking him to Argentina for at least two years and that he would be moving soon. Needless to say, I was devastated. I felt like my heart was mortally wounded. My entire body and mind were contorted in such pain, I wanted to be dead. I kept looking at a huge vein on the back of my right wrist and I wanted to slash it wide open just to divert the pain and watch my life ebb away. However, I kept telling myself, *"Actions have consequences – what would you tell the people at work if you went in with a big gash on your wrist? How will they feel toward you? Do you want to justify such behavior to others? Do you want to deal with their reactions of discomfort on top of what you're already trying to manage?"*

We've all heard of the concept of networking in conjunction with career advancement, and I've found that principle to be of paramount importance in assisting me with such types of deeply painful circumstances. So rather than trying to take my life, I began to call people whom I know and who love me and are concerned about my well-being. I also wrote an e-mail to my therapist telling him I had a "bad shock where my boyfriend is concerned" and asked him to please contact me if and when he could. Ironically, Dr. Dubin had gone to bed, but something told him to get up and check his e-mail, which he did, and he called me very late, for which I was deeply grateful.

I cried and told him my heart was broken, I felt totally abandoned and I simply could not go on. I told him I wanted to be dead and I could not tolerate the pain of this circumstance. I also told him I was hurting so badly I wanted to cut my wrist. He responded brilliantly – not by telling me I needed to get to a hospital – but by telling me to do absolutely nothing. "Don't do anything; do nothing." This was probably one of the best pieces of advice I've ever received because it was a profound thought to anchor to – "*Do nothing.*" And since everything felt like nothing anyway because I lost what I most cherished at the time, it became easy to just surrender into nothingness, which prevented me from indulging in any form of action that would have irreversible consequences.

So I called my friends and received much love and support; I received back what I try to give at all times in my life and that is love, kindness, forgiveness, compassion and nurturing. It is my hope that anyone who is in a suicidal frame of mind will stop and realize that when in that state of mind, if we cannot dissipate the thoughts by focusing on something positive, then the very best thing to do during those times is ... ABSOLUTELY NOTHING.

At such times sleep can be extremely healing as can long, slow, deep breathing. Also, it is critical to allow our emotions to flow. Let the tears come because they cannot hurt us and they are healing and cleansing. Because others can be intolerant of our emotionality, I excuse myself when I know that strong emotions are present and either go outside or to the ladies' room and let them come with their full intensity until they run their course.

I've often found these strong emotions are just as Dr. Dubin has said. They are like sounds that come and go; they never last interminably. If we are not afraid of them, since they are a part of ourselves and we do not need to be afraid of who or what we are, we can embrace them and let them ebb and wane just as sounds come and go, being careful not to take any actions based on our emotions or feelings. Our actions need to be a result of our thinking and what we choose to do or focus on. We can be held accountable for our actions; we cannot be held accountable for strong feelings caused by our brain biochemistry and resulting perceptions. And there is no shame in having intense emotions or confusing negative thoughts that come and go like sounds.

We are in control of what we choose, consciously, to focus on. This is where the question, *"What is the best use of my attention right now?"* can serve to remind us, on an ongoing basis, that we CAN control where we direct our awareness. I found that awareness and acceptance is the key to change. We cannot change what we are not aware of and what we have not accepted. Therefore, it is critical to maintain a vigilant awareness of our thoughts and body state, almost like diabetics who have to check their glucose levels. We can stay on top of our moods if we accept that (1) they vary intensely and often with no warning; and (2) they are ever-changing and no one mental state is going to be with us forever. This acceptance is critical to adopting the ability to have an impact and incorporate changes in the way we think and what we do to help modulate the height of the mountains and depth of the valleys.

I like to think of this ride as that of a sine wave in electronics, when an audio signal is introduced to an oscilloscope, which measures the sound frequencies. I've noticed that for every peak there is a valley that is equal to and opposite the peak. This is like a law of physics that states, "For every action there is an equal and opposite reaction." Therefore I know I will never stay way far down or way far up for extremely long periods of time. The key is to regulate the ups and downs to prevent them from being so steep, high or deep. I have coined a phrase I've found rings true every single time I begin to slip into what one might call a funk: *If you weather the downs and storms with dignity and grace, the next up will bear a surprise and a blessing beyond your wildest dreams.*" That's not to say we'll go zooming back up to a manic state; what it means is the good we do toward others even though we may not be feeling too good about ourselves always comes back as a form of rewards for faith and sowing positive seeds.

This is what Dr. Dubin calls "Stay the path of greatest advantage." It may sound trite to say, but it does take two mountains to make a valley so if we can choose to focus on the energy of the upswings, that choice puts a momentum in place that's almost like "banking" the good times. It is extremely difficult when we are down to remember those periods of peak performance and their maximum benefit. However, in order to remain on our path of greatest advantage, we must adopt what Dr. Dubin has told me over and over again, and that is a strategy of meta-cognitive awareness or mindfulness. It is like taking the stance of getting outside ourselves and watching the emotions, feelings and thoughts come and go as if we were watching a movie about someone else. This mindfulness allows us to become detached from the experiences so they have less impact upon our ability to direct our attention to that which will bring about a more positive state.

If we know we are in a troubled state of mind, we must be careful to refrain from creating negative subjective realities by such thinking as, *"I'm always going to be this way; I'm a mess; I'm useless and no good; everything is hopeless; I'd have to die to feel better,"* and so forth. The more we allow ourselves the luxury of "pity parties," the more we slip into negativity.

I like to think of this bipolar characteristic as "an adventure which only one in 100 people get to take." I would not trade my capacity for experiencing life to its fullest for anything and I view being bipolar as a gift that brings keen and rich understandings of life that many people are not privileged to experience.

Another strategy I employ is to sow the seeds of adventure. We all need something to look forward to and I like to use my creative energy when in a positive upswing to generate potential good things in my life. This can be something as simple as planning a dinner date with a friend for a week or so down the road; or it can be something more complex such as scheduling a vacation several months in advance or purchasing tickets to a concert or ballet; or joining a group such as The Writers' League of Texas and keeping up with their activities. This is the kind of thing I did when I wrote to the Delilah Radio Show about how Neil Diamond's song saved my life; or writing to the Oprah Winfrey Show about my weight loss story. If we don't plant those seeds of adventure, we cannot possibly expect good things to happen to us. It was never written in Scripture, "The Lord helps those who help themselves," but the saying is true regardless.

Maintaining an assertive attitude in life and an attitude of faith, or being motivated to answer the call to that which stirs inside of us, will provide us with an outlet for our attention if we should be feeling empty, lost or despondent. By planting these seeds of adventure, we set into motion the ability to achieve joy in life that can override our fears and self doubts.

I discovered one strategy to help bring about order to my chaotic mind is to embark upon little tasks of organization, or by bringing about order to my external reality. Sometimes just taking time to sort out papers on my desk, or clean out a jewelry drawer, or dust the furniture, or vacuum or even take out the trash provides an external action to anchor our thoughts and quiet them down so they are not racing or spiraling out of control.

I have another saying regarding fear and faith that partially came from a priest's homily that my sister Heidi shared with me. My psychiatrist who manages my medication, Dr. Robert Cantu, once told me that where there's faith, there's no fear. "*If fear knocks and faith answers, then fear goeth before the fall*

– faith knocks it down ... Therein lies the fall of fear!" If we can continuously anchor to positive affirmations and act as if we have no fear, it is amazing how we can modulate and modify intense feelings of panic, self-doubt and confusion.

Another thing Dr. Cantu told me that resulted in a huge change in my life was, *"You have to ACT your way into good thinking."* I had been having an extremely difficult time with a mixed state of rapid swings from depression to mania and back such that everything around me was perplexing, and all that I tried to do seemed like scaling Mount Everest. I worked very hard to eat right, get exercise, get enough sleep, do my relaxing deep breathing and everything, but I could not stabilize. This inability sent me careening into an overall depression because I was beginning to believe I could not meet the challenges of my work and I was, in fact, a failure.

I was ready for suicide when Dr. Cantu made that statement to me. I had been fighting for four months not to go manic and I kept crashing back down way below into the depression caused by an inability to perform in the way I know I am capable of performing. I was bothering people at work because I simply could not "get it" and needed constant help, which was an ongoing blow to my self-esteem. I knew I needed something outside medication that could help divert my attention to something positive and joyful.

I always had dogs in my life, and at one time had eight Border collies. By this point, I was down to the last one who had grown extremely feeble, frail and confused. I knew Clyde's days were numbered, which did not help my mood any because I lived 10 years after the death of my husband wondering what I would do when all the dogs were gone. That day was rapidly approaching and I grimaced at the thought of life with no dogs.

I went with my friend Trena and her daughter Megan to Buchanan Border Collies on Mother's Day a few months before and paid for and reserved a male Border collie puppy. However, I was not able to commit to picking one out and taking him home. When Dr. Cantu made that statement to me, *"You have to ACT your way into good thinking,"* I decided to go out to the Buchanan Border Collie Web site and look at available puppies.

I was under a huge anointing to take some kind of action to turn my life around as I was off all bipolar medications. I tried a couple that caused severely uncomfortable side effects and did no good at all, and was afraid at the time to try any more. I believed Dr. Cantu was right in his assertion. When I opened the Web site, little "Storm" was the featured puppy at the top of the page and I clicked on the link to see more of his pictures. Something about that puppy was different from all of the rest I had browsed over the previous three months. Something about him called to my heart.

I called Trena and asked her to look at him and, of course, she thought he was a cutie. I called the owner of the kennel and asked him about puppy "Storm." He told me Storm was the most affectionate of all of his current pups and he was always first to greet him; he told me he was "a pistol." I told him I wanted to make the hour-and-a-half drive up the next day to meet him, so since I paid for a puppy I had first choice over the other customers.

The next day we drove up to meet little Storm, and I was already calling him "Stormy." When Jim handed me that five-week-old little bundle of joy, Stormy literally drank in my entire neck and upper chest and then laid his head on my collar bone as if to say, *"I've found my mommy!"* I couldn't decide right away as I didn't want to be impulsive, even though I had paid for him. I knew Clyde had only a few more days to live and I wanted him to meet Stormy so he would know his mommy was okay and had a little friend to continue life with.

After about an hour and a half, I decided I wanted Stormy to be my little "dog-child," and I was ready for life with a tiny Border collie puppy. I had to wait another week before I could bring him home, and the following week we went back up to get my new "baby." Thus began what people now call "Post-Stormy Holly." Much has been written about the therapeutic value of animals and pets, and I will emphatically assert this little warm bundle of fuzz totally changed my life. It is a big sacrifice and a lot of expense to incorporate a high-energy, demanding Border collie into my life, but the rewards are huge. I had to experience the trauma, pain and grief of losing little Clyde six days after I brought Stormy home, but the joy of this tiny ball of youth and energy greatly diminished that sense of loss as I was able to do all the things Dr. Dubin had been teaching me in the previous months.

I was able to divert my attention to a positive focus and to work at making Stormy the best possible companion I could, which is an ongoing process and project. I was able to see myself accepting him and some of his rambunctious misbehaviors with kindness and nurturing and firm discipline which allowed me, at Dr. Dubin's encouragement, to become more accepting of my own weaknesses. Whenever anti-life thoughts creep into my awareness, I divert my attention to Stormy and am glad I am alive to be a good "mommy" to this precious new creature; I am acting my way into good thinking.

Having such a loving and devoted companion in my life even paved the way for the courage to go back on only 5 milligrams of Abilify per day, which helped me tremendously 18 months before. I wanted to be a good and positive influence on Stormy and I knew I needed additional help so I committed to again try the Abilify which has proven to be the best medication decision I ever made.

It is hard to tell what resulted in the healing and success I've experienced because there are so many factors involved, but I can say without reservation that if someone came up with an ultimate "cure" for bipolar disorder that would make me never experience another high or another low, but rather render me very "middle-of-the-road," I'd turn it down because I would take the excitement and the challenge of this ride any day over a life of dullness and boredom.

Printed in the United States
97557LV00004B/421-459/A